Capturing Campaign Dynamics:
The National Annenberg Election Survey

Capturing Campaign Dynamics: The National Annenburg Election Survey

Design, Method, and Data

Daniel Romer

Kate Kenski

Paul Waldman

Christopher Adasiewicz

Kathleen Hall Jamieson

Annenberg Public Policy Center
University of Pennsylvania

New York   Oxford
OXFORD UNIVERSITY PRESS
2004

Oxford University Press

Oxford   New York
Auckland   Bangkok   Buenos Aires   Cape Town   Chennai
Dar es Salaam   Delhi   Hong Kong   Istanbul   Karachi   Kolkata
Kuala Lumpar   Madrid   Melbourne   Mexico City   Mumbai
Nairobi   São Paulo   Shanghai   Taipei   Tokyo   Toronto

Published by Oxford University Press, Inc.
198 Madison Avenue, New York, New York 10016
http://www.oup-usa.org

Oxford is a registered trademark of Oxford University Press

Library of Congress Cataloging-in-Publication Data
Capturing campaign dynamics : the national Annenberg election survey : design, method,
    and data / Daniel Romer . . . [et al.].
        p.   cm.
Includes bibliographical references and index.
ISBN 0-19-516504-7 (pbk.)
    1. United States. Congress—Elections, 2000. 2. Elections—United States.
3. Voting—United States. 4. United States—Politics and government—1993–2001.
I. Romer, Daniel.
JK1968 2000b
324.97'0929—dc21   2003040463

Printing number: 9 8 7 6 5 4 3 2 1

Printed in the United States of America
on acid-free paper

*We dedicate this book to the memory of
Ambassador Walter Annenberg,
who made the National Annenberg
Election Survey possible.*

CONTENTS

ACKNOWLEDGMENTS

The 2000 National Annenberg Election Survey is a product of the efforts of a great many people. The survey was designed by Richard Johnston, along with Michael Hagen, Paul Waldman, Daniel Romer, and Kate Kenski. Mary Macintosh of Princeton Survey Research coordinated the implementation of the survey with Christopher Adasiewicz, who wrote the codebooks and created the data files on the CD-ROM. The interviews were conducted by Schulman, Ronca & Bucuvalas, Inc. John Stromer-Galley created the CD-ROM. Michael Hennessy and Frank Diebold provided helpful comments on the statistical and method content of the book. The entire project was directed by Kathleen Hall Jamieson.

PREFACE

The National Annenberg Election Study (NAES) of the 2000 presidential election is a landmark in the history of American political opinion polling. Never before has so intense a study been conducted of the public's day-to-day reactions to the political events of a U.S. presidential election and its extended contestation in the courts. The rolling cross-sectional (RCS) survey design perfected by Richard Johnston and his colleagues in their studies of Canadian national elections served as a model for the study. The unprecedented opportunity to examine trends and relationships in the resulting dataset led members of the Annenberg Public Policy Center to evaluate the strengths and weaknesses of alternative ways to summarize and analyze the data. This exploration led to the creation of this book, which not only contains an electronic copy of the entire NAES dataset but also provides background and overviews of several methods for analyzing the data. It is hoped that this overview will help newer as well as seasoned analysts take advantage of both graphical and regression procedures to answer questions about the wealth of information provided by RCS surveys and multiple panels conducted throughout the election year.

The majority of the book is based on a course taught by Dan Romer and Kate Kenski on the analysis of the RCS design at the Annenberg Summer Institute for Methods and Statistics at the University of Pennsylvania. The course was designed as a practical guide to analyzing the survey rather than a rigorous examination of the statistical underpinnings of data analysis. The presentation assumes that the reader is familiar with statistical concepts such as significance testing and the use of linear regression analysis. Nevertheless, important concepts are reviewed when necessary, and an appendix of technical terms is provided as a reference for readers. Whenever possible, examples of analysis strategies are illustrated using data from the NAES. In some chapters, analyses are suggested that readers might try on their own to demonstrate their mastery of the procedures. Because chapters were written by different members of the study team, we credit them for the chapters to which they contributed. A brief overview of the plan of the book will help readers find the material that is most useful to them.

In Chaper 1, Kathleen Hall Jamieson and Kate Kenski discuss the motivating premise of the NAES that a more complete record of the public's reaction to U.S. presidential elections will help to answer important questions about the influence of campaign events on the electorate. Despite the skepticism often expressed about the importance of election campaigns, Jamieson and Kenski provide compelling evidence for the usefulness (and limits) of the NAES in understanding events over the course of a presidential campaign.

In Chapter 2, Paul Waldman provides an overview of the content of the entire survey and the various files that are included in the accompanying CD-ROM. In addition, he describes other files that provide helpful methodological information for the use of the dataset, such as demographic weights and response rates for the survey. He also discusses practical considerations surrounding the use of these measures.

In Chapter 3, Kate Kenski reviews important concepts in survey and research design. She then shows how they apply to the design of different survey methodologies for the study of elections. In particular, the strengths and weaknesses of the RCS design are discussed in relation to other survey methods, such as simple cross-sectional and panel studies.

In Chapter 4, Kenski discusses the underlying strategy of the RCS design and the specific sampling and interviewing protocols that ensure comparable samples and questioning on each day of the survey. These procedures enable researchers to study change attributable to events during the election campaign as opposed to changing features of the survey methodology.

In Chapter 5, Kenski reviews the importance of graphical analysis of survey data. In particular, graphic displays permit the researcher to identify trends in the data and potential violations of assumptions that might be made in subsequent data analysis. She also discusses some strategies for smoothing data to identify trends over time.

In Chapter 6, Dan Romer reviews the use of linear and logistic regression for the analysis of cross-sectional data. He reviews the assumptions one makes in using these analyses to identify causal relations in survey data. He also discusses strategies for studying aggregate changes that unfold over time and the effects of voter experiences that might moderate these effects.

Chapter 7 by Kenski and Romer reviews strategies for the analysis of panel data. The NAES contains several panels that were designed to permit the study of important election events such as presidential debates. Strategies to permit stronger causal inferences from this design are discussed using examples from the NAES.

Chapter 8, by Romer provides an overview of the use of time series analysis for the NAES. This analysis uses data aggregated at the daily level to study effects of events during the election campaign or relations between variables measured on a daily basis. Many of the analytic techniques are borrowed from the literature on economic forecasting and may be more novel for readers than the approaches discussed in earlier chapters.

As noted earlier, a brief appendix of technical terms is provided so that readers can easily find definitions of concepts. The appendix is organized by chapter and by topic to help readers see the connections between concepts.

The codebook for the datasets found on the CD-ROM was written by Christopher Adasiewicz who also helped to coordinate the implementation of the survey.

NAES data are provided in the format used by the Statistical Package for the Social Sciences (SPSS), and most of the analyses we present use this program. However, we do not discuss specific details for using SPSS or other statistical programs for data analysis. Readers who are unfamiliar with SPSS or other statistical packages should consult the manuals of those programs for information about the procedures needed to run those programs.

We do not recommend the use of any particular statistical package for analysis of the NAES. Indeed, the data are also provided in tab-delimited format for easy importation into any statistical package. For the analysis covered in Chapter 8, readers will want to use packages that have specific procedures for time series analysis. SPSS can accommodate all of the analyses if the package includes the Trends module. Other packages that can also be used for time series data include the Statistical Analysis System (SAS), Eviews, and Matlab.

—Daniel Romer

Capturing Campaign Dynamics:
The National Annenberg Election Survey

Why the National Annenberg Election Survey?

Kathleen Hall Jamieson

Kate Kenski

DO CAMPAIGNS MATTER?

The presupposition of the NAES is that understanding campaign dynamics is important because campaigns do matter. Campaigns matter because they elect and because they forecast the positions the president will champion and the leadership capacities he or she will display in office. Much of the survey research on elections has asked: What determines individual voting decisions, and what determines who is elected? While important, these questions ignore the fact that campaigns are designed to elect someone who will lead. Survey questions about the character and competence of a candidate are not simply a vehicle for assessing comparative strategic advantages in gaining votes but are also a means of ascertaining what the public expects of the person who is elected. Nor is an understanding of issue positions simply of value in surmising why one candidate gained more votes, either popular or electoral, than the other. Conducting elections that forecast governance should be a goal of a democracy. Understanding what the public has and has not learned increases understanding of the expectations the citizenry brings to a presidency and at the same time invites us to identify ways to increase learning in campaigns.

What voters know about the candidates and their positions matters because the relationship among campaigning, voting, and governance makes it possible for the citizenry to hold those it elects accountable. By devoting considerable space to questions about what the public learned about candidates and their stands on issues, the NAES presupposes that accurate learning about both candidate similarities and differences is as important a goal for elections as actually deciding who wins or loses. The presence of an extensive battery of issue questions makes it possible to ask: Where did the campaigns confuse and where did they clarify the candidates' stands, and what did voters believe that the campaign of the winner had forecast for governance?

Of course, outcome matters as well. Scholars have long debated whether campaigns really make a difference to the outcome of elections. The first few decades of political research tended to find that there were two types of voters: those who decided before the campaigns began and those who decided at the last minute. Most fell into the former category, leaving researchers with the conclusion that few were truly affected by campaigns. According to Katz (1971), "Despite the many differences among countries and from election to election, typically about 80 percent, or more, of the voters have made up their minds about their vote before the campaign begins, that is at least several months prior to the election" (306).

Many models from political science suggest that one need not use information collected during a campaign to forecast the winner (for an overview of these models, see Holbrook 1996). Using economic indicators and presidential approval ratings prior to general election campaigns, the winners of several presidential elections have been predicted accurately. The 2000 presidential election is one of those elections in which the models failed. By most accounts, Gore should have won decisively.[1] Broder (2001) observes that

> a number of these political scientists have developed the notion that all that posturing and planning by candidates and managers, all the debate preparation, all the frantic flying from media market to media market and all the money spent from Labor Day to Election Day basically are wasted motions. Presidential elections, they maintain, are determined by fundamental factors, such as the performance of the economy earlier in the election year or the approval rating of the incumbent president or the degree of competition within the incumbent party's primaries.
>
> Because all these are measurable before Labor Day, they say, they can predict with confidence the outcome of the vote. It turns out they can't. These scholars' models missed Gore's minuscule 50.2 percent margin in the two-party popular vote by a statistical mile.

Some scholars argue that campaigns have an effect on voter choice by directing public opinion toward an equilibrium of candidate support that is determined prior to the campaign. "Campaigns do matter; they play a very important role in shaping public opinion during an election year and they contribute to the ultimate outcome," notes Holbrook. "But at the same time it is important to recognize that the political and economic context of the election can place parameters on the potential effect of the campaign" (1996, 158).

With the increased means of targeting voters and the weakened state of political party identification over the past few decades, researchers have found that greater numbers of the voters are making decisions during campaigns. In their investigation of when citizens decide, Chaffee and Rimal (1996) found that: "The determining factors are likely to arise from specific

---

[1] The March 2001 volume of *PS: Political Science & Politics* (vol. XXXIV, no. 1) contains articles that discuss how political science models fared in predicting the 2000 election.

circumstances, such as the number of candidates, availability of key information, and campaign tactics" (277). The variables that affect time of voting decision vary from one election to another. A similar conclusion was reached by Gopoian and Hadjiharalambous (1994), who found that looking across five presidential elections, "the events associated with particular campaigns are the major determinants of the composition of the late deciding electorate of a specific election" (71). Because there is always the possibility that a campaign will affect vote choice, the prospect of studying campaigns should not be dismissed before the campaigns have begun.

Popkin (1991) maintains that campaigns matter because they provide information about political candidates to voters. He states: "There is no denying that misperception is always present in campaigns. But it is also clear that campaign communications do affect choices, and that they generally make voters more, not less, accurate in their perceptions of candidates and issues" (40).

Many variables can be used as a test of whether or not campaigns matter. Do campaigns enhance citizens' interest in government and public affairs? Do Americans learn about candidate issue positions during political campaigns? Do campaigns affect vote choice? Regardless of the criterion used to determine whether or not campaigns matter, if one does not have data collected daily, some of these effects may be missed.

Locating Decisive Moments

Historians of presidential campaigns have long speculated about the importance of certain moments that may have turned the outcome in one direction rather than another. Unspoken in their analysis is the assumption that the outcome of presidential campaigns is not a foregone conclusion, that some moments are consequential where others are not, and that determining which moments mattered is important in making sense of who and how we elect and what it all means for those who govern and are governed.

Locked away in private archives are surveys conducted daily for past presidential candidates, but the kinds of daily tracking available from public polls provide answers to very few questions. For example, unanswered questions concerning the 1960 presidential campaign abound: Did Eisenhower's noncommittal response to a press conference question about Nixon's influence damage Nixon's chances? Did Kennedy's intervention to release Martin Luther King, Jr., from jail swing substantial votes his way? These are the sorts of information one might hope to glean from a well-done daily survey of the national public.

More questions follow from these: Did the Democratic ad exerpting Eisenhower's press conference create an impact separable from that of the press conference statement itself? Was any effect on black voters created by the news play of the action to free King or by the campaign communication that followed, or was any impact created from a synergy of news and ads? Larger social issues were at play in 1960 as well. How widespread was public awareness of, interest in, and responsiveness to Nixon's Quaker heritage and Kennedy's Catholic one? Did public acceptance of a Catholic or a Quaker president increase as the campaign progressed? Did any change in acceptance of a non-Protestant president extend beyond Catholics and Quakers?

Depending on their point of view, different scholars have featured the importance of different events in Kennedy's election. Unsurprisingly, the communication scholars who produced research for Sidney Kraus's *The Great Debates* (1962) saw the first debate as potentially decisive. In contrast, scholars focused on Kennedy's civil rights legacy emphasized the importance of the King endorsement (Wofford 1980).

Had a daily survey been in the field in the general election of 1960, could it have sorted any of this out? First, some history. Asked in a nationally televised press conference if he could give us an example of a major idea of Richard Nixon's that he had adopted, incumbent president Dwight D. Eisenhower responded, "If you give me a week I might think of one. I don't remember." That moment was then replayed in ads by Kennedy against Nixon in the '60 campaign (Jamieson 1996). Did that magnified moment move votes, and if so, were the numbers sufficient to give Kennedy the presidency?

Other factors favoring a Kennedy victory may also have been at work. That the black vote would go to Kennedy in 1960 was not a foregone conclusion. The Eisenhower administration had, after all, approved the first major civil rights act since reconstruction and had backed desegregation efforts with federal troops. At the same time, blacks who were overwhelmingly Baptist identified with a religious group fearful of the prospect of electing a Catholic president.

Had Kennedy carried the same percentage of the black vote that Stevenson garnered in 1956, he would have lost the election. In Illinois, for example, which Kennedy carried by 9,000 votes, over a quarter of a million blacks voted for the Massachusetts Senator.

Many historians believe that a shift toward Kennedy was precipitated by his call to Coretta King and his brother's call to a local judge—actions that, taken together, were credited by many in the civil rights movement with securing Martin Luther King's release from jail, where he was being held on charges stemming from a civil rights protest. What role if any did news coverage play? After all, once outside prison King stated, "I am deeply indebted to Senator Kennedy, who served as a great force in making my release possible. For him to be that courageous shows that he is really acting upon principle and not expediency." Did it matter that King's father told his congregation and with it the press, "I had expected to vote against Senator Kennedy because of his religion. . . . It took courage to call my daughter-in-law at a time like this. He has the moral courage to stand up for what he knows is right. I've got all my votes and I've got a suitcase and I'm going to take them up there and dump them in his lap." Did it matter that two million pamphlets containing endorsements from King were distributed outside black churches? What of the possible impact of ads carried on black radio? In one, civil rights leader Dr. Ralph Abernathy said that it was time "for all of us to take off our Nixon buttons because Kennedy did something great and wonderful when he personally called Mrs. Coretta King and helped free Dr. Martin Luther King, Jr. . . . Mr. Nixon could have helped but he refused to even comment on the case. Since Kennedy showed his great concern to humanity when he acted first without counting the cost, he has my whole-hearted support. This is the kind of man we need at this hour" (Jamieson 1996).

The religious dynamic in 1960 has also produced reams of speculation. In the two Eisenhower elections of the 1950s, the Catholic vote split 50-50 between the parties (Campbell, Converse, Miller, and Stokes 1966). One open question in 1960 was: Would Kennedy draw higher than expected numbers of votes from Catholics and drive Protestants even more into the embrace of the Republican party? Ultimately, Catholics voted 80-20 for Kennedy in 1960. "Calculating the normal vote to be expected of Catholics," Campbell and colleagues (1966) concluded that "one would expect at least a 63 percent Democratic margin among Catholics. The difference between 63 percent and the 80 percent which Kennedy achieved can provisionally be taken as an estimate of the increment in Democratic votes among Catholics above that which the normal Protestant Democratic presidential candidate could have expected" (87–88).

Working from a model inhospitable to communication effects and relying on data incapable of capturing them, Campbell and his colleagues could not address such questions as: Did Kennedy succeed in reframing questions of religion into ones of tolerance? Did messages from conservative Protestant ministers, arguing that a vote for Kennedy was a vote for the Pope, energize Catholic voters? What, if any, was the effect on Catholics and Protestants of Kennedy's speech to Baptist ministers at the Greater Houston Ministerial Association? To what extent was the impact of that event magnified by the repeated airing of it in predominantly Catholic areas that had defected to the Republicans in 1956? Higher than expected Catholic turnout in those regions may have been produced by simple religious identification. Alternatively, the Kennedy message may have capitalized on religious identification in ways that produced increased turnout and a vote shift to the Democrat.

Would a survey such as the National Annenberg Election Survey (NAES), a survey designed to capture campaign dynamics, have helped address the questions raised by the 1960 campaign? The answers indicate both the potential and the limitations of the NAES. The NAES uses a daily rolling cross-sectional (RCS) design to track changes in public opinion. The details of the design will be discussed in subsequent chapters. If consumption of news was tracked, exposure to the Eisenhower press conference assessed, and the media placement of the Democratic ad replaying the Eisenhower press conference logged, a daily sample of three hundred voters might have been sufficient to sort out the effects of the press conference and the ad. Tracking changes in public acceptance of a Catholic or a Quaker as a prospective president would also have posed no problem. Similarly, the impact of the King endorsement on the population of white voters could have been assessed.

However, confirming the effect of King's endorsement on the black vote would have proven impossible. Not only was this a relatively small population, but since potential black voters were widely disenfranchised in the South, the number able to vote was disproportionately low. Answering the question, "Did the King endorsement give Illinois to Kennedy?" poses the same problem we faced in Florida in the 2000 election. The size of the sample we drew in 2000 from any one state at any one point in time was simply too small to permit generalization to the state as a whole. And the number of African American voters drawn from within that sample created the equivalent of anecdotal evidence.

Even if done well and improved upon every four years, the NAES will leave unanswered a large number of tantalizing questions. However, three characteristics of contemporary politics make it possible to use the NAES to help sort out the impact of some forms of communication such as ads, news, and debates. First, ad effects can be teased out because in the most recent presidential general elections about half of the country received no paid presidential advertising. Second, debate effects can be isolated because a large part of the potential audience does not watch most of any debate. Third, the influence of news can be assessed because there are large differences in the amount of news watched and read by different parts of the public. If those effects change over time, daily tracking may capture movements in public opinion. So, for example, by comparing those who reported watching the first general election debate of 2000 to those who consumed news but not the debate, we can answer the question: Did the debate affect perception of Gore, or was the change in that perception reported in the national surveys only evident in nonviewers? Did the effect of debate-viewing decay over time? By examining Gore's standing day to day in the time period leading up to the first debate, we also can answer the question: Was his standing dropping in response to news coverage that preceded the debate, or did the decline begin with his first head-to-head confrontation with Bush?

DO COMMUNICATION DYNAMICS EXIST, AND, IF SO, CAN THE ROLLING CROSS-SECTIONAL DESIGN FIND THEM?

By giving us the tools to assess campaign dynamics, the design of the 2000 NAES allows us to study ways in which changes in exposure affect the other factors at play in an election. Scholars have argued that many individuals do not pay much attention to politics in between elections. As Election Day draws near, people begin paying more attention to politics. How much do

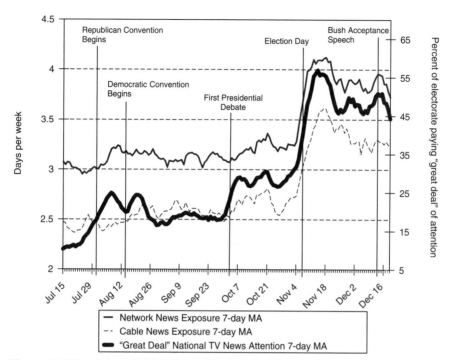

Figure 1.1 Network and Cable News Exposure and National Television News Attention from July 18 to December 19 (MA, moving average)

people in the United States watch and read campaign news during presidential elections? Does exposure vary over time, or is it constant? Is it the same for different types of media? From December 1999 to January 2001, the period covered by the NAES, exposure to news and attention to stories about the presidential candidates varied dramatically. NAES respondents were asked how many days in the past week they had watched network news and cable news. They were also asked to make a qualitative assessment about how much attention they had paid to national television news stories about the presidential campaign (pre-election) or presidential politics (post-election) in the past week. Figure 1.1 shows the responses to these television news exposure and attention questions across the general election and beyond at the daily level. Seven-day centered moving averages are used to smooth the data and reveal important campaign dynamics.[2] Interestingly, many people watched more television news and paid more attention to stories about presidential politics after Election Day, when the election was still undecided, than immediately before.

---

[2] The process of smoothing data will be discussed in Chapter 4.

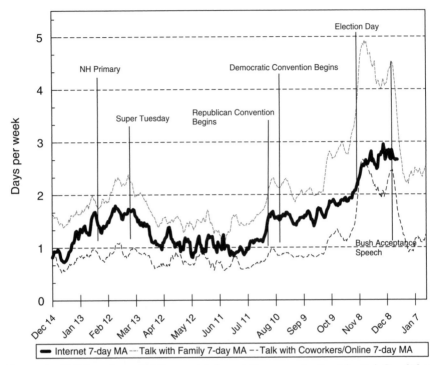

Figure 1.2 Talking about Politics and Internet Exposure to Presidential Candidate Information Across 2000 (MA, moving average)

What about other types of exposure to information? How did exposure to Internet information about the presidential candidates and talking about politics vary across the election? Since attention to television news about politics increased during the campaign, it would not be surprising if political conversation also increased as Election Day approached. Figure 1.2 makes further use of the data by looking at Internet use and talk about politics from December 14, 1999, to January 19, 2001. Respondents were asked how many days in the past week they had seen information about presidential politics online,[3] discussed politics with their family or friends, or discussed politics with people at work or on the Internet. Internet exposure to information about the candidates and talking about politics increased as Super Tuesday approached and then dropped off by mid-April. Increases appeared as the party conventions drew near and then leveled off for a spell. As Election Day approached, Internet use and talking about politics increased again. After Election Day failed to produce a decisive presidential winner, Internet use and talking about politics increased greatly. These examples demonstrate

---

[3] This question was asked to respondents who reported having Internet access.

that media exposure and talking about politics were not stable variables across the presidential campaign. The rolling cross-section (RCS) design has made it possible to capture the dynamic nature of these phenomena.

While communication dynamics exist, so too do unanticipated moments that elicit communication. An RCS design makes it possible to capture these moments as this book will explain. Who would have foreseen that the fate of a Cuban child, a decision about releasing oil from the petroleum reserve, or a conviction for driving under the influence of alcohol would play roles in the 2000 election? Making sense of such occurrences requires a survey that is in the field daily. If perceptions of the state of the economy are assumed to play an important role in the process by which voters make decisions, then having the ongoing capacity to capture shifts in the public perception of the economy is important as well.

More than forty years ago, Carl Hovland observed that cross-sectional surveys were unlikely to find short-term persuasion and opinion change (Hovland 1959). They are also unable to tie the impact of specific events to shifts in attitude. For example, writing about the 1988 campaign Abramson, Aldrich, and Rohde (1991) argued that "the vice-presidential candidates had an effect on the candidates, and vice versa" (530). They drew their evidence from the fact that in September and November of that year Bush dropped four points in favorability among Gallup respondents, Dukakis and Quayle dropped six, but Bentsen's ratings jumped by five points. What their data can't tell them is what role, if any, the debates played in producing those changes.

But even when the method involved located communication effects, scholars who weren't looking for them, missed them. Becker, McCombs, and McLeod (1975) showed that the pioneering Columbia researchers Lazarsfeld, Berelson, and Gaudet (1944) and Berelson, Lazarsfeld, and McPhee (1954) overlooked the fact that among voters who were exposed to media messages in opposition to their predispositions, substantial persuasion occurred. In addition, early studies showed an agenda-setting effect, although the scholars conducting the studies didn't interpret it as such. In fact, media exposure increased. If communication in campaigns mattered, most cross-sectional designs were ill equipped to capture or explain that fact. In 1984 the National Election Studies (NES) planning committee responded to these concerns with a weekly RCS design.[4] Decades later, those who looked

---

[4] The American National Election Study (1984), was conducted by The Center for Political Studies of the Institute for Social Research, under the general direction of Warren E. Miller. Santa Traugott was the director of studies. Board members during the planning phase of the 1984 NES included Ray Wolfinger (chair), Richard A. Brody, Heinz Eulau, Morris P. Fiorina, Stanley Kelley, Jr., Donald R. Kinder, David R. Mayhew, Warren E. Miller (ex officio), David O. Sears, and Merrill Shanks. The 1984 NES planning committee included several NES board members (Kinder, chair; Brody; Kelley; Miller, ex officio; Sears; and Wolfinger) and three other scholars, Stanley Feldman, Ethel Klein, and Steven J. Rosenstone.

for communication effects through the lens provided by an RCS design found them. In their path-breaking studies of Canadian elections, Richard Johnston, André Blais, Henry E. Brady, and Jean Crête (1992) confirmed that the RCS could detect debate effects. Drawing on the lessons he and his colleagues learned in their Canadian work, Richard Johnston wrote the protocols for the NAES and supervised their implementation.

Begun in November 1999 and carried through inauguration day 2001, the National Annenberg Election Survey was an attempt to transcend the limitations of cross-sectional surveys with a daily assessment of the knowledge, dispositions, beliefs, and behavior of the U.S. electorate. The survey was designed to ascertain how elections work and to permit scholars to draw inferences about the ways in which they forecast governance. In the following chapters and the accompanying CD-ROM, Dan Romer, Kate Kenski, Paul Waldman, and Chris Adasiewicz explain the design, uses, and analyses of the NAES. The 2004 NAES will be put in the field in November 2003.

REFERENCES

Abramson, Paul R., John H. Aldrich, and David W. Rohde. 1991. *Change and continuity in the 1988 elections.* Washington, DC: Congressional Quarterly Inc.

Becker, Lee B., Maxwell A. McCombs, and Jack M. McLeod. 1975. The development of political cognitions. In *Political communication,* ed. S. Chaffee. London: Sage.

Broder, David S. 2001. Why election predictors bombed. *Washington Post,* April 8, p. B7.

Berelson, Bernard, Paul Lazarsfeld, and William McPhee. 1954. *Voting.* Chicago: University of Chicago Press.

Campbell, Angus, Philip E. Converse, Warren E. Miller, and Donald E. Stokes. 1966. *Elections and the political order.* New York: John Wiley & Sons.

Chaffee, Steven H., and Rajiv Nath Rimal. 1996. Time of vote decision and openness to persuasion. In *Political persuasion and attitude change,* Diana C. Mutz, Paul M. Sniderman, and Richard A. Brody, ed. 267–91. Ann Arbor: The University of Michigan Press.

Gopoian, J. David, and Sissie Hadjiharalambous. 1994. Late-deciding voters in presidential elections. *Political Behavior* 16(1):55–78.

Holbrook, Thomas M. 1996. *Do campaigns matter?.* Thousand Oaks, CA: Sage.

Hovland, Carl. 1959. Reconciling conflicting results derived from experimental and survey studies of attitude change. *American Psychologist* 14:8–17.

Jamieson, Kathleen H. 1996. *Packaging the presidency.* New York: Oxford University Press.

Johnston, Richard, André Blais, Henry E. Brady, and Jean Crête. 1992. *Letting the people decide: Dynamics of a Canadian election.* Stanford, CA: Stanford University Press.

Katz, Elihu. 1971. Platforms & windows: Broadcasting's role in election campaigns. *Journalism Quarterly* 48:304–14.

Kraus, Sidney. 1962. *The great debates.* Bloomington: Indiana University Press.

Lazarsfeld, Paul, Bernard Berelson, and Hazel Gaudet. 1944. *The people's choice.* New York: Columbia University Press.

Miller, Warren E., and the National Election Studies. 1999. National Election Studies, 1984, Continuous Monitoring Project [dataset]. Ann Arbor: University of Michigan, Center for Political Studies [producer and distributor].

Popkin, Samuel L. 1991. *The reasoning voter: Communication and persuasion in presidential campaigns.* Chicago: The University of Chicago Press.

Wofford, Harris. 1980. *Of Kennedys and kings.* New York: Farrar, Straus and Giroux.

2

Survey Procedures, Content, and Dataset Overview

Paul Waldman

INTRODUCTION

The 2000 National Annenberg Election Survey is the largest public opinion study of the American electorate ever conducted. For fourteen months during the 2000 presidential campaign and after the election, U.S. residents were interviewed by telephone about their perceptions and behaviors relevant to the campaign as well as the political system generally. Interviews were conducted with over 79,000 respondents; because some respondents were interviewed multiple times, in total more than 100,000 interviews were conducted. The surveys were commissioned jointly by the Annenberg School for Communication and the Annenberg Public Policy Center of the University of Pennsylvania.

The centerpiece of the 2000 National Annenberg Election Survey (NAES) is the national rolling cross-section study, which ran continuously from mid-December 1999—just before the height of the presidential primary election season—through mid-January 2001, after the dispute over whether George W. Bush or Al Gore won the election and just before Bush's inauguration. A total of 58,000 respondents were interviewed in the national rolling cross-section.

Additional surveys were also conducted around primary elections in early 2000, also using a rolling format. As a result, the CD-ROM includes separate datasets containing Iowa residents, New Hampshire residents, South Carolina residents, Michigan residents, those in states holding primaries on Super Tuesday (March 7), and those in states with primaries on what we refer to as Second Tuesday, the March 14 primaries held in six states.

After their interview for a cross-section study, some respondents were reinterviewed to form pre-post panels around key campaign events: the presidential primary elections, the summer Republican and Democratic presidential nominating conventions, the fall Bush-Gore debates, and the November general election. The CD-ROM thus contains three groups of datasets: the national rolling cross-section, the supplemental primary studies, and the panel studies. See Table 2.1 for sample sizes in each component.

TABLE 2.1 Sample Sizes

National Rolling Cross-section	Rolling Cross-section	58,373
National panels	Pre-post Republican Convention	1,197
	Pre-post Democratic Convention	1,230
	Pre-post first debate	1,514
	Pre-post second debate	670
	Pre-post third debate	2,052
	Pre-post general election	6,508
Pre-primary rolling cross-sections	Iowa	3,173
	New Hampshire	3,814
	Super Tuesday	6,627
Pre-primary cross-sections	Second Tuesday	1,591
	South Carolina	1,171
	Michigan	388
Pre-post primary panels	Iowa	1,596
	New Hampshire	1,900
	Super Tuesday	3,853
	South Carolina	503
	Michigan	145
Add-on studies	November 1999 cross-section	2,486
	New Hampshire post-primary cross-section	1,835
TOTALS	Respondents	79,458
	Interviews	100,626

SAMPLING AND INTERVIEWING PROTOCOLS

Fieldwork for all cross-section interviews and reinterviews, with the exception of interviewing for the South Carolina and Michigan state-specific studies, was conducted by Schulman, Ronca & Bucuvalas of New York and Ft. Myers, Florida. Interviewing for the South Carolina and Michigan studies was conducted by Princeton Data Source of Fredericksburg, Virginia. All fieldwork was conducted under the direction of Princeton Survey Research Associates. Interviews were conducted in Spanish at the respondent's request. In the national cross-section, approximately 2.3% of the interviews were conducted in Spanish.

Rolling Cross-Section Sampling

Each respondent was initially interviewed for the NAES as part of a cross-section study. Respondents were selected for cross-section study samples via a two-stage process. First, households were selected by randomly generating telephone numbers. Area code, exchange, and bank, representing the first eight digits of a ten-digit phone number, were randomly generated proportional to telephone company estimates of the count of residential numbers in each combination of area code, exchange, and bank. The last two digits of each phone number were generated entirely at random.

Second, at each sampled number that was determined to represent a household, and at which the household agreed to participate, interviewers randomly selected one of the adult residents to interview. Upon calling a household, interviewers asked to speak with any adult, who was then asked how many adults live in the household. If two adults lived in the household, either the younger or older adult was randomly chosen to be interviewed. If three adults lived in the household, one of the three was randomly chosen by age: youngest, middle, oldest. If four or more adults lived in the household, either the adult with the most recent or next birthday was chosen to be interviewed.

To maximize response rates and thus the randomness of the survey, we were extremely aggressive in seeking out respondents. The ongoing nature of the survey allowed us to make repeated attempts to reach the households that our sampling protocol had generated. Interviewers called each sampled telephone number up to twenty times over fourteen days until (1) the number was determined out of service or not a number linked to a residence, (2) the number was determined linked to a residence but no one at the residence agreed to participate, (3) it was determined that no one at the residence was eligible to be interviewed, (4) an interview was completed at the residence with an eligible respondent, or (5) the number was not resolved by the time fourteen days had elapsed from the date of the first call to the number.

If a household refused to participate, it was scheduled to be called back by a specially trained interviewer who would attempt to elicit participation. Additionally, if a respondent started but stopped an interview, additional attempts were made to recontact the respondent and complete the interview.

All cross-section studies, with the exception of the South Carolina and Michigan pre-Republican presidential primary election cross-sections, were fielded as rolling cross-section samples. New randomly generated telephone numbers were added on a strict schedule to the pool of numbers interviewers were calling to attempt to complete interviews. On each day of fieldwork, a set count of new numbers was added, proportional to the desired count of interviews completed daily. The intention was to maximize the representativeness of any single day's interviewing sample by stabilizing the proportion of respondents interviewed who completed an interview after having been called only a few times and those who completed after having been tried numerous times.

Consequently, the day on which a respondent was interviewed may for purposes of analysis be considered a random event. With the exception of the first few days of interviewing, each day of the survey contains an approximately proportional number of respondents reached on the first attempt, the second attempt, and so on as any other day of the survey. This unique feature of the rolling cross-section method makes the data a true time series.

Reinterview Sampling

To construct our panels, we randomly selected reinterview samples from the cross-section samples. For example, the sample of respondents interviewed August 4–13 for the post-Republican presidential nominating convention reinterview is a random subset of the respondents interviewed July 21–30 for the national cross-section.

In cross-section interviews, respondents' first names were collected. For reinterviewing, interviewers asked for respondents by name and confirmed that the right respondent was selected by asking sex and age and comparing these with the data recorded in the cross-section interview. Interviewers called each sampled reinterview respondent up to twenty times to attempt to complete an interview. Respondents sampled for reinterviews were attempted in random order.

Response Rates

The question of response rates is of significant concern to any researcher employing survey data, particularly data gathered via telephone. While in-person surveys generate substantially higher response rates, carrying out a survey of the size and scope of the NAES using in-person interviews would be prohibitively expensive and time-consuming. Response rates for the NAES were comparable to those obtained by most contemporary telephone surveys in both the cooperation rate—the proportion of respondents who agreed to participate in the survey once they had been successfully reached by an interviewer—and the overall response rate, which accounts for both refusals and those potential participants interviewers were unable to contact despite repeated attempts. The cooperation rate for the national sample was 53%, while the response rate was 31%. It should also be noted that the samples obtained by the NAES are very similar to the populations from which the samples were drawn in nearly all respects (see "Sample Weighting").

Researchers interested in response rates for the various components of the survey should consult the file on the CD-ROM labeled "Response rates.pdf." This file utilizes the "response rate calculator" devised by the American Association for Public Opinion Research (AAPOR), with figures for the NAES included. The AAPOR calculator provides four separate formulas by which response rates may be calculated.

Daily Interviews

During the height of the presidential primary campaign, on average one hundred national cross-section interviews were completed daily, and these were supplemented by hundreds of interviews daily for state-specific cross-sections and reinterviews to form pre-post presidential primary election panels.

From mid-July through Election Day, on average three hundred national cross-section interviews were completed daily, plus hundreds of reinterviews daily around the presidential nominating conventions and Bush-Gore debates, to form pre-post panels. Those researchers interested in tracking daily changes during the campaign might concentrate on this period, where sample sizes are largest.

During November and much of December 2000, the period of the disputed Florida vote, on average one hundred national cross-section interviews were completed daily, and this was accompanied by reinterviews of 6,500 respondents interviewed before the November election, to form a pre-post general election panel.

SAMPLE WEIGHTING

Public opinion researchers often choose to apply weights to their data to account for discrepancies between the sample obtained through interviewing and the actual makeup of the population from which the sample is being drawn. A weight variable is provided in the NAES dataset if researchers choose to use it. However, before applying weights a number of cautions should be noted.

First, the use of weights is only appropriate when reporting simple data presentations, such as the percentage of respondents who answered a particular question in a particular way. However, when conducting multivariate techniques such as regression analysis, any or all of the variables can be held constant in the analysis without resorting to weighting.

Second, the weight provided in the NAES was defined for the entire survey period of the relevant dataset, for example, the entire rolling cross-section, the entire Iowa sample, the entire New Hampshire sample, and so on. However, due to sampling variation, weights for smaller time periods may be different, since each finite time period represents its own sample with slightly different characteristics. If a researcher chooses to examine, for instance, responses during the month of October 2000, he or she would have to calculate weights that reflect the makeup of the sample assembled during that period. If weights are to be applied to different subsamples, they must be calculated anew.

The weight variable in the dataset accounts for the number of adults in each respondent's household (since more adults decreases the chance that a particular individual will be selected) and the number of voice lines in the respondent's household (since more lines increases the chance that an individual will be selected), along with the commonly used demographic variables of gender, age, race, education, and region.

If researchers wish to calculate weights for subsamples, they should consult the file labeled "Weighting targets.xls" on the CD-ROM. This file contains tables for each of the data sets, summarizing both the characteristics of each dataset and the characteristics of the American population based on the latest census data available at the time the surveys were conducted. It should be noted that these census data are 1998 projections of 2000 population; if researchers would like to update them with data from the 2000 census, they should visit www.census.gov to obtain updated figures.

As can be seen from the tables in the Excel file, the sampling of the 2000 NAES was highly accurate in reflecting the demographic makeup of the population, with one significant exception common to telephone surveys: the education variable. The sample contains fewer individuals of lower education than the population and more individuals of high education. Researchers reporting simple analyses of variables that are expected to correlate with education should thus consider applying weights. Nonetheless, preliminary analyses indicate that even on variables that correlate highly with education—for example, the political knowledge batteries—applying the weight variable produces extremely small differences in results.

The use of weights is not an uncontroversial topic among public opinion researchers, and the creators of the 2000 NAES take no position on whether researchers should or should not apply weights when performing their own data analysis. We do, however, strongly recommend that the application of weights be done with care to ensure that the proper weight is applied to the proper subsample.

MISSING DATA

Although the occurrence of missing data is quite infrequent in the NAES, researchers should be aware of the different types of missing data present in the files. Because the presence of missing data can introduce biases into analyses, researchers should either recode the data or consider using maximum likelihood estimation procedures (which estimate the effects of missing data) or multiple imputation procedures (see Allison 2001 for a discussion of these approaches).

All questions in the data files have codes for missing values. If a respondent answered "don't know" to a question, the response is coded as 998. If a respondent refused to answer a question—an extremely infrequent occurrence, but one that emerges on a few items such as income—the response is coded as 999. If a particular question was not asked of a particular respondent, it is coded as 991. This occurred either in the case of items in which the sample was randomly split to receive different sets of questions or in cases where a previous response eliminated the need to ask a question. For instance, if a respondent during the primaries indicated that he did not recognize Steve Forbes, he would not be asked to give Forbes a thermometer rating, and would therefore be coded 991 for the thermometer question.

THE CD-ROM

The CD-ROM contains two groups of files. The first group is the data files, in both SPSS format and a tab-delimited format, which can be imported into other statistical packages. The second group is the codebook files, which contain all the pertinent information concerning the survey questionnaire. Table 2.2 details the names and contents of each data file.

There are two codebook files on the CD-ROM, both of which may be read with Adobe Acrobat. The principle file researchers will be using is entitled "Main Codebook." It contains detailed information on every question asked in the NAES. The second file is entitled "Main Codebook Annex B." This file contains the various versions of the questionnaire as they were asked by the telephone interviewers, so that researchers can view the order in which questions were asked.

Using the Main Codebook, researchers can examine the text of questions, response categories, the timing of questions, and form splits where they occurred. This information is organized into a variety of tables for reference. The codebook contains an introduction that details the format of the tables and the manner in which entries should be read. Although the codebook is quite lengthy at over seven hundred pages, its organization should enable users to quickly find the items in which they are interested.

In addition, the CD-ROM contains a simple search engine, called NAES Search, that allows for quick keyword searching of the codebook.

THE QUESTIONNAIRE

Throughout the fourteen months of interviewing and across the different interviewing components, the questionnaires administered to respondents were a mix of questions common to large segments of the fieldwork and questions specific to small subsets. For example, core sets of questions about evaluations of candidates and the respondent's positions on policy issues were asked for most interviews. But highly event-tailored questions were asked around conventions and debates. And after Election Day, roughly half of the questionnaire was devoted to the disputed Florida vote.

As the 2000 election progressed, the survey designers attempted to reconcile two conflicting needs: on one hand, to maintain as many questions as possible throughout the period the survey was in the field so as to maximize the utility of the time series, and on the other hand, to respond to campaign events and issues as they arose. Consequently, while the majority of

TABLE 2.2 Data Files

		Contents	File Name
Cross-section studies	*National Rolling Cross-Section*	Interviewing December 14, 1999–April 3, 2000	Nat CS 19991214–20000403 Data.sav
		April 4–July 17	Nat CS 20000404–20000717 Data.sav
		July 18–September 4	Nat CS 20000718–20000904 Data.sav
		September 5–October 2	Nat CS 20000905–20001002 Data.sav
		October 3–November 6	Nat CS 20001003–20001106 Data.sav
		November 8–January 19, 2001	Nat CS 20001108–20010119 Data.sav.
		Iowa pre-presidential primary election cross-section	IA CS Data.sav
		New Hampshire pre-primary	NH CS Data.sav
		Super Tuesday states	Super CS Data.sav
		Second Tuesday states	Sec CS Data.sav
		South Carolina pre-Republican presidential primary	SC CS Data.sav
		Michigan pre-Republican presidential primary	MI CS Data.sav
Panel studies		Iowa pre-post presidential primary election panel	IA Panel Data.sav.exe
		New Hampshire pre-post primary	NH Panel Data.sav.exe
		Super Tuesday states	Super Panel Data.sav.exe
		South Carolina pre-post Republican primary	SC Panel Data.sav.exe
		Michigan pre-post Republican primary	MI Panel Data.sav.exe
		Pre-post Republican convention	GOP Conv Panel Data.sav
		Pre-post Democratic convention	Dem Conv Panel Data.sav
		Pre-post October 3 Bush-Gore Debate	3 Oct Deb Panel Data.sav
		Pre-post October 11 debate	11 Oct Deb Panel Data.sav
		Pre-post October 17 debate	17 Oct Deb Panel Data.sav
		Pre-post general election	Elect Panel Data.sav
		New Hampshire post-primary cross-section	NH Post CS Data.sav

the questions remained on the survey through all or most of the survey period, many other questions were asked for finite periods of time. For instance, in late 1999 it was not apparent that prescription drug coverage for senior citizens would be a topic of discussion during the campaign; when it emerged as an issue in the summer of 2000, questions were added about the respondent's position and his or her knowledge of the candidates' positions.

The conflict between maintaining a time series and addressing new issues arises because of an inherent limitation of telephone interviewing: There is only so long a researcher can reasonably ask a subject to remain on the phone. After a certain point, respondents tend to become impatient and seek to terminate the interview. Consequently, NAES interviews were limited to thirty minutes. To allow for a greater number of questions to be asked, at various times the sample was split into groups that would receive different sets of questions on some topics. The "Main Codebook" file on the CD-ROM contains a detailed explanation, in Section X, of the various splits that were used.

This approach has benefits and drawbacks. While the number of questions increases, the number of respondents answering each of the questions in the split variable groups declines. Whether this presents a problem for those analyzing the data depends on the nature of the changes being examined and whether time is used as an independent variable. For instance, in its later stages the national cross-section interviewed approximately 300 respondents per night, meaning that a question asked of half the sample would have only 150 respondents per night. At this rate, it would be difficult to identify a change in responses that occurred on one particular day. However, if one were looking for changes in responses that occurred over a period of weeks or months, the smaller sample would not present any problems.

Table 2.3, the Variable Categories table, shows the categories of variables included in the survey. Some of these categories contain only a few variables, while others contain dozens. The variable names in the data file use these letters as prefixes, along with the letter C or R, for cross-section and reinterview. For example, all the demographic variable names in the cross-sections begin with the letters "cW." Refer to the codebook file on the CD-ROM for specific variable names, descriptions, and response categories.

Evaluations of Candidates, Political Figures, and Groups

One of the key goals of the 2000 NAES was to track the evolution of opinions of the presidential candidates as the campaign progressed. To that end, a variety of questions probed respondents' views on the candidates, ranging from the general to the specific. Respondents were asked to rate the candidates on a "feeling thermometer," a scale ranging from 0 to 100. If respondents did not know enough about a candidate to give a rating, they were coded as 102. This response can be used to create an awareness vari-

TABLE 2.3 Variable Categories

0	Sampling		C	Evaluations of groups
A	Evaluations of candidates and political figures (favorability, traits, political ideology, one-word descriptors)		D	Candidates' biographies (perceptions of presidential and vice presidential candidates)
B	Policy issues (respondent's positions, perceptions of candidates' positions and candidates' competencies, knowledge of background facts)		E	Media use
	BA	Economy	F	Debates (presidential primary, Bush-Gore, and Cheney-Lieberman)
	BB	Taxes	G	Presidential nominating conventions
	BC	Social Security	H	Advertising, TV appearances, and speeches
	BD	Education	J	Contact with presidential campaigns
	BE	Health insurance	K	Political participation (interest, discussion, advocacy for candidates)
	BF	Abortion	L	Evaluations of campaign discourse
	BG	Crime	M	Orientation to government (evaluations of institutions, political efficacy)
	BH	Money in politics	N	Presidential candidate chances (of winning the primary and general elections)
	BJ	National defense	P	Presidential candidate endorsements
	BK	Immigration	R	Voting behavior and general attitudes (registration, intended and actual voting in the presidential primary and general election, general attitudes and behaviors)
	BL	Gay rights	S	Election outcome and disputed Florida vote
	BM	Other civil rights	T	Expectations of Bush presidency and approval of transition
	BN	Energy	U	U.S. House and Senate (incumbents and challengers: favorability, name recall, vote choice)
	BP	Poverty	V	Political orientation
	BQ	Elian Gonzalez	W	Demographics
	BR	South Carolina Confederate flag	X	Random assignment to question modules
	BS	Environment	Y	Interviewer attributes
	BT	Other		

able that measures how well a candidate was known. If respondents were unaware of the candidate, they were not asked the following group of questions, which asked how well a series of trait descriptions described each candidate, including "honest," "inspiring," "knowledgeable," and "cares about people like me." Respondents also assessed how conservative or liberal they found each candidate. As with other categories, in the primaries these questions were asked about Al Gore, Bill Bradley, George Bush, John McCain, and Steve Forbes.

For the less competitive primary candidates—Gary Bauer and Alan Keyes—the NAES asked questions about vote intention, endorsements, and candidate contact. Other candidates—Elizabeth Dole, Lamar Alexander, Dan Quayle, Bob Smith, Orrin Hatch—dropped out of the race before the survey went in the field in the fall of 1999. As the candidates who remained dropped out of the primary race, questions about them were dropped from the survey.

Although space did not allow for a full battery of questions regarding every potentially important political figure, respondents were asked to give a favorability rating to Gary Bauer and Alan Keyes during the primaries and to Bill Clinton, Pat Buchanan, Ralph Nader, Ross Perot, and vice presidential candidates Joe Lieberman and Dick Cheney.

To widen the degree to which each respondent's political outlook could be assessed, questions were also asked about their feelings toward a range of groups, including labor unions, corporations, drug companies, the National Rifle Association, the feminist movement, and various demographic and religious groups.

Policy Issues: Measuring Knowledge and Opinion

One of the key questions the rolling cross-sectional design enables us to answer is how much Americans knew about the candidates as the campaign progressed. When combined with demographic and behavioral variables including media use and political discussion, these measures will enable researchers to investigate the process by which citizens learn about candidates over the course of the campaign.

To that end, we included a series of questions about the candidates' positions on issues that confront the federal government. Respondents were read an issue position, then asked whether the candidate supported or opposed it. The list of issues contains some that are more commonly known and some that are more obscure, some that were prominent during the campaign and some that were not. Consequently, the issue battery enables researchers to construct issue knowledge scales that include both easy and difficult questions, allowing for discrimination between people at different knowledge levels.

We also sought to ascertain how familiar voters were with the candidates by asking questions about their biographies, for example, which candidate was a state governor, which had been a prisoner of war in Vietnam, and which had been a professional basketball player. Respondents were asked to compare Bush, McCain, and Forbes with each other and Gore and Bradley with each other during the primaries, then asked to compare Bush and Gore during the general election. In the general election, voters were asked to compare Bush and Gore on who would "do a better job" on various issues, regardless of their choice for president. Other Republican candidates—Elizabeth Dole, Lamar Alexander, and Dan Quayle—dropped out of the race before the survey went into the field. A decision was also made that the electoral chances of candidates Alan Keyes, Gary Bauer, and Orrin Hatch were too remote to warrant multiple questions. Therefore, we included them in questions about vote intention, endorsements, and contact with candidates, but did not ask about their issue positions.

To provide a measure of knowledge unrelated to the candidates, we asked a set of questions testing awareness of background facts related to policy issues, including the most common tax bracket, the amount of the minimum wage, whether the trade deficit had risen in the year prior to the survey, the proportion of pregnancies that end in abortion, the number of Americans without health insurance, and the cost of ethanol subsidies. These questions were asked only during the primaries.

The survey also includes a rating made by the interviewer of each respondent's political knowledge, on a scale of A (excellent) to F (very poor). Although this measure is obviously subjective, it has been used in past surveys, including the National Election Studies (NES), and has been found to provide a reasonable summary of a respondent's political knowledge.

To integrate data on people's beliefs about where the candidates stood with data on their own opinions, we asked a matched set of questions covering the same issues to explore the respondents' opinions. These questions used identical wording as the candidate questions. We also asked a battery of questions about government priorities that allow for a comprehensive analysis of each respondent's political beliefs and perspectives. Based on research conducted by Merrill Shanks and his colleagues, these issue questions explore respondents' views by asking four types of questions. The first asks how serious a problem the respondent finds various conditions, such as the number of Americans without health insurance or the amount of money Americans pay in taxes. The second set asks whether the government should or should not take a specified action related to the issue. The third asks how much effort the respondent believes the government should put into addressing a given issue—more than it currently does, less than it does, the same amount, or none at all. The fourth set of questions asks the respondent whether the government should spend more, less, the same amount, or no money addressing the problem.

In sum, this portion of the survey contains five types of questions:

- The respondent's own positions on policy issues
- Perceptions of presidential candidates' positions on policy issues
- Evaluations of candidates' competencies in policy areas
- Knowledge of candidate biographies
- Perceptions of background facts relevant to policy issues

In addition, respondents were asked standard questions about their political orientations: their party identifications and whether they consider themselves conservative or liberal.

Media Use

A central goal of the 2000 National Annenberg Election Survey was to enable analysis of media effects over the course of a campaign. In the past, researchers using post-election cross-sectional surveys have been largely unsuccessful in locating media effects, despite the common belief in the media's power and influence. The designers of the NAES believed that part of this difficulty results from the fact that by the time a post-election survey goes into the field, a campaign has gone through many twists and turns; by watching the campaign evolve, media effects may be more apparent.

Although self-reported measures of media use have shortcomings that are well known to survey researchers, in the context of a telephone survey there is little choice but to ask people how much they use various news media. Like many other surveys, the NAES asks respondents how many days in the week prior to being interviewed they used the following news sources: newspaper, national television news, cable news, local television news, talk radio, and the Internet. Those who read the newspaper or listened to talk radio were asked which newspaper and which radio host. In addition, respondents were asked how much attention they paid to stories about the presidential campaign in each of these media.

In addition, there are a few questions touching on media issues that appear in other sections of the survey. For instance, respondents interviewed after the election graded the news media's overall performance and answered questions specific to media coverage of the Florida conflict.

Advertisements

Although previous research has indicated that survey respondents are somewhat unreliable in their ability to recall political advertisements they have seen, the 2000 NAES attempted to gain some measures of exposure to political ads. For a period during the general election, respondents were asked general questions about ads for Bush and Gore—whether they had seen any, which candidate they had seen discussed more in the ads, and whether they recalled the ads saying more positive or more negative things about each candidate. During the primaries, respondents to the primary rolling cross-section studies (Iowa, New Hampshire, and Super Tuesday) were asked questions about specific advertisements that were receiving heavy buys and generating news discussion.

Campaign Events: Debates and Conventions

One of the questions commonly posed by journalists and researchers is whether campaign debates make a difference. Although primary debates are generally not shown on national broadcast networks and audiences for general election debates have steadily declined, the events are nonetheless given great attention in the press both before and after they occur. The NAES allows exploration of debate effects in both the primary and general election campaigns.

The 2000 primary campaign saw an unusual number of debates on both the Republican and Democratic sides. The survey asked all respondents during the primary period whether they had heard or read anything about the primary debates and, if they had, whether they had watched any. In addition, as each debate occurred respondents interviewed over the next few days were asked whether they had heard anything about the debate and whether they had seen it. Questions of this type were asked for eight Republican primary debates and seven debates between Al Gore and Bill Bradley, including a joint appearance the two made on *Nightline*.

The general election debates were given substantially more attention by the NAES. Respondents were asked whether they watched each debate, how much of it they watched, whom they believed performed better, whether each candidate performed as well as they had expected, and which network they viewed the debate on. Respondents who did not see any of a debate were asked whom they heard had won. These questions were asked for all three debates between Al Gore and George Bush, while for the debate between Dick Cheney and Joe Lieberman, respondents were asked only whether they saw the debate, how much of it they watched, and whom they believed performed better.

Researchers interested in debate effects should also look to the panel studies conducted around these events and review the examples contained in Chapter 7. Many respondents were interviewed multiple times before and after the conventions, the debates, and Election Day. Further details on these panel studies may be found on the CD-ROM.

When other important televised events occurred, the survey asked respondents whether they had seen them. These included Bush and Gore's appearances on Oprah Winfrey's talk show and President Clinton's 2000 State of the Union speech.

Campaign Participation

The designers of the NAES elected in a few cases to adopt question wording that had proved fruitful in the NES. As in a number of other areas of the survey, this duplication will allow interested researchers to explore methodological issues surrounding the NES and the NAES, including testing the volatility over time of variables that on the NES are necessarily assumed not to be time-dependent and comparing responses on a national telephone survey to a national in-person survey (most of the NES interviews are conducted in person). Many of the questions in the area of campaign participation were taken from the NES.

It should be noted that while in these cases there is at least one question with identical or nearly identical wording to the NES, in most cases there are additional variants of the question particular to the NAES. For instance, while the NES asks: "Did you go to any political meetings, rallies, speeches, dinners, or things like that in support of a particular candidate?" the NAES varied the question according to the time being asked. A question with the same wording preceded by "During the campaign . . ." was asked through the cross-section, while in post-primary panel reinterviews, respondents were asked whether they had done so "in the presidential primary campaign." In other cases, respondents were asked whether they had participated in a given way in the week prior to being interviewed; those interviewed after Election Day were asked whether they had participated in this way at all during the campaign.

The questions with identical or nearly identical wording to the NES participation battery are whether the respondent tried to convince someone else how to vote (k13, k14, k15); attended political meetings or rallies (k16, k17, k18); did any other work for the parties or candidates (k19, k20, k21); made a campaign contribution (k22, k23, k24); and wore a button, put a sticker on his or her car, or placed a sign on his or her lawn (k25, k26, k27).

Campaign Contact

The survey sought to answer the question of what kind of a difference campaign contact made in voters' opinions and choices. This was of particular interest in the New Hampshire and Iowa primaries, where voters receive an extraordinary amount of attention not only from the campaigns but from the candidates themselves. While most citizens will never encounter a presidential candidate in person, many residents of these two states will have the opportunity to meet and talk with numerous candidates as their primary votes are sought. Over one in ten of our New Hampshire respondents of whom we asked the question met a presidential candidate during the 2000 primary season.

Of course, many more will be contacted by the campaigns in other ways: with a knock on the door, a phone call, or a piece of direct mail, among others. Because interest groups on both the left and right are becoming increasingly involved in voter contact, we asked respondents not only whether they had been contacted by the campaigns in these ways but also whether other groups had contacted them as well.

Political Interest and Discussion

Researchers have used various measures to assess individuals' level of political awareness and engagement. Although the debate on the best means of doing so is far from resolved, the NAES allows the question to be approached from a variety of angles. Those who favor political knowledge as a surrogate for involvement have ample measures from which to choose in the NAES. More direct questions were also asked; respondents told how much they "follow what is going on in government and public affairs" and described their interest in the 2000 campaign and how much they cared which party won the election.

A series of items on political discussion was also included, tapping discussion both among intimates (family and friends) and those with whom the respondent was not as close (at work or online). In both cases, respondents were asked not only how often they engaged in political discussion but also how much disagreement those discussions contained. These items will allow researchers to gauge the degree of political concordance and dissonance in the social environments in which respondents are situated.

Evaluations of Campaign Discourse

Because the 2000 National Annenberg Election Survey is focused in significant part on the role of communication in politics, the survey includes a number of items in which respondents gave their impressions of the campaign itself. They described how much the candidates were discussing issues, how much they were talking about their own plans, and how much they were criticizing their opponents; whether the 2000 campaign was more negative than those of the past; and whether Bush or Gore was waging the more negative campaign. They also gave grades to the candidates and the news media for how responsibly they were acting and told whether they felt they had learned enough to cast a vote. Given the recent attention to the subject of negative campaigning, these items should be of interest to many researchers.

Orientation to Government

Another topic of recent interest is what we refer to as orientation to government, combining trust in government, cynicism, and political efficacy. Respondents answered a range of questions, some of which are in similar formats to those that have been asked on past surveys. Trust questions included how often one can trust the federal government to do the right thing and how much confidence one has in various branches of government. Cynicism questions included whether presidents keep their promises, whether candidates say what they think the public wants to hear, and whether candidates vote the way their contributors want. Efficacy questions included whether "people like me" have a say over who is president, whether politics too complicated to understand, and whether officials care what "people like me" think.

Assessments of Candidate Chances

Previous research in electoral campaigns, particularly in primaries, has pointed to the importance of momentum in moving votes. That is, perceptions of candidates can be swayed by which candidate is perceived to be ahead and which behind, which gaining and which faltering. To capture the dynamics of this process, the NAES included items asking respondents to assess each candidate's chances of victory. During the primaries, respondents were asked the two sets of questions. The first asked the respondents to rate each candidate's chances of gaining his party's nomination on a scale of 1 to 100. The second posited potential general election match-ups (for example, if John McCain were to face Bill Bradley in the general election) and asked for a rating on the same scale. In the general election, the question was asked about Bush and Gore. Of course, as with all questions in which multiple candidates were mentioned, the order in which the candidates' names appeared was rotated.

Knowledge of Endorsements

Presidential candidates aggressively seek a variety of endorsements, including those of newspapers, interest groups, and other politicians. The effect of these endorsements is obviously mitigated by the degree to which voters are actually aware of who endorsed whom. To allow for analysis of the effects of endorsements, the NAES asked respondents whether they were aware whom a variety of parties had endorsed. Voters in New Hampshire and Iowa were asked about specific newspaper endorsements (for example, the *Concord Monitor* and the *Manchester Union-Leader*) in addition to endorsements made by interest groups and politicians during the primary season, while voters in the rest of the country were asked a smaller set of endorsement questions. During the general election, respondents were asked whether they knew whom a number of interest groups and political figures had endorsed. They were also asked if they knew whom the newspaper they read had endorsed. Preliminary analyses of these data indicate that endorsements can influence vote choice, particularly in primaries; researchers will no doubt want to investigate this question further.

Voting Behavior

In recent years, many states have moved to liberalize their voting systems in an effort to boost voter turnout. Some states have instituted "early voting," allowing people to cast their ballots before Election Day at polling stations. Others have liberalized their absentee voting rules; while in prior years voters would have been required to provide the state a reason they had to vote by absentee, in these states voters must now simply request an absentee ballot. Oregon has gone the farthest in this direction, eliminating polling places completely and conducting almost all voting by mail. Table 2.4, the Early and Liberal Absentee Voting table, lists the states with liberal absentee rules and those enabling voters to vote early at polling stations.

Because of this expanding feature of American voting, researchers should take care when analyzing survey results on voter preference. While most respondents to the survey vote at traditional polling places and are thus telling what they will or might do, others are relating what they already have done.

TABLE 2.4 Early and Liberal Absentee Voting in 2000

Liberal Absentee States	Early Voting States	States with Both Liberal Absentee Voting and Early Voting
Alaska	Nevada	Arizona
California	Tennessee	Arkansas
Kansas	Texas	Colorado
Maine	Virginia	Hawaii
Massachusetts		Idaho
Montana		Iowa
Nebraska		New Mexico
Utah		North Carolina
Vermont		Oklahoma
Washington		Oregon
Wyoming		Wisconsin

As Figure 2.1 shows, as Election Day approached an increasing number of respondents said they had voted prior to being interviewed. For an analysis of these early voting patterns, see Chapter 5.

Because some respondents had already voted before being interviewed and some had not, a somewhat complex protocol was used to assign respondents to questions about their vote—how likely they were to vote, the method by which they intended to vote, and of course for whom they intended to vote. Figures 2.2 and 2.3 show how the questions proceeded.

Researchers interested in studying the primary campaign have a number of options available in the 2000 National Annenberg Election Survey. In ad-

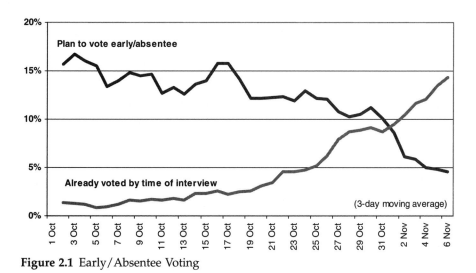

Figure 2.1 Early/Absentee Voting

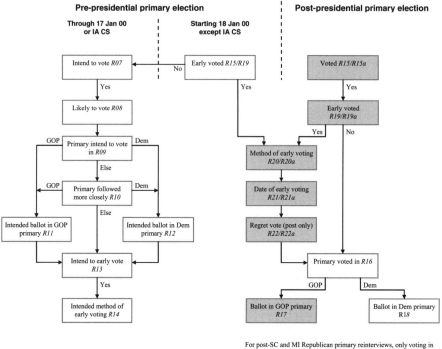

Figure 2.2 Intended and Actual Voting in Presidential Primaries. For post-SC and MI Republican primary reinterviews, only voting in the Republican primary was measured (shaded items: R15a, R17, R19a-R22a).

dition to the Iowa, New Hampshire, South Carolina, Michigan, Super Tuesday, and Second Tuesday oversamples, the rolling cross-section contains thousands of respondents interviewed prior to their presidential primaries. As the primary campaign progressed, questions on voting behavior were altered when a respondent's state had held its primary campaign. Therefore, when examining primary data one should keep in mind the dates of each state's primary. Table 2.5, the Primary Dates table, details the 2000 primary schedule.

House and Senate

The NAES contains a number of items in which respondents are classified according to their congressional district and the nature of the congressional races occurring in their district and state. Respondents were asked open-ended recall questions seeking the name of their representatives and senators, and their challengers if there was to be an election. Respondents also answered favorability questions using the "feeling thermometer" and told

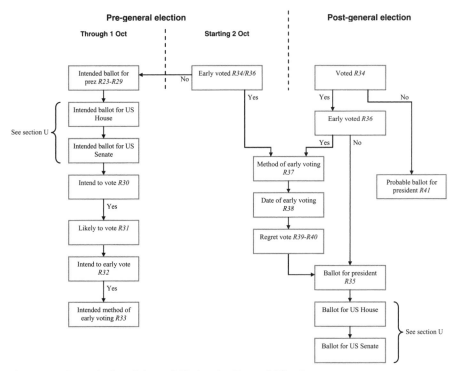

Figure 2.3 Intended and Actual Voting in General Election

their vote intentions if they were interviewed before the election and their actual vote if they were interviewed after the election.

After the Election

When the 2000 election ended in uncertainty and the battle moved to Florida, the NAES devoted a substantial portion of its interviewing to assessing people's responses to the unfolding events. As such, the NAES will allow interested researchers to analyze public opinion of the Florida controversy on a day-by-day basis. A number of different types of questions were asked, some for only a short time and others continuing the length of the controversy. As each development occurred (e.g., the rulings of the various courts involved), respondents were asked whether they approved of the outcome. They were also asked about their opinions not only of the performance of the two campaigns but also of some of the other actors involved. Opinions on some disputed details were assessed (including whether machine counts or hand counts are more accurate), and respondents were quizzed on their understanding and opinions of the Electoral College. Respondents were also asked their opinions of the news media's performance on Election Night and about the meaning of the 2000 election: whether it showed that every

TABLE 2.5 Presidential and Congressional Primary Dates

| | PRESIDENTIAL PRIMARY ELECTION | | | |
State	Republican and Democratic Balloting on Same Day	Republican Balloting Only	Democratic Balloting Only	Congressional Primary Election
AL	June 6			June 6
AR	May 23			May 23
AZ		February 22	March 11	September 12
CA	March 7			March 7
CO	March 10			August 8
CT	March 7			September 12
DC	May 2			
DE		February 8	March 27	September 9
FL	March 14			September 5
GA	March 7			July 18
IA	January 24			June 6
ID		May 23	March 7	May 23
IL	March 21			March 21
IN	May 2			May 2
KS	April 4			August 1
KY	May 23			May 23
LA	March 14			November 7*
MA	March 7			September 19
MD	March 7			March 7
ME	March 7			June 13
MI		February 22	March 11	August 8
MN		April 25	March 12	September 12
MO	March 7			August 8
MS	March 14			March 14
MT	June 6			June 6
NC	May 2			May 2
ND		February 29	March 7	June 13
NE	May 9			May 9
NH	February 1			September 12
NJ	June 6			June 6
NM	June 6			June 6
NV		May 25	March 12	September 5
NY	March 7			September 12
OH	March 7			March 7
OK	March 14			August 22
OR	May 16			May 16
PA	April 4			April 4
RI	March 7			September 12
SC		February 19	March 9	June 13
SD	June 6			June 6
TN	March 14			August 3
TX	March 14			March 14
UT	March 10			June 27
VA		February 29	April 17	June 13
VT	March 7			September 12
WA	March 7			September 19
WI	April 4			September 12
WV	May 9			May 9
WY		March 10	March 25	August 22

*Louisiana has a unique congressional election system in which there is no primary election. Instead, all candidates run in the general election; if no candidate receives 50% of the vote, a runoff is held in December.

vote counts, whether it harmed the United States, and what it said about democracy.

Once the Supreme Court made its decision and Al Gore conceded, respondents were asked about their expectations of the Bush presidency: whether he would succeed in getting his proposals passed, whether he would keep his promises, and whether he could work with Democrats and bring the country together.

Demographics

The battery of demographic questions on the NAES contains most of what can be found on typical telephone surveys, with standard questions on age, education, income, race, religion, employment, marital status, and so on. We also asked some questions that may be less common, including whether the respondent was employed by the government, had any family members who had served in the military, and had health insurance. As in most surveys, the demographic battery was asked at the end of the interview, since some respondents find these questions intrusive and are more likely to terminate the interview if they are asked them at the beginning.

It should be noted that the brief explanations of the variable categories contained in these pages do not by any means describe the full breadth of the 2000 National Annenberg Election Survey. Researchers should use the search engine and codebook to find all the items pertinent to the research questions they are asking.

REFERENCE

Allison, P. D. 2001. *Missing data.* Thousand Oaks, CA: Sage Press.

3

Research Design Concepts for the Rolling Cross-Section Approach

Kate Kenski

In this chapter and the next, we will introduce the reader to the rolling cross-sectional (RCS) design and illustrate the types of research that can be conducted with the 2000 National Annenberg Election Survey (NAES). These chapters assume reader familiarity with basic research methods and statistics.[1] However, we review several concepts that are important for analyzing the NAES. We then synthesize the RCS approach and compare it to two other observational research designs commonly used in the study of political campaigns: the repeated cross-sectional design and the panel design.

BASIC CONCEPTS IN RESEARCH DESIGN

Before we discuss the tradeoffs of different research designs, a review of some basic but important concepts is in order. These concepts are important for evaluating which type of design should be used in one's research. Our research should begin, of course, with a question or set of questions that we want to answer. Sometimes research questions are **descriptive.** Their purpose is to describe the characteristics of a population. How prevalent is A in the population? How many adults in the United States listen to political talk radio? Other research questions are **associative** and deal with the relationships of variables. Is A associated with B? Are respondents' levels of education associated with their exposure to political information on the Internet? Many research questions deal with the **causal relationship** between variables. That is, does A affect or produce changes in B? Does newspaper reading increase respondents' levels of political knowledge about the presidential candidates?

We refer to the concepts of interest as **variables.** A **variable** is an entity that takes on two or more values. These values can be quantitative or qual-

---

[1] Individuals who have not taken an introductory research methods course should consult texts such as Babbie (1995), Cook and Campbell (1979), Schutt (1996), and Spector (1981).

itative. A **constant,** on the other hand, is an entity that has only one value. It does not vary. When conducting research, we often want to know how concepts relate to one other. Constants are not helpful in trying to figure out how concepts relate to each another. For example, we might have a research question about the relationship between gender and political participation. If we conduct a study in which we survey only women, we cannot answer questions about the relationship between gender and participation because gender in the study is a constant. In order to look at the relationship between gender and participation, we also need to interview men as well so that we can compare men's responses to those made by women.

Researchers often identify variables in their studies as either **independent** or **dependent.** An independent variable refers to one that is thought to be the cause or predictor of another. A dependent variable refers to a variable that is the result or outcome. For example, we may ask: Does watching late-night comedy increase one's cynicism about the political process? Here, watching late-night comedy is hypothesized to produce an effect, increased cynicism. Late-night comedy is the independent variable, and cynicism is the dependent variable.

In the social sciences, causal inferences (Does A cause B?) are usually made in probabilistic rather then deterministic terms. We do not restrict our interest only to those matters where A always causes B. We are interested in whether A tends to cause B or is likely to cause B. Unlike descriptive or associative inferences, the case for causality is often difficult to make. Researchers frequently look to John Stuart Mill's criteria for making causal inferences. "Mill held that causal inference depends on three factors: first, the cause has to precede the effect in time; second, the cause and effect have to be related; and third, other explanations of the cause-effect relationship have to be eliminated" (Cook and Campbell 1979, 18).

The first criterion in assessing causality is time. Does A precede B? Temporal sequencing of variables is not always readily apparent and is more evident in some cases than in others. For example, in answering the question, "Are women less knowledgeable about politics than men?" we can be certain that gender precedes political knowledge. It is unlikely that one's level of political knowledge will produce an effect on one's gender. In other situations, the temporal sequencing of variables is difficult to determine. Does political knowledge affect political participation? Or, does political participation affect political knowledge?

The second criterion is association. Is A associated with B? If two variables are not related to one another, then one cannot produce an effect on the other. The level of association between variables can be determined by analyzing how the variables covary. Variables are said to **covary** when the variation in one is related to the variation in the other. Results from cross-tabulations or correlations between two variables let us know how strongly if at all two variables are associated.

The third criterion, ruling out alternative explanations, is the most difficult to achieve. The list of alternative explanations can be endless. But some alternatives are more plausible than others, and it is to these that researchers devote most of their attention. Suppose we hypothesize that A causes B, and we have met the criteria of temporal sequencing and association. A comes before B in time, and A and B are highly associated. Could there be another explanation, other than A causing B? One might be that a third variable, C, causes both A and B. Suppose C occurs before both A and B. Because C is causing both A and B, it makes it look as if A and B are related. In this situation, C is producing a spurious relationship between A and B. Ruling out alternative explanations involves eliminating potential **confounding variables.** Confounding variables are those that may obscure the relationship between the variables of interest in a given study.

While researchers studying a topic probably have a good sense of many of the potential confounding variables, it is possible that some variables have not been considered. There is rarely a final word in research. Since our knowledge of the world is constantly evolving, the cautious researcher will recognize that there are limitations to every study. It is unlikely that a scholar has thought of everything. No research strategy is perfect. But careful design can increase the likelihood that research will improve our understanding of the world.

Intervening variables help explain the mechanics of the causal relationship between two variables. The independent variable causes variation in the intervening variable, which in turn produces variation in the dependent one. For example, we might want to explore the relationship between respondents' sex and levels of political participation. Because political participation can be defined in different ways, we specify a particular type of participation that we are interested in, such as giving money to the campaigns of candidates. What is the relationship between gender and donating money to candidates? Does being female influence whether one gives money to political candidates? In the NAES data collected between October 6 and November 6 (N = 4,390), there is an association between gender and giving money to a presidential candidate. More men than women contributed money to presidential candidates (8.1% of men compared to 5.5% of women). This difference was statistically significant (chi-square = 11.537, df = 1, p = .001).

Is there something innate about women that makes them less likely to give to political campaigns? Or, are there other variables that might help us explicate the relationship? We know that men and women differ in their socioeconomic status. Men tend to make more money than women on average—a finding confirmed in the NAES. We might hypothesize that men give more money to political candidates because they have more disposable income than women do. We can check this contention by looking at the correlation between gender and donating money while controlling for income. If the relationship between gender and participation is no longer significant, then evidence suggests that being male affects giving money to presidential candidates because of income differentials between men and women. Results from the NAES support this claim. When controlling for income, the correlation between gender and giving money is not significant.

MAKING VALID INFERENCES

In order to gather data about the variables in which we are interested, we develop instruments to measure those variables. These measures are not the true concepts themselves but reflections of the concepts. **Operationalization** is the process by which we define the variable through our selection of an instrument. Spector (1981) warns: "Choice of instruments is as important as any step in an investigation, but too often little attention is given to instrumentation" (20). When analyzing secondary data, the choice is often not up to us. But we can still scrutinize whether the measures in a survey meet our research needs.

We create survey questions to capture the concepts as completely as possible. Often scholarly debates occur over whether or not the measures captured the concepts better than other measures that could have been used. If measures are to be useful, they must be reliable. The **reliability** of a measure is its ability to be replicated. If our survey instruments are inconsistent in the responses that they elicit, then they are of little use. A measure that gives us different results time after time is one that is not reliable and thus does not get at the essence of the concepts that we want to capture. Also, a measure that is not reliable is not going to be valid.

Validity is the ability to measure the essence of the concepts that we want to capture. A valid measure is one that does a good job of getting at the true meaning of our variable. It measures what we want to measure. The truth, of course, is always elusive to some extent. And while we are never sure that we have captured it in its entirety, we try to make sure that we are as close as possible. Cook and Campbell (1979) use the terms *"validity* and *invalidity* to refer to the best available approximation to the truth or falsity of propositions, including propositions about cause" (37).

The **content validity** of measures is crucial. Content validity is sometimes called face validity. On their face, do the measures used in the study seem to measure the concepts in which we are interested? Wording questions properly enhances the validity of one's study.[2]

Problems can occur when questions are not worded consistently across respondents. If interviewers, for example, stray from the survey scripts and change the wording of the questions when they are interviewing different people, then the reliability of the responses can be undercut. Problems can also occur when the wording of questions is vague. When the meaning of

---

[2] For more information about the wording of questions, see Sudman and Bradburn (1982).

words is ambiguous, respondents can interpret the meaning of the question in multiple ways. Ambiguous wording in a question challenges the validity of the question because the respondents may have a different idea in mind than the one that researcher wanted to test. For example, for a brief period, the NAES included a question that was supposed to capture whether people felt it was their civic duty to vote. Respondents were asked: "When you vote do you usually get a feeling of satisfaction from it, or do you only do it because it's your duty?" What is the content validity problem with this question? It is unclear whether people make a clear distinction between duty and satisfaction. Must these options be mutually exclusive? Because those who vote because they feel it is their duty might in turn feel satisfied from performing that duty, arguments could be made that the validity of this item is questionable.

Technical jargon should be avoided in the question wording, especially when conducting research on a large or diverse population. Question wording should be simple so that it can be understood by a wide variety of potential survey participants from different educational and cultural backgrounds. Researchers should pay attention to how questions are framed. The wording should be as unbiased as possible, meaning that it should not lead the respondent toward a particular answer.

Even the ordering of questions should be considered before a survey is put into the field. The ordering of questions should be randomized so that it does not affect the outcome of the responses. When possible, consideration should be given to the ordering of responses within questions as well. For example, if one candidate's name always comes before another's, does the ordering benefit or penalize any of the candidates? The NAES randomized the order of several questions to avoid problems that a fixed order might produce.

Sometimes there are socially desirable answers to particular questions. Efforts should be made to minimize social desirability bias. For example, people know that voting is a socially desirable activity. Thus when asked if they have voted, many respondents say they have when in fact they have not. To minimize the social desirability bias about voting, the NAES voting question lets respondents know that many people do not get a chance to vote. NAES respondents were asked: "In talking with people about politics and elections, we often find that they do not get a chance to vote. Did you happen to vote in the November election?" Even with the preface that many people do not get a chance to vote, respondents are still likely to say that they have voted when they have not. Although the Federal Election Commission reports that 51.3% of the voting-age population in the United States voted in the 2000 general election, 75.3% of NAES respondents interviewed between November 8 and November 22 said that they had voted in the general election (N = 2,293).

Much survey research involves the use of interviewers. Interviewers should be trained before conducting interviews to ensure that they do not influence the responses that the survey participants give. "When interviewers are used, it is important to avoid having them influence the answers respondents give, and at the same time to maximize the accuracy with which questions are answered" (Fowler 1993, 6). There is often a gap between a measure and the true meaning of a concept that the measure is attempting to represent. In short, there is often some error in our measurements. Sometimes the error is random, meaning that it does not occur in a systematic way. When **random error** occurs, any single response is as likely to be higher than the true value in the population as it is likely to be lower than it. For example, the NAES asked respondents how many days in the past week they watched late-night comedy shows, such as David Letterman or Jay Leno. Looking at the national cross-sectional data from October 3 to November 6 (N = 10,808), respondents watched late-night comedy an average of 0.65 days per week (SD = 1.45).[3] Many (76.8%) reported that they had not watched late-night comedy in the past week. If the errors in the survey participants' responses were random, the respondents would be as likely to overreport how much they actually watched late-night comedy shows as they were to underreport how much they watched. Random errors are a concern because they can affect the precision of our estimates. **Bias** is another type of error, but one that is much harder to deal with. When something is biased, it systematically throws off our estimates. When this occurs, it is difficult to adjust because we are never sure about the exact magnitude of the bias.

When conducting research that involves causal inferences, researchers should be concerned with different types of validity. Cook and Campbell (1979) identify four types: construct, external, statistical conclusion, and internal. These types of validity influence our confidence in making causal inferences. Some of the specific threats to validity that will be mentioned fall into more than one of these four categories. These categories are used to give readers a general overview of potential threats to the validity of their studies.

External validity is the ability to generalize a study to the population that it was intended to reflect. When conducting surveys, we frequently use randomization so that we can generalize our findings. Population parameters are the characteristics of the population that we want to study. We often want to ask questions about populations that are large. Most of the time, it is simply not possible to interview everyone in the population, as is done when a **census** is taken. Therefore, we sample members of the population that we wish to study.

A **sample** is a subset of a population. There are different ways to sample members from a population. Some sample methods are better than others

---

[3] The data used in this example are unweighted. Before making a generalization about the viewing habits of adults in the United States, researchers may want to consider weighting the data.

when trying to generalize from a sample to a population. The NAES sample is a **random sample** of adults in the United States, meaning that the sample is a random subset of the population of adults in the United States. According to Fowler (1993),

> The key to good sampling is finding a way to give all (or nearly all) population members the same (or a known) chance of being sampled, and to use probability methods for choosing the sample. Early surveys and polls often relied on samples of convenience or on sampling from lists that excluded significant portions of the population. These did not provide reliable, credible figures. (4)

In any research design, there are always limitations or threats to making valid inferences. The generalizability of a study depends in part on the **sample frame.** The sample frame is the list of members from a population who have a chance of being selected into the sample. The NAES was conducted using random digit dialing (RDD). Households were randomly selected. Procedures were established for randomly selecting adults from the households for interviews. The sample frame consisted of individuals who were living in households that had telephones. Individuals without telephones were not interviewed. "Nationally, this is about 5% of the households; in some areas, particularly central cities or rural areas, the rate of omission may be greater than that" (Fowler 1993, 24). This puts a constraint on the population to which we can generalize.

Selecting a sampling procedure that gives each person in the population a known chance of being interviewed is important for obtaining a representative sample of the population. Once a sample frame has been selected, an equally important issue is nonresponse. Having a good sampling strategy does not by itself justify claiming that the sample is representative of the population to which we want to generalize. Generalizations from our data can be sabotaged by **nonresponse bias.** Nonresponse bias occurs when individuals who have been selected for interviews do not answer the survey and differ from those individuals who do answer it. Researchers typically report response rates or cooperation rates with their studies. Response rates usually refer to the number of people interviewed divided by the number of people sampled. Cooperation rates refer to the proportion of people who were interviewed to people who were contacted. There are different formulas for response and cooperation rates that take into account partial and completed interviews.[4] High response and cooperation rates are desirable. If the response rate of a study is high, then nonresponse bias is less likely to be a problem.

---

[4] The American Association for Public Opinion Research's *Standard Definitions* should be consulted for more information about response and cooperation rates. This information can be found on the AAPOR website: www.aapor.org.

Researchers sometimes try to compensate for these limitations by weighting the data. "Whenever an identifiable group is selected at a different rate from others, weights are needed so that oversampled people are not overrepresented in the sample statistics" (Fowler 1993, 25). If a study underrepresents a segment of the population, survey weights can be constructed to give cases from the underrepresented segment more weight. While weights may be important when conducting descriptive analyses of populations, there is disagreement over whether these weights are necessary when trying to assess the relationship between variables. There is also debate over how such weights should be constructed. Should weights be based solely on demographic characteristics? Should they be based on how many telephone lines, including cell phones, a respondent has in his or her household? After all, a respondent who lives in a household with multiple telephone lines has a greater chance of being selected into the survey. Should researchers interested in vote choice weight the data by party identification? Some researchers claim that party identification is a stable characteristic, while others argue that party identification is an attitudinal concept that has the potential to fluctuate over the course of a campaign. The issue of weighting is an important one and should be considered by the researcher before she conducts data analysis. The examples used in this book, however, are created from unweighted data so that the reader can replicate them with little difficulty.

Statistical conclusion validity deals with the ability of the study to make conclusions about the covariation of the variables. Were there enough cases in the study to detect an effect that one hypothesized? This is the issue of statistical power. Zaller (2002) argues that power analyses are missing from many published works. He states: "To judge from most published work, whatever survey they are analyzing is plenty big enough to answer the question they are asking. If they get a null result, the normal assumption is that the hypothesis under investigation is weak or wrong" (298). The size of a sample affects the precision of the estimates that can be drawn from it. As sample size increases, the sampling error around estimates decreases. Detecting large effects is easier than detecting small ones. If the effect that one wishes to detect is likely to be small, then one may have to increase the sample size of the study. If there is a lot of variation in the population characteristics that one wishes to detect, then bigger samples will be needed.

The validity of our assertion that one variable causes another depends on whether or not these variables covary. Assuming that one has enough power to detect the effects, is there evidence to suggest that the variation in one variable is related to the variation in another? Cook and Campbell (1979) note:

> In many studies, a decision about covariation is made by comparing the degree of covariation and random error observed in the sample data to an a priori specified risk of being wrong in concluding that there is covariation. This risk is specified as a probability level (usually 5%), and we speak of setting α at .05. (40)

The statistical conclusion validity is further enhanced when the magnitude of the variation is large.

Construct validity deals with issues of confounding. Are we appropriately describing or naming the cause of a presumed effect? Some of the issues around question wordings discussed earlier could be considered construct validity problems. The Hawthorne effect is an example of a construct validity problem. This effect occurs when people in a study change their attitudes or behavior because they feel important or special for taking part in the study. "[T]he mere knowledge that one is in a study may affect behavior even if observations are not being made" (Spector 1981, 27). In short, it is not the event or treatment that has brought about the change but some other process instead. Researchers may not be aware of the intervening process that is producing the effect.

Internal validity is the truthfulness of a claim that one variable causes another. Assuming that we have determined that two variables are associated, is there enough evidence in our data to suggest that A produces an effect on B? Harkening back to Mill's criteria for supporting causal inferences, have we ruled out possible alternative explanations? There are many ways that the internal validity of our causal assertions can be threatened. We discuss just a few of them here.[5]

One threat to internal validity is history. History refers to events that take place during our study that happen at the same time as our purported causes. In searching for campaign effects, researchers often want to see if campaign events produce change in voters' opinions about the candidates. Assuming that effects are found, history hinders our ability to attribute the changes to the campaign events if other events take place during the same time period. Because the opinion changes may have been caused by other events, it is difficult to make solid claims that the campaign events produced the difference in opinions.

In the course of a study, researchers sometimes change the wording of questions. When the wording of questions changes during a study and a change in respondent answers is observed, it is difficult to know whether the change occurred because of some event or because the wording of the questions shifted. This threat to internal validity is also a threat to the construct validity of the measures.

Another threat to internal validity is maturation. "This is a threat when an observed effect might be due to the respondent's growing older, wiser, stronger, more experienced, and the like between the pretest and posttest and when this maturation is not the treatment of research interest" (Cook and Campbell 1979, 52). When the pretest and posttest are conducted over a short period of time, it is unlikely that maturation will pose a great threat to the internal validity of the study.

---

[5] Cook and Campbell (1979) provide detailed explanations and examples of different types of threats to the validity.

The internal validity of a study can be hurt by selection bias. Selection bias occurs when the people in groups differ. For example, we might want to test whether watching the presidential debates enhanced people's scores on the political knowledge items about the issue positions of the presidential candidates. We could compare those people who said that they watched the debates to those who did not. However, debate watchers may differ from nonwatchers. People who watch debates are likely to be more interested in politics, more partisan, and more educated than their counterparts, for example. This creates a selection bias problem.

A related selection bias in panel studies is differential subject loss. Panel studies often experience some attrition in study participation. Differential subject loss occurs when the people who drop out of the study are different from those who remain. When effects are observed, we do not know if they would have occurred if the people who dropped out of the study had remained in it.

In studies where the same individuals are interviewed over time and are given the same questions, testing effects may occur. Repeated testing allows respondents to become familiar with the questions. This may affect their performance on the items.

A related problem is interaction of testing and treatment. This problem occurs when the event that we supposed would affect members of the population has an effect on study participants because they took the pretest. For example, the NAES includes several knowledge questions about the issue positions of the presidential candidates. Some respondents were interviewed more than once. The initial interview may have made the respondents more sensitive to information about particular issue positions. If we observe that the accuracy of their responses to these questions has improved, we will not know whether the improvement is attributable to some campaign event, to their familiarity with the questionnaire, or to an interaction of having taken the pretest and being influenced by the campaign event because of it. To the extent that this problem hampers the generalizability of the effect, interaction of testing and treatment may be considered an external validity concern. To compensate, the NAES includes the national RCS data, which can be used as a control for the panel data.

To maximize the validity of a study, researchers should take into account the various threats to which particular research designs are more vulnerable. When conducting surveys, Fowler (1993) contends that researchers should pay attention to three things: (1) the sampling strategy, (2) questionnaire writing, and (3) interviewing techniques. For research to be successful, carefully planning is required at many levels.

RESEARCH DESIGNS THAT CAPTURE CHANGE

Different designs have been employed to explore the issue of whether or not campaigns produce effects. In any type of research, the causal direction of the variables of interest can be subject to debate. Some research designs, however, make stronger cases for the hypothesized relationship of variables than do others.

The notion of capturing campaign effects suggests that the researcher will study some phenomenon at a minimum of two points in time. After all, in order to see change and attribute it to some event, one has to know what the state of something was prior to the event that is thought to have caused the change.

It is not always possible to collect data over time. A **cross-section** refers to data that have been collected at a single point in time. Some research methods can be used to test inferences about causality from cross-sectional data. While the case for the association between two variables can be made from cross-sectional data, inferences about causality are much harder to make since we are not often sure which variable preceded the other. The strength of the causal inferences that can be made from a single cross-section design is much weaker than inferences that can be made about data that have been collected at more than two time points.

The study of effects can be performed through experimental as well as nonexperimental or observational research designs. Experimental research designs are those studies in which the researcher manipulates the stimuli that the study participants receive. This manipulation is called the treatment and is the independent variable of the study. "Experimental research is explanatory in nature: experiments are conducted primarily to test hypotheses, not to describe some large population or to explore previously uncharted social patterns" (Schutt 1996, 220).

Observational studies, in contrast, are those in which the researcher does not manipulate or intrude upon an environment. When one wants to generalize about a large population, nonexperimental approaches are often preferred. Observational studies, however, have their drawbacks. Because data collected in the field in an observational study are not manipulated, inferring causality is challenging. "For the most part, experimental studies are considered to be more powerful than nonexperimental designs in uncovering causal relationships among variables. This is due to the fact that through control and randomization, potential confounding effects can be removed from a study" (Spector 1981, 20). Through the collection of observational data over time, researchers can strengthen their case that one variable has produced an effect on another.

In analyzing observational data, we often try to control for extraneous factors that might hide the relationships of the variables in which we are interested. But as previously discussed, there are many potential threats to the validity of causal inferences. It is difficult, if not impossible, to control for everything. Experiments have the benefit of randomly assigning study participants to treatments. Assuming that the randomization has worked and the groups are comparable in everything other than the treatment given, when effects are found, they can be attributed to the manipulation. In studying campaign effects, however, it may be difficult to create realistic manipulations. While effects may be witnessed in the laboratory, the setting is often unnatural, hindering the researcher's ability to generalize the effects to the larger population.

In studying campaigns, most of the time we are not merely interested in whether it is possible to produce effects. We want to know whether actual events produced effects on potential voters. The rest of this chapter is devoted to comparing the rolling cross-section design to two commonly used longitudinal designs that are used in observational studies: the repeated cross-sectional design and the panel design.

The **repeated cross-sectional design** is one in which data have been collected at two or more points in time. The collected data are different samples drawn from the same population. The repeated cross-sectional design is "appropriate when the goal is to determine whether a population has changed over time" (Schutt 1996, 133).

In the **panel design,** the same individuals are interviewed at two or more points. This design allows researchers to track changes in individuals over time. In this design, measures on the pretest are compared to the measures on the posttest to see if significant differences appear. When differences are found, it is often assumed that the observed change was produced by the event or treatment that happened between the panels.

The NAES includes several panel datasets. During the primary season, panel studies were conducted around the Iowa caucuses, the New Hampshire primary, the South Carolina Republican primary, the Michigan primary, and the Super Tuesday primaries. During the general election campaign, panels were placed around important campaign events including the Republican convention, the Democratic convention, and each of the three presidential debates. A panel study was also conducted around the general election; the same respondents were interviewed before and after the general election.

While the panel design has the capacity to capture change at two or more time points, high costs often prohibit tracking the same individuals several times across the course of an election. Not only can this approach be expensive, but repeated interviewing of the same study respondents can produce participation fatigue and attrition. Repeated cross-sections do not cause the same levels of fatigue as do panel designs. In both designs, researchers have to plan when the waves of data collection will take place. They must have a good sense of when potentially consequential campaign events are likely to happen.

Many election studies have not been designed to capture campaign dynamics. Even when studies manage to conduct interviews at two time points, this collection is not sufficient to capture the ebb and flow of political campaigns. Holbrook (1996) observes:

> One of the problems with studying campaign effects at the individual-level is that most public opinion surveys are not designed with this purpose in mind. The main data source used by students of elections, the biennial National Election Study (NES), is primarily designed to study the effect of

partisanship, issues, and personalities on voting behavior. The primary drawback to the NES is that it lacks a dynamic component that would allow for a clear analysis of how campaign events produce changes in political attitudes. In addition, the NES includes very few survey items that are specifically intended to capture the effects of political campaigns. (34)

While data collected at two time points may be able to demonstrate change in a population or change in individuals, it is difficult to attribute these changes to any single event.

The **rolling cross-section (RCS) design** allows researchers to track dynamics in a population. The RCS "is a design that facilitates detailed exploration of campaign dynamics. Its essence is to take a one-shot cross-section and distribute interviewing in a controlled way over time" (Johnston and Brady 2002, 283). Although RCS design is referred to as a distinct approach in this chapter, it is actually a special case of the repeated cross-section design. The RCS design involves taking a series of cross-sections over a period of time. Each cross-section is equally spaced across the time period of interest. In the NAES, cross-sections took place each day. What makes the rolling cross-section unique is the sampling protocol used to ensure that each cross-section is truly random. The details of this protocol and why it works are explained in Chapter 4. Because each cross-section is random, researchers can aggregate the data to create time series.

The RCS approach is relatively new. It was first used in the 1984 American National Election Study (ANES) and again in an ANES 1988 study of the Super Tuesday primaries. This design was adopted for the Canadian Election Study (CES) in 1988. While the 1984 ANES used weekly cross-sections, the 1988 CES was the first to employ a daily cross-section design.[6]

Figures 3.1 and 3.2 illustrate the types of dynamics that can be analyzed by tracking public opinion across the course of the election. Respondents were asked whether the federal government should spend more money on Social Security benefits, the same as now, less, or no money at all. Figure 3.1 shows the percentage of respondents surveyed July 15 to November 6 that thought the government should spend more money on Social Security. Using a seven-day moving average to smooth out some of the sampling variation, this figure shows that beginning the second week of October, support for increasing government spending on Social Security began to decrease somewhat. Nevertheless, a majority of respondents across this time period supported an increase in Social Security spending.

Figure 3.2 tracks the electorate's understanding of the presidential candidates' positions on investing Social Security contributions in the stock market. Respondents were asked whether the candidates favored allowing workers to invest some of their Social Security contributions in the stock market. Bush favored the position, while Gore opposed it. Figure 3.2 shows that the

---

[6] For more information about this important study, see Johnston et al. (1992).

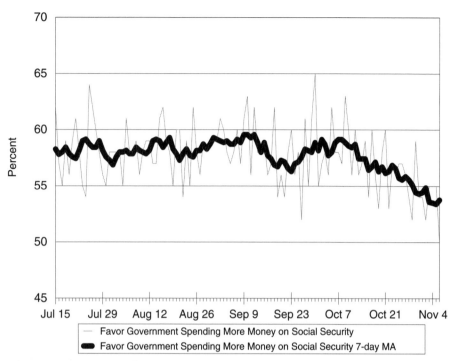

Figure 3.1 Percentage of the U.S. Adults Stating from July 15 to November 6 that the Federal Government Should Spend More Money on Social Security Benefits (MA, moving average)

percentages of adults answering the candidate issue positions correctly increased across the course of the general election.

Tracking the effects of campaigns across time is a function of the study design. Capturing campaign dynamics requires information about a population across a number of time periods. In the next section, we compare the RCS design to others commonly used to ascertain campaign effects.

THE RCS APPROACH AND THE REPEATED CROSS-SECTIONAL DESIGN

The RCS and repeated cross-sectional designs are similar. Both of these designs allow researchers to generalize about large populations when appropriate sampling strategies have been used. Generalizations made from the RCS approach and repeated cross-sectional designs are restricted to the population level. Some generalizations can also be made about subgroups within the population, assuming that the sample sizes are large enough. Because these designs do not track the same individuals over time, researchers cannot test hypotheses about individual-level changes.

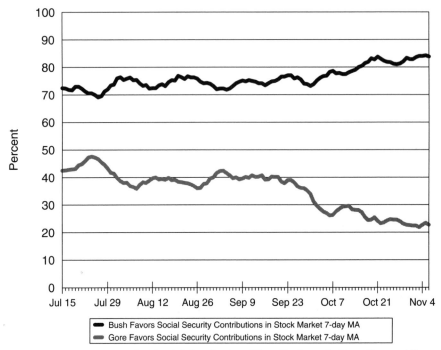

Figure 3.2 Percentage of U.S. Adults Stating That Bush and Gore Favor Allowing Workers to Invest Social Security Contributions in Stock Market (MA, moving average)

The RCS approach is essentially a specific type of repeated cross-section design. Repeated cross-sections are used to identify changes in a population between two or more points in time. The repeated cross-sectional design itself does not specify how far apart in time the waves of cross-sections should be conducted. The timing and frequency of the cross-sections are up to the researcher.

In campaign research, repeated cross-sections are usually scheduled before and after an event takes place so that the researcher can argue that the event produced some change in the population under study. Each cross-section is composed of individuals randomly selected from the population. When a *single* cross-sectional study takes place over the course of several days, interviews completed at the beginning of the interviewing process may not be comparable to those completed toward the end of the process. When a single cross-section is being conducted, a list of individuals randomly selected from the population is drawn. The researchers contact individuals on the list throughout the course of the study. Some individuals will respond to the researchers' interview request quickly. Others are harder to reach and will have to be contacted several times before they are interviewed. Because individuals who answer the survey immediately upon being contacted may differ from those who are interviewed only after repeated contact, time within the single cross-section may be related to specific characteristics of the survey respondents.

The rolling cross-section design, on the other hand, requires that interviews take place on a set schedule across the time period of interest. The unit of this schedule can vary from study to study. For any particular study, the schedule must remain constant. The NAES was run on a daily release schedule. Rather than working from a single list of randomly selected members of the population, several lists are generated and are released into the field at specified intervals (daily for the NAES) so that the date of the interview is a random event. The smaller the unit of the release schedule, the more sensitive the study is to changes in the environment, assuming that the sample size is large enough. Because of the nature of political campaigns, using the day as the unit of the release schedule makes sense. Many things happen in the news environment daily.

Researchers who rely on repeated cross-section designs may miss important campaign events depending when the cross-sections have been conducted. If a lot of time passes between the repeated cross-sections, it may be difficult to attribute any effects to a specific event.

Because the rolling cross-sectional surveys are in the field for a long and consistent period of time during campaigns and each individual cross-section is random, the data generated from this design can be grouped into larger cross-sections if desired. For those researchers who want to compare the scores of individuals at one period with the scores of other individuals in the population at another period, data from the time points of interest can be grouped and compared. Before conducting analyses on the primary variables of interest, however, the newly constructed cross-sections should be compared to make sure that the demographic variables are comparable.

To demonstrate using the NAES data as repeated cross-sections, the overall evaluations of Gore and Bush were compared before and after the first presidential debate. For those interested in campaign events, the first presidential debate is a likely focus for a repeated cross-sectional study. The first presidential debate was on October 3. Data collected five days prior to the debate (N = 1,599) are compared with data collected five days after the debate (N = 1,511). To ensure that these cross-sections were comparable on sociodemographic variables, t-tests were performed comparing them on gender, age, and educational composition. No significant differences were found on these variables.

NAES respondents were asked to give overall evaluations of the presidential candidates. These evaluations are sometimes called feeling thermometer ratings. Respondents were asked the following:

> For each of the following people in politics, please tell me if your opinion is favorable or unfavorable using a scale from 0 to 100. Zero means very unfavorable, and 100 means very favorable. Fifty means you do not feel favorable or unfavorable. If you don't know enough about the person to rate him or her, just tell me and we will move to the next one.

Respondents were then asked to evaluate Al Gore and George Bush. Their responses were used to create a new variable based on the difference between these evaluations. This variable is called "Gore minus Bush." When Gore's evaluation is higher than Bush's evaluation, the variable is positive. When Bush is performing better, it is negative. Did the scores on this variable before the debate differ significantly from scores given after the debate? In the five days prior to the debate, the average difference between respondents' Gore and Bush scores was -2.68 (N = 1,514). The average "Gore minus Bush" score was -2.20 in the five days after the debate (N = 1,440). An independent samples t-test revealed that the difference in the ratings between these two time periods was not statistically significant.

A look at a time series of this variable a few weeks prior to the first presidential debate to a few weeks after the third presidential debate gives a better understanding of the difference between Gore and Bush's evaluations. While the only conclusion that can be reached from the repeated cross-section approach is that there was no difference between them, the RCS approach shows that Gore's evaluations began to fall in mid-September. Around the third week of September, respondents generally gave Bush higher evaluations than they gave Gore. Around the third debate, the difference between Bush and Gore's evaluations grew, with Bush outperforming Gore. After the third debate, Gore's rating began to rise (see Figure 3.3).

The disadvantages of the RCS approach compared to a simpler repeated cross-sectional design are that it requires more planning in the sampling scheme and it costs more than conducting a few cross-sections. The major advantage of the RCS approach compared to a repeated cross-sectional design that only contains a few waves of data is that the RCS approach is more likely to capture changes when they are not necessarily expected.

THE RCS APPROACH AND PANEL DESIGNS

The RCS approach and panel designs share the goal of trying to capture changes. The nature of the designs, however, allows different types of generalization to be made. While data collected with the RCS and repeated cross-sectional designs can tell us whether a population has changed over time, data collected with panel designs can tell us whether individuals have done so. There are often times when we would like to argue that group-level data tell us something about individuals' behavior. Making inferences about individual-level process from group-level data, however, is problematic. Researchers who make inferences about individual process from group data commit what is called an **ecological fallacy.**[7] Panel designs have an advan-

---

[7] For more information about ecological inferences, see Achen and Shively (1995), King (1997), and Langbein and Lichtman (1978).

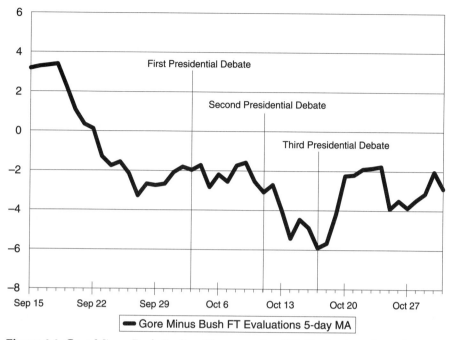

Figure 3.3 Gore Minus Bush Feeling Thermometer (FT) Evaluations from September 15 to October 31 (MA, moving average)

tage over the RCS and repeated cross-sectional designs if the purpose of the research is to monitor changes within individuals. Generalizations should not be made about individual processes when using RCS and repeated cross-sections.

The internal validity threat of history is always a concern to designs that track changes over time. When we observe changes in individuals or in populations, we can never be absolutely certain that a particular event produced the effects. Because the RCS design gives us a wider view of the campaign, we can make stronger claims about when changes occurred. Theoretically, the panel design could also be implemented with the same rigor across the course of the campaign. But in practice, the cost of such an endeavor would be prohibitive. "Keeping track of panel members is expensive, and the likelihood of subject attrition is high. In addition, panel members who are interviewed frequently may tire of the process, which is called 'subject fatigue'" (Schutt 1996, 134).

Because the NAES panels are placed at only two points in time, they can only tell us whether individual changes occurred. They cannot tell us whether the changes were in the process of happening prior to the events around which the panels were placed. "The most obvious shortcoming of this design is that one cannot be certain that some factor or event other than the treatment was responsible for the posttest change" (Spector 1981, 29).

Using the NAES panel data collected around the first presidential debate, the differences in respondents' evaluations of Gore's honesty can be compared at the individual level. Respondents in this panel were initially interviewed between September 21 and October 2. The post-debate follow-up interview took place between October 4 and October 10. Looking again at the first presidential debate, the trait ratings of Gore's honesty are analyzed. Respondents were asked to evaluate the presidential candidates on a series of traits through questions such as, "Does the word 'honest' describe Al Gore extremely well, quite well, not too well, or not well at all?" Answers were recoded so that "extremely well" and "quite well" responses were grouped together and compared to "not too well" and "not well at all" responses. A paired samples t-test of Gore's honesty ratings revealed that respondents lowered their ratings of Gore from the first panel wave to the second (N = 1,424). About 55.6% of respondents in the pre-debate panel said that "honest" described Gore well compared to 51.3% in the post-debate panel. This 4.3% difference was significant with $p < .001$. If the only data that we collected were panel data, we might have concluded that the first presidential debate had lowered public opinion about Gore's honesty.

How does using the RCS data enhance our understanding of the effects of the first presidential debate? An advantage of the RCS design is that it allows researchers to construct a time series to get a stronger sense of where public opinion was prior to the event. "The advantage of the time series is that one can see the direction in which trends were heading at the time of intervention or treatment. A treatment might inhibit or stop a trend which would not be reflected in a single pretest-posttest comparison" (Spector 1981, 31). Figure 3.4 tracks the percentage of respondents who say that "honest" describes Al Gore well. This graph shows that opinions about Gore's honesty were on the decline well before either the first or second presidential debate took place. We cannot conclude that the first presidential debate had no effect on individual-level processes. Because the RCS presents evidence to suggest that the changes in the population were already in motion, however, the claim that the debate caused individuals to lower their opinions about Gore's honesty is weakened.

"Endogenous change is a major problem with before-and-after designs. In panel designs with a single pretest and posttest, any change may be due to testing, maturation, or regression" (Schutt 1996, 245). In an election study in which the panels are conducted over a short period of time, the likelihood of maturation being a threat to internal validity is small.

Testing effects, however, may occur with panel designs. As mentioned earlier, panel designs may sensitize survey participations to the concepts being explored in the survey. Sometimes events may affect survey respondents because the respondents have become sensitized by the pretest questions, creating a testing and treatment interaction. When this problem occurs, the generalizability of our study is stunted. Panel designs do not require having a post-event comparison group that has not received the pretest. Such

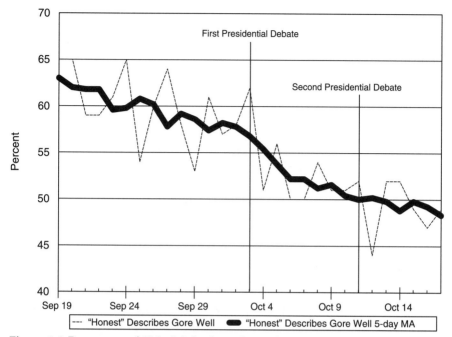

Figure 3.4 Percentage of U.S. Adults from September 19 to October 17 Who Say "Honest" Describes Gore Quite Well or Extremely Well (MA, moving average)

comparison groups are often a good idea. Because observed changes may be attributed to respondents having been asked questions prior to an event, a comparison group that has not received the pretest and therefore could not have been affected by the pre-event interview is useful. Testing effects from the panels can be explored with the NAES panels by using the national cross-section as a group that did not get the initial set of questions. Before conducting such tests, however, researchers should make sure that the national cross-section respondents are similar on a wide variety of characteristics to those in the panel studies.

Panel attrition is another potential drawback to the panel design. When respondents drop out of a study, the generalizability of the study is diminished if the individuals who drop out are different from those individuals who remain. When we compare the demographics of the first presidential debate panel to that of the national cross-section interviewed at the same time as the debate panel pretest (September 21 to October 2), we find that the RCS and panel are statistically equivalent on average household income and proportions of females and blacks. Participants in the panel, however, are more likely to report being older, married, educated, and interested in politics.

When studying campaign dynamics, one potential shortcoming of the panel approach is that researchers often fail to anticipate important events before they occur. Panels can be placed around known events such as conventions and debates. But if unanticipated events occur, the researcher is out of luck. Some campaign events happen without being forecast.

CONCLUSION

No research design is flawless. There are always potential threats to the validity of one's research. Each design comes with its own set of constraints. Before selecting a research design, the tradeoffs of the various designs should be considered. Understanding the level of analysis to which one wants to make causal inferences is important. "The units of analysis for a study represent the level of social life on which the research question is focused, such as individuals, groups, towns, or nations. We do not fully understand the variables in a study until we know what units of analysis they refer to" (Schutt 1996, 88). If researchers wish to make inferences about individual-level causal processes, then panel designs should be employed. While the most innovative feature of the NAES is its rolling cross-sectional data, many panels are also contained within the study for those wishing to study individual-level changes.

Capturing campaign dynamics requires a research design that tracks members of the population across the course of the campaign. Presidential candidates create and participate in various campaign events through the campaign season. Campaigns generate advertising and direct mail that target members of the electorate at different times throughout the course of the campaign. News about the candidates is generated every day. While simple repeated cross-sectional designs and panel designs can capture change, the RCS approach offers researchers data over a longer period of time, giving researchers a wider context in which to understand their results.

As Holbrook (1996) notes, "Understanding the effect of any process is difficult if the focus is only on what comes out at the end of the process. Only by expanding the analysis to include studying the dynamics of public opinion during the campaign period can one gain an appreciation for the effect of the campaign" (46). This is precisely the goal of the National Annenberg Election Survey.

REFERENCES

Achen, Christopher H., and W. Phillips Shively. 1995. *Cross-level inference.* Chicago: University of Chicago Press.

The American Association for Public Opinion Research. 2000. *Standard definitions: Final dispositions of case codes and outcome rates for surveys.* Ann Arbor, Michigan: Author.

Babbie, Earl. 1995. *The practice of social research.* 7th ed. Belmont, CA: Wadsworth.

Cook, Thomas D., and Donald T. Campbell. 1979. *Quasi-experimentation: Design & analysis issues for field settings.* Boston: Houghton Mifflin Company.

Federal Election Commission. 2002. Voter registration and turnout 2000 [Online]. Available: *www.fec.gov* (consulted 10/8/02).

Fowler, Floyd J. 1993. *Survey research methods.* 2d ed. Newbury Park, CA: Sage.

Holbrook, Thomas M. 1996. *Do campaigns matter?* Thousand Oaks, CA: Sage.

Johnston, Richard, and Henry E. Brady. 2002. The rolling cross-section design. *Electoral Studies* 21:283–95.

Johnston, Richard, André Blais, Henry E. Brady, and Jean Crête. 1992. *Letting the people decide: Dynamics of a Canadian election.* Stanford, CA: Stanford University Press.

King, Gary. 1997. *A solution to the ecological inference Problem: Reconstructing individual behavior from aggregate data.* Princeton, NJ: Princeton University Press.

Langbein, Laura Irwin, and Allan J. Lichtman. 1978. *Ecological inference.* Beverly Hills, CA: Sage.

Schutt, Russell K. 1996. *Investigating the social world: The process and practice of research.* Thousand Oaks, CA: Pine Forge Press.

Spector, Paul E. 1981. *Research designs.* Beverly Hills, CA: Sage.

Sudman, Seymour, and Norman M. Bradburn. 1982. *Asking questions: A practical guide to questionnaire design.* San Francisco: Jossey-Bass.

Zaller, John. 2002. The statistical power of election studies to detect media exposure effects in political campaigns. *Electoral Studies* 21:297–329.

4

The Rolling Cross-Section Design

Kate Kenski

This chapter provides details on the rolling cross-sectional design in general and the NAES in particular. Data from the NAES are used to illustrate how we implemented the RCS design. As mentioned in Chapter 3, the rolling cross-section is a series of repeated cross-sections using a sampling plan to ensure that each of the cross-sections is composed of randomly selected members from the population under study. Because the composition of each cross-section is random, researchers can treat the date of interview as a chance event. "Properly done, the date on which a respondent is interviewed is as much a product of random selection as the initial inclusion of that respondent in the sample" (Johnston and Brady 2002, 283). In the case of the NAES, this process allows analysts to aggregate the individual cases to the daily level (or higher aggregates) and look for changes that take place in the electorate over the course of the election season.

Interviews with randomly selected individuals take place throughout the course of a rolling cross-sectional study. The unit of analysis can be either the individual at a single point in time or the population over time. The primary unit of analysis for studying populations over time must be determined before an RCS study begins.

The date of interview is a central concern of the rolling cross-section design. Prior to conducting an RCS study, researchers have to decide what type of schedule they wish to implement. The unit of the schedule can vary from study to study. In one study, researchers may want to track changes that happen on a weekly basis. In another, changes that happen day to day may be the focus. For any particular study, once the unit of the schedule has been chosen, it should remain constant throughout the study.

The NAES rolling cross-sectional design used day as the unit for the schedule. The NAES team chose day because many things happen in the news environment daily. A larger unit, such as week, could have been chosen. To capture campaign dynamics and attribute changes in public opinion to particular campaign events, however, day was selected as the unit of the sampling schedule. Generally, a study using a smaller unit for its release schedule will be more sensitive to changes in a dynamic environment than a study that uses larger units. Researchers who prefer to use week as their unit of analysis, moreover, can aggregate data collected on a daily release schedule into weekly sections. If the study has been conducted under a weekly schedule, however, researchers cannot break those data into days.

RCS SAMPLE DESIGN

Once a schedule has been chosen, a random sample of members from the population is drawn. Rather than working directly from this initial list of randomly selected members of the population, this list of randomly selected individuals is broken up into several smaller lists called **replicates.** The NAES sample was acquired through random-digit dialing procedures. A list of randomly generated telephone numbers in the United States was made.[1] This list was then broken into several replicates. Each replicate contained fifty telephone numbers. Just as a telephone number's chance of being selected for the initial list was random, so was the number's chance of being placed into a particular replicate.

A certain number of replicates are released into the field each day, depending on how many interviews researchers want to complete. Schulman, Ronca & Bucuvalas (SRBI), the firm that conducted the RCS fieldwork for the NAES, determined that a 6:1 ratio of sampled telephone numbers to completed interviews was generally needed to produce a target number of interviews. The number of replicates released each day varied across the NAES study. More replicates were released into the field on days when important events were happening or were likely to occur than on days when little was going on in the campaign environment.

Figure 4.1 shows the number of interviews that were completed each day from December 14, 1999, to January 19, 2001. Averages of between fifty and three hundred interviews were conducted each day for the national RCS study. During the intense periods of the presidential primary campaigns, one hundred national cross-section interviews were completed each day on average. At the end of the primary season around the beginning of April and up until the beginning of July as word of vice presidential prospects leaked to the press, this average fell to around fifty interviews per day. Because the general election was of great interest, the NAES allocated more resources to the collection of data around the general election rather than around slower periods, such as the summer when the number of campaign activities were relatively low. In July, the target number of interviews increased, and more replicates were released into the field each day. Around three hundred national cross-section interviews were completed daily from mid-July through the general election. During November and much of December 2000, one hundred national cross-section interviews were completed

---

[1] See Chapter 2 or the NAES codebook for more information about the telephone procedures used to construct the NAES sample.

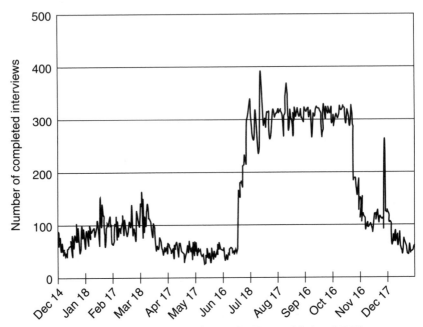

Figure 4.1 Number of Interview Completions by Day in National RCS

each day on average. These averages do not include interviews that were done as a part of the panel studies or add-on cross-section studies noted in the NAES codebook.

Selecting a target sample size for each day (or whatever the unit of the release schedule is) depends on three things: (1) the size of the effect that one wants to detect, (2) the project's budget, and (3) the capacity of the call-house(s). Research projects always contain practical as well as theoretical constraints. Implementing a highly sensitive research design can be expensive, especially if the effects that one wants to detect are small. The larger one's sample size, the more precise one's estimates. Each daily cross-section comes with sampling variation. This sampling variation is reduced when the sample size increases.

If one is conducting research on a subset of the population, then the power of that effect on that subpopulation should be determined. If one wants to look at African Americans, for example, then one should make sure that there are enough cases to find an effect when analyzing the NAES or any dataset. Zaller (2002) observes:

> It would also seem that the scholars who consume surveys should make more use of power analysis in their studies, especially in studies which turn up null or trace effects. That is, they should estimate the probability of rejecting the null hypothesis with respect to the particular size of effect

they expect, given the model they are using, the characteristics of the variables in it, and the amount of data they have. (323)

Compared to most election studies, the total sample size of the NAES is massive. Nevertheless, to detect small effects for some hypotheses, even the NAES may not be large enough.

SAMPLE RELEASE AND CLEARANCE

For RCS designs to work, strict procedures must be worked out so that each telephone number has the same chance of being selected and of producing a completed interview as any other telephone number. Serious effort was made to increase the response rates without compromising the assumption underlying a random sample. For example, people who were initially called on a weekend day were not to be pursued more aggressively than people who were initially called on a weekday. The NAES followed a special protocol so that the sample of respondents interviewed on any single day would be as representative of the population as possible. In the 2000 NAES, a total of eighteen call attempts were made for every telephone number that was released into the field. The call backs took place over a period of two weeks. If it was determined that a telephone number was out of service or was a nonresidential number, interviews at that number were not pursued. After a telephone number was released into the field, call attempts were made as follows:

Days 1–4:   Two attempts each day
Days 5–14:   One attempt each day

There was also a refusal conversion protocol. If a respondent made an initial refusal on days 1–6 from the phone number's release into the field, the person was called back for potential conversion four days from the initial refusal. If the initial refusal was made on days 7–9, the person was called back on day 10. If the initial refusal took place on days 10–13, the respondent was called back for conversion the next day. And finally, if the initial refusal took place on day 14, then a callback for conversion was made on the same day. If a completed interview did not take place after fourteen days of a telephone number having been released into the field, no further contact was initiated.

What is important to note here is that there were strict procedures in place so that no telephone number was treated differently from any of the other numbers selected. Telephone numbers released on Tuesdays were not handled differently from telephone numbers released on Fridays. This protocol ensures that the probability of being interviewed is a random event. By stabilizing the proportion of respondents who completed an interview after having been called only a few times and those who completed an interview after being called numerous times, the representativeness of the daily cross-sections is maximized.

Why is it important that the date of the interview be a random event? If the date of interview is random, then the characteristics of the sample on any given day will not vary systematically. Figure 4.2 shows that if we plot the data across time, there are no systematic patterns of variation in the demographic characteristics, such as gender or race, which should remain stable across the campaign. If we have been consistent in our sampling and interviewing strategy, we would not expect, for example, the number of female or white respondents in the sample to increase. Because these characteristics do not change in a predictable way, we do not have to worry that they are potential confounding variables to our analyses. When we observe that some variables change in systematic ways across the campaign, we can attribute these patterns to genuine changes in the electorate with greater confidence.

The NAES design allows us to challenge the assumptions of what is and is not stable during the course of the campaign. For example, partisan stability across the campaigns has been questioned. Some polling organizations weight their data by party identification. If party identification fluctuates across the campaign in a nonrandom way, however, this strategy may not be wise. Figure 4.3 shows the percentage of the electorate that identified as Independent from mid-July to the end of December. It demonstrates that this

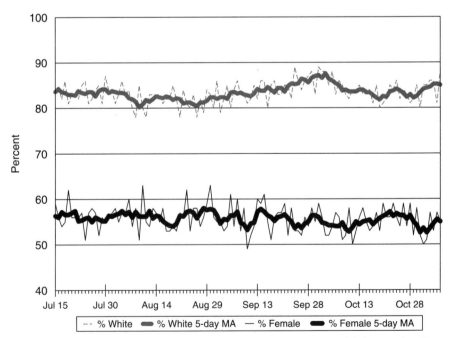

Figure 4.2 The Gender and Racial Composition of National RCS from July 15 to November 6 (MA, moving average)

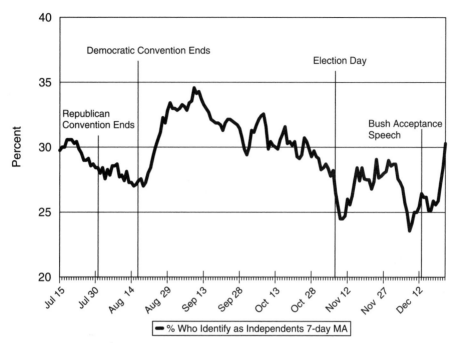

Figure 4.3 Percentage of Respondents Who Identify as Independents During the General Election (MA, moving average)

percentage was not stable over time. Surveys that are weighted by party identification may be operating under some misconceptions about party identification. Party identification may not be as stable as once thought and could be considered an indicator of the respondents' attitudes toward candidates at a given moment in the campaign. Because we know that the sample characteristics on things that should remain stable, such as gender and race, are in fact stable when we plot them, we are able to make the claim that party identification changes over the course of the campaign and is not steady.

CALL DISPOSITIONS

A total of 373,016 telephone numbers were called over the course of the nation cross-section study. This total includes 12,944 calls that were made during the initial phase of the study, which began November 8, 1999. Interviews that took place prior to December 14, 1999, were used to test survey questions and work out the kinks in the process of releasing the replicates. It was during this time that the call-house, SRBI, determined how many replicates were needed to complete the target number of interviews for each day.

Random-digit dialing, of course, produces many telephone numbers that fail to yield completed interviews. When first contacting individuals at a randomly generated number, 22.6% of these numbers were not residential lines or were not in service. Disposition data are shown in Table 4.1. The table shows that only 4.7% of first call attempts produced completed interviews. There are a number of reasons why individuals must be contacted several times before an interview is completed. A large percentage of initial call attempts resulted in the person answering the telephone telling the survey firm to call back at some other time (21.6%).

Of those telephone interviews that were completed, the average number of calls made to complete the interview was 3.71 (SD = 2.99). The median number of calls was 3. Figure 4.4 shows the percentage of completed interviews by the number of dials made. There is a pattern of decreasing yield as the number of dials to a telephone number increases. Most of the interview completions take place in the first few dial attempts. Fewer completions take place the longer a telephone number has been in the field. The farther away in time it is from a number's initial release into the field, the less likely the number will yield a completed interview.

This pattern is important because respondents who answer the survey in the initial few calls may be different from those who are harder to reach. Because new numbers are released into the field each day, the completed interviews are composed of many people who are reached after a few dials as well as a few people who are reached after many call attempts. When an RCS study begins, the first couple of weeks of interviews will not have this mix of people contacted after a few calls and those contacted after several calls. On the first day of the study, for example, completed interviews will

TABLE 4.1 Disposition of Calls for the NAES National Cross-Section

Disposition	Disposition of First Call	Disposition of Final Call
Not in service/nonresidential number/ line problems	84,157 (22.6%)	126,746 (34%)
Updated number	87 (0.0%)	
No answer/busy	113,191 (30.3%)	44,357 (11.9%)
Answering machine	64,550 (17.3%)	13,705 (3.7%)
Respondent unavailable for all of field/ not competent	3,091 (0.8%)	12,781 (3.4%)
Call back	80,707 (21.6%)	55,278 (14.8%)
Refusal	8,205 (2.2%)	52,184 (14%)
Ineligible	1,091 (0.3%)	5,346 (1.4%)
Break-off	362 (0.1%)	1,760 (0.5%)
Complete	17,575 (4.7%)	60,859 (16.3%)
Total	373,016	373,016

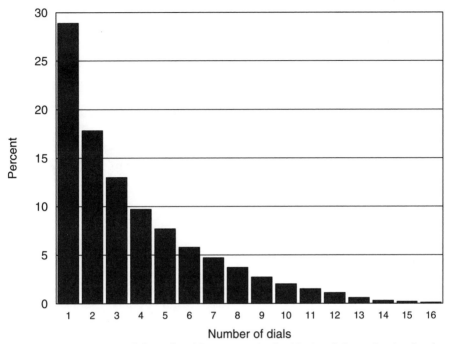

Figure 4.4 Percentage of Completed Interviews in the National Cross-Section by the Number of Dials Made

only consist of those individuals who have been called once or twice, based on the NAES protocol. This is why the first few weeks of the NAES data collection are not included for analysis.

Figure 4.5 demonstrates that there is some variation from day to day in the average number of dials made before an interview is completed. The first day of interviews was November 8, 1999. The graph shows that the average number of dials made before interviews were completed was the lowest on November 8 than on any other date.

It should be noted that there were thirteen days in the 2000 NAES when replicates were not released and calls were not made because these days fell on national holidays. Telephone calls were not made on:

1999: December 24, December 25, December 31

2000: January 1, January 2, July 3, July 4, November 7, November 23, December 24, December 25, December 31

2001: January 1

Before conducting across-time analyses, researchers should be aware that data are missing on these dates.

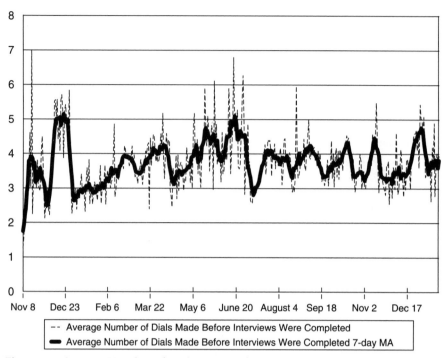

Figure 4.5 Average Number of Dials Made Before Interviews Were Completed from November 8, 1999, to January 19, 2001 (MA, moving average)

CONCLUSION

RCS design is a special type of repeated cross-sectional design that uses strict calling protocols. By releasing new lists of people to be interviewed into the field on a regular schedule, this design is able to ensure that each of the cross-sections is composed of randomly selected members from the population under study. If done correctly, the RCS design should rank at the top of studies that generate the possible random sample for capturing campaign dynamics.

The NAES target sample size varied throughout the study. On those days when large samples were desired, additional replicates were released into the field. Because the general election was of great interest, it was made a priority in resource allocation and sample size. The larger the sample size, the greater the precision of the estimates generated. When conducting an RCS study, the size of one's sample may be constrained by the research budget. Interviewing large numbers of individuals is expensive. Therefore, researchers with specific hypotheses should perform power analyses to see whether conducting such studies is worth their time, given the resources available.

REFERENCES

Johnston, Richard, and Henry E. Brady. 2002. The rolling cross-section design. *Electoral Studies* 21:283–95.

Zaller, John. 2002. The statistical power of election studies to detect media exposure effects in political campaigns. *Electoral Studies* 21:297–329.

Visualizing Data Across the Campaign

Kate Kenski

Charts and graphs can give insight into patterns and relationships that
are not readily apparent when relying solely on statistical summaries.
Cleveland (1993) argues that "[v]isualization is critical to data analysis. It
provides a front line of attack, revealing intricate structure in data that cannot be absorbed in any other way. We discover unimagined effects, and we
challenge imagined ones" (1). This chapter emphasizes the importance of
graphing data when studying campaign dynamics. There are many ways in
which researchers can use visual techniques to help them better understand
their data and convey that understanding to others. This chapter suggests a
couple of ways that information can be graphically displayed. We begin by
discussing how researchers can be misled when they do not look at their
data through visual techniques. Next, we turn our attention to the process
of aggregating and smoothing data. And finally, we illustrate some of the
advantages of using visual approaches with one's data.

REASONS FOR VISUALIZING DATA

Visual techniques can uncover campaign dynamics in ways that statistical
summaries of data often cannot. Charts and graphs can bring us closer to
our data and help us explain our findings to others. Tufte (1983) argues,
"Graphics *reveal* data. Indeed graphics can be more precise and revealing
than conventional statistical computations. Consider Anscombe's quartet: all
four of these data sets are described by exactly the same linear model (at
least until the residuals are examined)" (13). Table 5.1 provides the data from
Anscombe's quartet. The quartet refers to four datasets. Each dataset has
eleven cases and two variables, X and Y. The individual values on each variable differ from dataset to dataset. Nevertheless, each has an X variable with
a mean of 9 (SD = 3.32), and a Y variable with a mean of 7.5 (SD = 2.03).
When a linear regression equation is calculated for each dataset, the equation is the same: $Y = 3.0 + .5X$.[1]

---

[1] The R-square statistic tells us how much of the variation in the dependent variable that the model explains. The R-square for each model is .67. The standard error of the regression for each dataset is 1.24.

TABLE 5.1 Anscombe's Quartet

1		2		3		4	
X	Y	X	Y	X	Y	X	Y
10.0	8.04	10.0	9.14	10.0	7.46	8.0	6.58
8.0	6.95	8.0	8.14	8.0	6.77	8.0	5.76
13.0	7.58	13.0	8.74	13.0	12.74	8.0	7.71
9.0	8.81	9.0	8.77	9.0	7.11	8.0	8.84
11.0	8.33	11.0	9.26	11.0	7.81	8.0	8.47
14.0	9.96	14.0	8.10	14.0	8.84	8.0	7.04
6.0	7.24	6.0	6.13	6.0	6.08	8.0	5.25
4.0	4.26	4.0	3.10	4.0	5.39	19.0	12.50
12.0	10.84	12.0	9.13	12.0	8.15	8.0	5.56
7.0	4.82	7.0	7.26	7.0	6.42	8.0	7.91
5.0	5.68	5.0	4.74	5.0	5.73	8.0	6.89

Based on the means, standard deviations, and regression equations, it is tempting to assume that each dataset is essentially the same. Visual techniques can highlight important aspects of the data that are not readily apparent by means, standard deviations, and other statistics. Figure 5.1 plots Anscombe's quartet and shows that the relationship between X and Y varies greatly from dataset to dataset. Each dataset looks quite different from the others. These plots show that a linear model does not suit some of these datasets. Dataset Two, for example, needs a curvilinear model to capture it more accurately.

Graphical displays of data can help us better understand phenomena. In his discussion of the Anscombe quartet, Diebold (2001) offers four reasons to look at graphics (53). First, "*Graphics helps us summarize and reveal patterns in data,* as, for example, with linear versus nonlinear functional form in the first and second Anscombe datasets." When we run correlations or ordinary least squares (OLS) regressions, we assume that the data have an underlying linear form. When we plot the data and see that nonlinear patterns are apparent, we must rethink our assumptions. Sometimes this means that we should transform the variables in some way, and other times it means that we need to rethink the types of statistical methods we are using.

Second, "[g]raphics helps us identify anomalies in data, as in the third Anscombe dataset," states Diebold. There is a single outlier in the top right corner of Dataset Three's graph. Such an outlier will pull the regression line toward it. When outliers appear, we should take steps to identify who or what the outliers are. Outliers can often give us new insight into our theories. In the event that we decide to delete outliers from our analyses and re-run our models, we must make sure that we note the deletion in our reports.

Third, Diebold notes, "Less obvious, but most definitely relevant, is the fact that graphics facilitates and encourages comparison of different pieces of data." By plotting these datasets next to one another as we did in Figure 5.1, for example, we can compare them instantaneously. One immediately sees that the datasets exemplify very different relationships.

Finally, Diebold explains,

> There is one more aspect of the power of statistical graphics. It comes into play in the analysis of large datasets, so it wasn't revealed in the analysis of the Anscombe datasets, which are not large, but it is nevertheless tremendously important. *Graphics enables us to present a huge amount of data in a small space, and it enables us to make huge datasets coherent.*

AGGREGATING DATA

The NAES data files contain individual-level data. Each case in these data reflects the responses of an individual respondent. To look at variations in the data over time, the individual cases can be aggregated to a larger, temporal unit, such as day. Many statistical packages have commands that allow researchers to convert data into larger units. To aggregate data to day, a variable is selected from one of the RCS datasets, in which many individuals have responded. So that the date of interview variable can become the

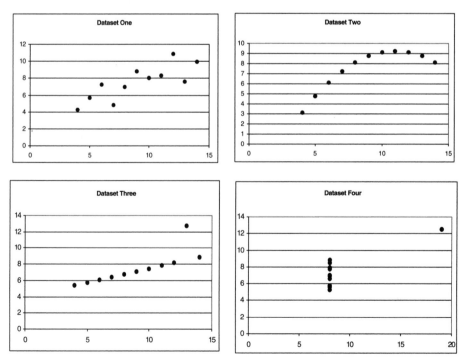

Figure 5.1 Scatter Plots of Anscombe's Quartet

new unit of analysis, a mean of the individual responses on the variable of interest should be calculated for each day. A new dataset can be made, where each case is now the date of interview rather than individual respondent.

Figure 5.2 shows the average feeling thermometer evaluations from August 7 to January 19 of Republican Dick Cheney and Democrat Joseph Lieberman, the vice presidential candidates. Overall, the public gave relatively favorable ratings to the VP candidates. Neither candidate had evaluation averages that went below 50, which was given to candidates for whom respondents felt neither favorable nor unfavorable. How were these data aggregated? The feeling thermometer evaluations for each candidate were aggregated for each day. For example, on August 7 there were 233 respondents who gave substantive answers to the Cheney feeling thermometer question, meaning that the respondents received the question and did not refuse to answer it. Their answers ranged from 0 to 100. These responses were averaged together so that a single number, 57.79, represents responses for August 7. The same was done for the Lieberman evaluations.

As mentioned in Chapter 4, data on some dates are missing in the NAES data because we did not interview people on national holidays. There are different strategies for handling missing data. One could chart the data and simply leave the missing dates out of the continuum. One could also take

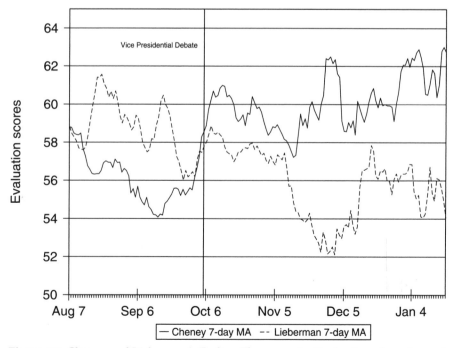

Figure 5.2 Cheney and Lieberman's Feeling Thermometer Evaluations from August 7 to January 19 (MA, moving average)

an average of the days surrounding the missing date and insert the average to hold the date's place in the continuum. For example, since November 7 is missing, one could take an average from the responses made on November 6 and 8 and insert the average before charting the data. Whichever strategy is used, researchers should report how they have decided to handle these dates in their data analysis reports. In the dataset used to create Figure 5.2, missing data appeared on November 7, November 23, December 24–25, December 31, and January 1. We inserted averages for the dates on which data were missing.

ILLUSTRATING THE RELATIONSHIPS BETWEEN SERIES

On October 5, the vice presidential candidates had a televised debate. Around this time, Cheney's evaluations rose, while Lieberman's fell slightly, as shown in Figure 5.2. While one can see that there is a relationship between these two series of evaluations, graphs can be used to illustrate differences between series even more strikingly. Figure 5.3 builds on the graph from 5.2, adding a line that shows the difference between the Cheney and Lieberman evaluations. The thick black line at the bottom of the graph shows the difference

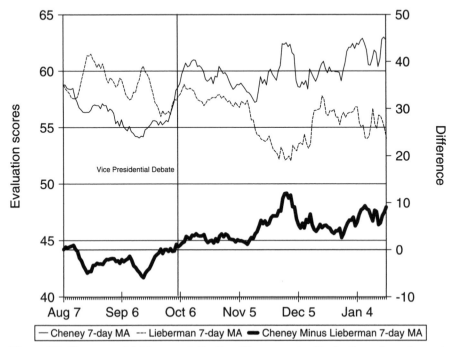

Figure 5.3 Cheney and Lieberman's Feeling Thermometer Evaluations from August 7 to January 19 (MA, moving average)

between Cheney and Lieberman's evaluations using the righthand side axis of the graph. When this line is above zero, it means that Cheney's evaluations were higher than Lieberman's. When it goes below zero, it means that Lieberman was rated more highly than Cheney on average.

SMOOTHING DATA THROUGH MOVING AVERAGES

Daily cross-sections are subject to sampling variation. The underlying patterns in data can be obscured by this variation, which decreases as one's sample size increases. Consequently, pooling data across days makes graphs more readable. "[O]therwise the real shifts would be scarcely detectable through the uninteresting day-to-day fluctuation induced by sampling error" (Johnston et al. 1992, 26). By pooling data across days, some of the random sampling variation is smoothed out of the graph, giving us a better sense of where the true population percentages lie.

One way to smooth data is by using moving averages, which pool data across days. Two commonly used moving average techniques are the centered moving average and the prior moving average. The centered moving average for a particular day is that day's value averaged with specified values around it. A five-day centered moving average, for example, takes the value of a particular day plus the values on the two days before it and the values on the two days after it and averages them. In Table 5.2, the five-day centered moving average for day 3 is the sum of the values for days 1–5 divided by 5: $(5 + 4 + 3 + 3 + 2)/5$. By performing similar calculations for the other days, a smoother pattern than the initial observations is revealed when the data are plotted.

The prior moving average for a particular day is that day's value averaged with a specified set of values before it. A five-day prior moving average, for example, takes the value of a particular day plus the values on the four days

TABLE 5.2 Hypothetical Example of Moving Averages

Day	Original Value	Five-day Centered Moving Average	Five-day Prior Moving Average
1	5		
2	4		
3	3	3.4	
4	3	3.2	
5	2	3.2	3.4
6	4	4.2	3.2
7	4	4.6	3.2
8	8		4.2
9	5		4.6

preceding it and averages them. Notice that the five-day moving average is the same as the centered moving average simply offset by two days.

There are no hard and fast rules about which type of moving average is preferable. It is important to note, however, that the centered moving average takes on the values of data following it. Since day 3 of a five-day centered moving average is influenced by the values that come before it, changes in the data may appear in the graph before they actually occurred. Let's suppose, for example, that some event occurred on day 8. This event increased the value of the variable. While the increase is not picked up in the prior moving average until day 8, it is picked up in the centered moving average on day 6. This does not make the centered moving average less useful. The dynamics will still be picked up in the data but at a slightly earlier point in time.

The more days that are used to create the moving average, the smoother that the data become. Figure 5.4 contains a seven-day centered moving average and a fifteen-day one. From July 18 to September 7, NAES respondents were asked a total of eighteen candidate issue position questions—nine questions about Bush and nine about Gore. These questions were used to create a knowledge index. The sampling variation in the initial observations covers up some of the important patterns in the data. Using the centered moving averages, it becomes clear that knowledge increased before the Republican National Convention began. Knowledge about the candi-

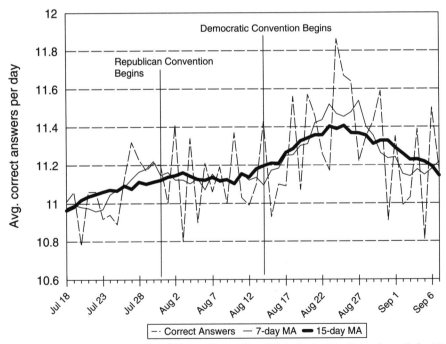

Figure 5.4 Knowledge Index of Major Party Candidate Issue Positions from July 18 to September 7 (MA, moving average)

dates then leveled off until the beginning of the Democratic National Convention, when knowledge increased again. About a week after the Democratic convention ended, the gains in knowledge began to recede.

Across how many days should data be averaged? The answer depends in part on the daily sample sizes. If they are small, one may need to pool more days to smooth out the sampling variation. But once again, there are no hard-and-fast rules. If one uses too many days to create the moving average, one risks oversmoothing the data to the point where important variation is obscured. Johnston et al. (1992) observe that "pooling has a disadvantage: where the true percentage is shifting, mixing values together from different days can mask the shift" (26). If one smoothes across as many days as possible, the value will take on the average of the variable, revealing a horizontal line that crosses the Y-axis at the mean of Y. For those wanting to capture campaign dynamics, this smoothing approach is not useful. As a general rule, it is better to have graphs containing some sampling variation than risk oversmoothing the data to the point where dynamics are concealed. The goal is to find a balance between sampling variation obscuring the dynamics at one extreme and merely reflecting the overall mean of the variable at the other.

To see if the patterns of knowledge acquisition differed by candidate, the candidate knowledge index was broken down into two indices: one for knowledge about Bush's issue positions and one for Gore's. Figure 5.5 tracks

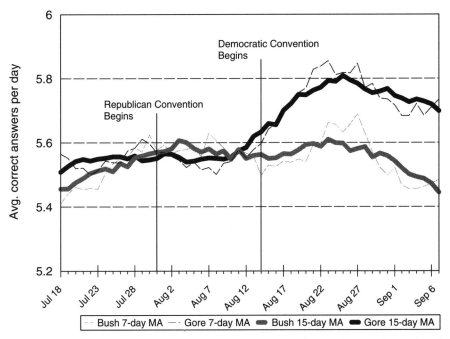

Figure 5.5 Knowledge of Bush and Gore's Issue Positions from July 18 to September 7

these indices around the convention periods using seven-day and fifteen-day centered moving averages. While the lines are not as smooth as they could be using the seven-day moving average, the campaign dynamics are revealed. While there are some changes in the respondents' understanding of Bush's issue positions, the greater changes appear in their understanding of Gore's. Knowledge about Bush increased as the Republican convention approached but then leveled off. Knowledge about Gore, however, increased most dramatically after the Democratic convention began. In transmitting knowledge about issue positions, the Democratic convention was more successful than the Republican convention.

ADVANTAGES OF THE VISUAL APPROACH

There are two major advantages from engaging in the task of graphing data. First, graphs may reveal relationship structures that were not assumed previously. And second, graphs can communicate information to one's audience more easily and efficiently than information given in tabular form. To illustrate these advantages, we will use data from the NAES on absentee and early voting during the general election campaign.

As we saw with the Anscombe's quartet, it is often not until data are graphed that we begin to understand their underlying structure. Cleveland (1993) explains that bivariate data in a scatter plot have two components of variation. "One component is a smooth underlying pattern. . . . Fitting such bivariate data means determining a smooth curve that describes the underlying pattern. The second component is residual variation about this underlying pattern—the vertical deviations of the points from the smooth curve" (8). Determining the underlying structure is important.

Election Day is thought to be the time when American citizens cast their votes for the political leaders of their choice. The notion that all American voters cast their ballots on a single day, however, is no longer accurate. In many states, citizens are given the opportunity to vote prior to Election Day by either balloting by mail or voting early at polling stations. Election Day is more accurately described as the last day when voting for candidates takes place. As this section will demonstrate through the graphing of responses from the NAES, campaign studies that fail to acknowledge that voting often takes place weeks before Election Day ignore an important campaign dynamic.

A unique feature of the NAES pre-election survey was that rather than assuming that they had not voted before Election Day, respondents were asked whether they had already voted at the time they were interviewed. This allows researchers to distinguish between voting intentions and behavior during the pre-election period. Ajzen and Fishbein (1980) argue that intentions and behavior are not synonymous; a large body of social psychological research confirms this distinction. As absentee and early voting grow in popularity, the distinction between voting intentions and voting behavior during the pre-election period becomes an increasingly important one.

How prevalent was voting before Election Day in the 2000 presidential campaign? The NAES post-election survey treated as a single cross-section shows that 15% of those who voted in the general election cast their ballots before Election Day. Around 46% of respondents in the national rolling cross-section lived in the twenty-six liberal absentee,[2] early voting, or voting-only-by-mail (VOBM) states (see Chapter 2 for details on these states). In those states that have liberal absentee, early voting, or VOBM policies, 23.5% of the electorate voted before Election Day.

Why should it matter to campaigns that 15% of U.S. voters cast their ballots early? If all absentee and early voting ballots were cast the day before the election, then absentee and early voting would not greatly affect how campaigns are conducted. If absentee and early voting takes place over the course of several weeks prior to Election Day, however, politicians would have to adopt different types of campaign strategies to ensure that they get their messages out before citizens have cast their ballots. The structure of absentee and early voting during the pre-election period, therefore, becomes important for us to understand.

We can use the pre-election national rolling cross-section to trace the prevalence of absentee and early voting from October to Election Day. What does a graph of absentee and early voting reveal? Figure 5.6 shows that over the course of October, the percentage of the electorate that has voted, defined as those who plan to vote or have already voted in the general election, increases. Because the daily samples are subject to sampling variation, a five-day centered moving average is used to approximate the underlying dynamics. The five-day moving average reveals that by October 23, fifteen days before Election Day, about 5% of the electorate had already voted. Nine days before Election Day, on October 29, 10% of the electorate had cast their ballots. By November 4, 15% of the electorate had balloted.

This example shows that plotting data can challenge our assumptions about campaign dynamics. Data from the NAES clearly show that voting does not take place on a single day. For many voters, the act of voting takes place weeks before Election Day. Campaigns that fail to recognize that some will vote before Election Day may end up wasting their resources on messages to people who have already cast their ballots. Political communication scholars who fail to recognize the prevalence of absentee and early voting miss out on understanding fundamental campaign dynamics.

In Figure 5.6, we used a five-day centered moving average to smooth the data in order to reveal an underlying pattern. While we can impose many types of structures on our data, Figure 5.6 revealed that the pattern under-

---

[2] Liberal absentee voting states are those states that give all potential voters the opportunity to cast absentee ballots without providing excuses, such as work, travel, or religious holiday conflict.

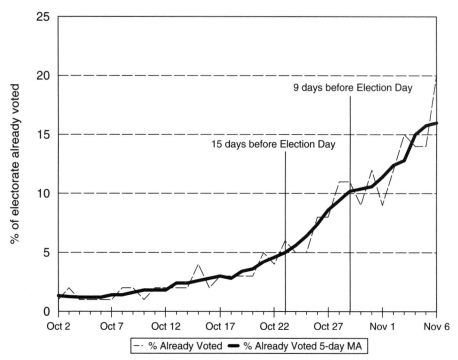

Figure 5.6 Percentage of Electorate That Voted Prior to Election Day (MA, moving average)

lying voting before Election Day was nonlinear. While the linear model is widely used, it does not always best reflect the true pattern underlying our observations.

Figure 5.7 shows two types of models that have been fit to the data: a linear trend, and an exponential curve.[3] The jagged line represents our initial observations. Our visual inspection of the data suggests that the exponential curve fits over the observations better than the linear trend, as there is less error between the initial observations and the exponential curve than there is between the initial observations and the linear trend.

Graphing data is an important component of the research process. Rather than just assuming that phenomena have a specific structure, data should be graphed to see whether the researcher's assumptions are valid. "Statistical graphs are central to effective data analysis, both in the early stages of an investigation and in statistical modeling" (Fox 1997, 35).

A second advantage of graphing data is that visual representations can capture dynamics in ways that are more striking than when dynamics are expressed in equations. The adage that "a picture is worth a thousand

---

[3] Trends will be discussed in more detail in Chapter 7.

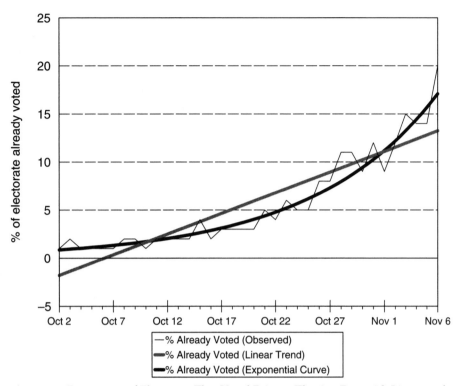

Figure 5.7 Percentage of Electorate That Voted Prior to Election Day with Linear and Exponential Fits to the Data

words" applies to data analysis. Pictures give us an intuitive understanding of data and allow us to better communicate our findings to others. While tables are of great interest to researchers studying a topic, they hold less appeal for those who are less knowledgeable or initially less interested in it. Graphs can often convey a wealth of information more easily than tables.

For example, campaign researchers want to know: Where did the electorate stand at a given point during the campaign? Because of absentee and early voting, researchers should not rely solely on the voting intentions variable when using the NAES data to figure out which presidential candidate was ahead or behind in the general election campaign. In 2000, those who cast their ballots before Election Day were more likely to vote for Bush. In the unweighted post-election sample from November 8 to January 19, 58.2% of early voters said they voted for Bush compared to 51% of Election Day voters (Chi-square = 8.761, df = 1, p < .003).

Since those who vote before Election Day were more likely to cast their ballots for Bush, pre-election analyses should take early voters into account. If one is interested in only those who are capable of being persuaded, then *voting intentions* may be the variable of interest. However, if one is interested

TABLE 5.3 Percentage of the Two-Party Vote Favoring Bush in the Last Days of the Campaign

Date	Voting Intention for Bush	Already Voted for Bush	Combined Intention/ Behavior for Bush
11/2/02	50% (N = 191)	52% (N = 25)	50% (N = 216)
11/3/02	49% (N = 199)	60% (N = 35)	51% (N = 234)
11/4/02	47% (N = 156)	56% (N = 25)	49% (N = 181)
11/5/02	49% (N = 189)	43% (N = 30)	48% (N = 219)
11/6/02	49% (N = 171)	63% (N = 41)	51% (N = 212)

in where the whole electorate stood at any given point in time, then one should combine the survey's voting intention and voting behavior variables.

Table 5.3 shows the daily percentages of the two-party vote favoring Bush in the last five days of the campaign. The voting intentions percentages tend to lean toward Gore. The early voting decisions tend to lean toward Bush. When combined, neither candidate is predominant.

Figure 5.8 tracks the percentages of the two-party vote choice for Bush from October 16 to November 6 using a seven-day centered moving aver-

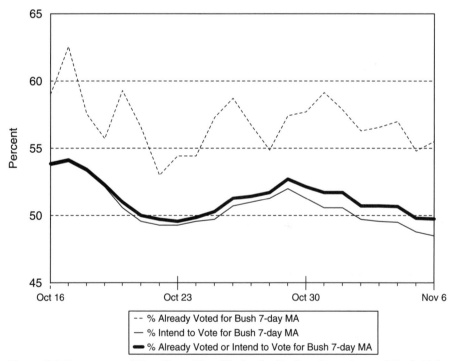

Figure 5.8 Percentage of Two-Party Vote Choice for Bush as Intention and Early Ballot from October 16 to November 6 (MA, moving average)

age. This graph demonstrates that as Election Day approaches, it becomes important for researchers to combine the voting intention and voting behavior measures if they want to capture where the electorate stands in its vote preference. While looking solely at the voting intention variable would suggest that Gore was over a percent ahead of Bush the day before Election Day, the combined intention/behavior measure suggests a statistical dead heat between the candidates.

There are a few drawbacks to the visual approach. While graphing techniques can give us greater insight into our data, they are not a replacement for hypotheses testing. There is a bit of subjectivity used when constructing graphs. Potentially, researchers could tell a story around the data, rather than bringing a story to the data and testing it. The problem with telling stories around the data is that when data are collected via random sampling, there is a possibility that the results appear by chance.

CONCLUSION

There are many ways that data can be visually displayed. We have discussed only a few techniques in this chapter. One does not necessarily need to aggregate data to look at the relationship between time and other variables. Nevertheless, aggregating data to the daily level can allow researchers to look at campaign dynamics in compelling ways.

Graphical displays of data can challenge the assumptions that we make and effectively communicate findings. When used in conjunction with other methods, graphing data across the campaign helps researchers better understand and explain campaign dynamics.

REFERENCES

Ajzen, Icek, and Martin Fishbein. 1980. *Understanding attitudes and predicting social behavior.* Englewood Cliffs, NJ: Prentice-Hall.

Cleveland, William S. 1993. *Visualizing data.* Summit, NJ: Hobart Press.

Diebold, Francis X. 2001. *Elements of forecasting.* 2d ed. Mason, OH: South-Western.

Fox, John. 1997. *Applied regression analysis, linear models, and related methods.* Thousand Oaks, CA: Sage.

Johnston, Richard, André Blais, Henry E. Brady, and Jean Crête. 1992. *Letting the people decide: Dynamics of a Canadian election.* Stanford, CA: Stanford University Press.

Tufte, Edward R. 1983. *The visual display of quantitative information.* Cheshire, CT: Graphics Press.

6

Linear and Logistic Regression Models for Cross-Sectional Analyses

Daniel Romer

In this chapter we outline the major strategies for analyzing the NAES using cross-sectional designs. In addition, we review the ways in which linear and logistic regression can be used to analyze these data.

The NAES opens four avenues of analysis using different designs: (1) the panel design involving respondents who were interviewed more than once during the study period; (2) the cross-sectional design involving respondents at only one time period; (3) the repeated cross-sectional design that is the same as the cross-sectional design but conducted at successive time periods or in **waves;** and (4) the rolling cross-sectional design that permits time series analysis with respondents aggregated potentially at each day of the year.

Although the panel study has many advantages, it is limited in its ability to assess changes as they occur in time. Furthermore, repeated assessment in the panel design can introduce biases that are less likely when respondents have not been previously interviewed. One solution to the bias and limits of the panel study is to conduct a separate study using different cross-sectional samples to allow estimates of changes during the election and to avoid the problems of repeated assessment. This design has different individuals at each wave in the data table. It can be conducted as a standalone survey or as a complement to the panel design.

THE REPEATED CROSS-SECTIONAL DESIGN

Table 6.1 contains the data matrix for a cross-sectional analysis in a hypothetical four-wave design. For purposes of illustration, we only show one dependent variable Y_{ti} and two independent variables X_{1ti}, X_{2ti} at each wave (t) as an example of the data layout. There could be any number of both dependent and independent variables in each cell of the design. The data points are identified by both cases (i) and waves representing successive time periods (t). Each case refers to a set of scores obtained from one respondent at one wave of data collection. Unlike the panel design, the cross-sectional design only includes observations on unique individuals at a single wave.

TABLE 6.1 Data Matrix in a Repeated Cross-Sectional Design with Four Waves

	WAVES (t)			
Case (i)	1	2	3	4
1	Y_{11}, X_{111}, X_{211}	Y_{21}, X_{121}, X_{221}	Y_{31}, X_{131}, X_{231}	Y_{41}, X_{141}, X_{241}
2	Y_{12}, X_{112}, X_{212}	Y_{22}, X_{121}, X_{222}	Y_{32}, X_{132}, X_{232}	Y_{42}, X_{142}, X_{242}
i	Y_{1i}, X_{11i}, X_{21i}	Y_{2i}, X_{12i}, X_{22i}	Y_{3i}, X_{13i}, X_{23i}	Y_{4i}, X_{14i}, X_{241}
n-1	$Y_{1n-1}, X_{11n-1}, X_{21n-1}$	$Y_{2n-1}, X_{12i}, X_{22n-1}$	$Y_{3n-1}, X_{13n-1}, X_{23n-1}$	$Y_{4n-1}, X_{14n-1}, X_{24n-1}$
n	Y_{1n}, X_{11n}, X_{21n}	Y_{2n}, X_{12i}, X_{22n}	Y_{3n}, X_{13n}, X_{23n}	Y_{4n}, X_{14n}, X_{24n}

There is no requirement that the number of cases at each wave be the same, although it is desirable to aggregate time periods with roughly similar numbers of cases. As a result, there are a total of nt unique cases in the design distributed over the T waves of data collection.

The rolling cross-sectional design of the NAES makes it possible to analyze changes on a daily basis. However, for this purpose, we recommend using the time series analyses that are described in Chapter 8. In this chapter, we assume more interest in either general relationships between responses in the survey at one time period (e.g., a month during the election cycle) or in more global changes assessed across time periods (e.g., successive weeks or months of the election cycle) than in daily trends. We will illustrate analysis strategies for both types of questions. First, because it is the model we will use most often to analyze cross-sectional data, we will review some basics of linear regression analysis.

THE LINEAR REGRESSION MODEL

To estimate models with time and other predictors, we use the most popular model in the social sciences, linear regression. The model is easy to estimate, and there is a unique solution for almost all data sets. In addition, it is easy to test the significance of the parameters.

The analysis uses an equation that relates a dependent variable to one or more of k independent and nonredundant variables:

$$Y_i = b_0 + b_1 X_{1i} + \cdots + b_k X_{ki} + e_i$$

There are $i = 1$ to N observations of each variable in the equation. As long as there are more observations than variables, one can solve the equation. The more observations one has, the more certain one can be about the range of values of the parameters (the values of b_k). Indeed, the standard error surrounding the estimates for the parameters is a function of $1/N$.

The last term in the model (e_i) is a random component that is not directly observed but is assumed to have a mean of 0 and a standard deviation that is constant across predicted values of Y. This term is called the *error* or *residual* in the equation because it is not predicted by any of X variables in the model.

The major aim of the regression model is to predict values of Y. The random component is simply the **residual** that remains after the predicted score Y_i is subtracted from the observed score Y_i:

$$e_i = Y_i - Y_i$$

CAUSAL MODEL REPRESENTATION OF LINEAR REGRESSION

Another way to represent a regression model is to use a causal diagram (Figure 6.1.)

The diagram tells us that the independent variables lead to the dependent variable with weights b_1 to b_k. A regression model does not imply causation, but we often use it to estimate "effects" that are assumed to represent causal relations between the independent variables and dependent variable. Even if we do not interpret the relations as causal, we often try to rule out reverse causal directions from Y to any of the Xs.

The curved arrows between the independent variables tell us that the variables may be related to each other. But these relations only indicate that the

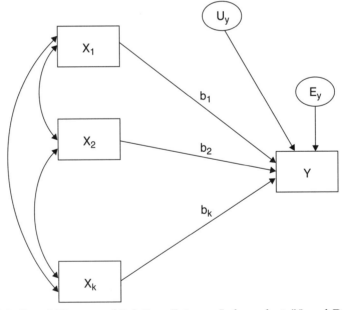

Figure 6.1 Causal Diagram of Relations Between Independent (X) and Dependent Variables (Y), Including the Contribution of Unknown Causes (U_y) and Measurement Error (E_y)

variables are potentially correlated with each other and do not specify a causal connection. The **b** weights represent the relation between each independent variable and the dependent variable holding constant correlations with other variables. One consequence of possible correlation between variables is that estimates of the weights will depend on the variables in the model. If a variable that is related to a predictor is left out of the model, the predictor's effect may be misrepresented.

The potential for unknown predictors is shown in the diagram by the presence of U_y. In causal model diagrams, unobserved variables are enclosed by circles while observed variables are in boxes. If U_y were correlated with any of the Xs, the weights could change. The model assumes that the effect of unknown components is represented by the constant term in the model **(b_0)**. There is often no way to know if the constant term contains variables that are correlated with the Xs, but researchers tend to include as many variables as possible in their models to reduce the chances that an important variable has been neglected. Short of this strategy, one must assume that any unknown predictors are uncorrelated with the Xs (as the diagram indicates).

The diagram also tells us that the measurement error in Y is uncorrelated with the predictors. This is an assumption in the model. **The analysis always produces an error term that is uncorrelated with the predictors, so one cannot test this assumption directly.** But if the assumption is incorrect, then the model will misrepresent the effects of one or more predictors. When this happens, the model will not replicate across samples unless the errors are stable.

ORDINARY LEAST SQUARES ESTIMATION OF THE LINEAR REGRESSION MODEL

We usually use a procedure called **ordinary least squares (OLS)** to estimate the regression model. This procedure estimates the parameters in the model such that the resulting error variation is minimized (i.e., the error variance). The error variance around the regression line is defined as:

$$V_e = \sum (Y_i - Y_i)^2 / (N - k)$$

The simplest OLS estimate of any score is the mean of that score. The mean is the best predictor of a score if no other information is available. It is also the estimate with the smallest error variance.

The total variance in the dependent variable is equal to the error variance plus the variance predicted by the model. A good measure of the ability of an OLS solution to fit the data is the ratio of the predicted variance divided by the total variance. This measure is called R^2 because it equals the square of the correlation between the predicted score and the dependent variable.

Even if a model has a good fit, it is not necessarily useful. When two or more independent variables are so highly related that there is nothing unique about them (they are essentially redundant), we have a situation known as **collinearity.** In this case, the model may fit the data quite well, but the parameters will also be uninterpretable. We usually see this happen when the parameters and their standard errors are extremely large. Another sign of possible collinearity is dramatic change in the direction of the parameters when collinear variables are added to the equation. If parameters exhibit dramatic sign changes or become extremely large as variables are added to the equation, then it is a good idea to see if some of the predictors are so highly related that they cancel each other in the prediction equation.

When we use OLS to estimate the parameters of the linear regression model, we make at least three assumptions.

1. Variance in the error is constant across predicted values of Y, a condition known as **homoskedasticity.** If the errors vary in size with predicted values of Y **(heteroskedasticity),** then the model cannot produce a single set of estimates of the standard errors.

2. The errors are uncorrelated with each other. That is, the error for one case is not related to the error of another case. This is the assumption of zero auto-correlation.

3. The analysis also assumes that the errors have a normal distribution. This permits us to use standard statistical tests for the parameters (e.g., **t** tests).

CODING OF PREDICTORS

One of the more important considerations in setting up a regression model is the coding of the independent variables. There are three basic types of independent variables in a regression model.

1. Quantitative variables represent ordered variation in a predictor. Some examples include party ideology, age, education, and ratings of candidate personality. We also can rescale any of these variables so that they have a mean of zero, in which case they are called **contrasts.**

The benefit of this rescaling is that it permits an interpretation of the **b** weight as a value relative to the average of the predictor. So, a score above zero adds to the dependent variable and a score below zero detracts from the dependent variable. Although rescaling is helpful in interpreting the **b** weights, it does not change the statistical significance of a predictor.

Some examples of quantitative variables include:

- 1, −1 for a two-level variable where 1 represents high values and −1 low values
- 1, 0, −1 for a three-level variable where 0 represents an intermediate value

- −1, 2, −1 for a three-level variable that peaks in the middle
- 1, 2, 3, 4 for increasing levels of a variable, such as attention to news about an election

   2. Dummy variables are indicators that represent a distinction between a category and everything else.

Some examples include the following codings:

- Male gender as +1 and female gender as 0
- Democrats as +1 and everyone else as 0
- Persons who saw a debate as +1 and everyone else as 0

This procedure can be used to make $J - 1$ predictions for any variable with J distinctions. For gender, there is only one possible dummy variable because it only takes one variable to distinguish between two categories. For political party there can be more dummy variables. Typically, one makes at least three distinctions among party types in the United States (i.e., Democrat, Republican, and Independent).

Each predictor adds the value of the **b** weight for the category when it is equal to 1 and adds nothing for the category when it has a score of zero.

   3. Interaction variables are products of either of the aforementioned variables. For example, we can multiply gender by political ideology to ask whether either variable predicts the dependent variable differently across values of the other variable. Some analysts call this a **moderator** effect.

For example, if one wanted to know whether the effect of party depended on gender, one could construct an interaction between the two variables. If gender were coded 1, 0 (male vs. female) and party were coded −1, 0, 1 (Republican, Independent, Democrat), then the interaction could be coded as gender X party which would be −1, 0, 1 for men and 0 for women.

CODING OF DEPENDENT VARIABLES

When we analyze a dependent variable, it is sometimes helpful to rescale the response or to combine responses across dependent variables. One combination takes differences between candidates as indicators of differential response to the candidates. For example, if we were interested in differential reactions to Bush and Gore on the favorability thermometer scale, we could take the difference between them as a measure of this reaction: Bush − Gore. A positive score would reflect a more favorable reaction to Bush than to Gore. A negative score would reflect the reverse.

Difference scores remove idiosyncratic uses of the thermometer scale by different respondents. Some respondents may use the lower end of the scale for all candidates, while others may use the upper end. But when we take differences, we only measure the relative standing of one candidate versus the other.

If we want to remove this kind of idiosyncratic use of the response scale for all candidates, we can take all the thermometer ratings a respondent provides and calculate the mean of these ratings. We can then take each rating (X_i) and subtract the mean (M) from it. In this case, the scores reflect each candidate's standing relative to the mean of all candidates:

$$x_i = (X_i - M)$$

Another strategy that removes not only the mean but also the tendency to use a wider range of the scale standardizes all the ratings that a respondent makes on a common scale with a mean of zero and a standard deviation of 1. This removes both the average level of response and the dispersion of response. This is the familiar standard score:

$$Z_i = (X_i - M)/S(X_i)$$

where S represents the standard deviation or square root of the variance.

EXAMPLES OF CROSS-SECTIONAL ANALYSES

Effects of Background Variables on Political Outcomes

One of the simpler uses of cross-sectional data examines the relation between stable background variables, such as demographic variables or party affiliation, and attitudes toward candidates or issues. For example, how do respondent party affiliation and political ideology influence attitudes toward candidates? To illustrate the use of an interaction term in a regression model, we will analyze thermometer ratings of Bush's favorability (cA01) using the respondent's party affiliation (cV01) and political ideology (cV04) as predictors. Based on theories of social identity (e.g., Turner 1987), we would expect that party members would be less inclined to evaluate a candidate on the basis of their own political ideology and more inclined to evaluate the candidate on the basis of membership in their party. On the other hand, we would expect Independents to evaluate either candidate of the major parties more on the basis of their own ideology than on party identification. This prediction involves an interaction between party affiliation and ideology such that the effect of ideology is stronger among Independents than among Democrats or Republicans.

We select for analysis a time range in the survey when the parties have made their choices of presidential nominee, namely, a four-week span beginning in early September. We can see if the predictors interact by examining the means of the dependent variable as a function of the predictors.

Figure 6.2 shows that Bush is rated most favorably by both conservatives and Republicans, as we would expect. However, political ideology has less impact on Bush's rating among Republicans and Democrats than among Independents (Figure 6.3). This interaction is understandable if party

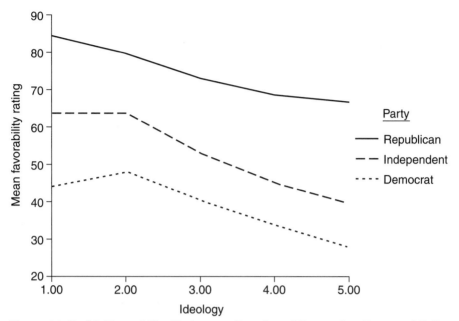

Figure 6.2 Bush's Favorability Rating as a Function of Respondent Party and Political Ideology (1 = Very Conservative, 5 = Very Liberal)

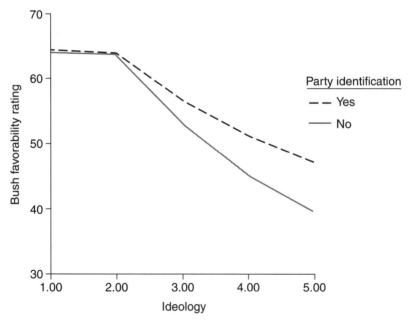

Figure 6.3 Bush's Favorability Rating as a Function of Respondent Party Identification (Democrat and Republican = Yes; Independent = No) and Political Ideology (1 = Very Conservative and 5 = Very Liberal).

affiliation increases loyalty to the party's nominee. The effect of party is also stronger among people who do not label themselves as conservative.

To test this interaction, we can create a new variable that is the product of political ideology (PI) and a dummy coded variable for independent party affiliation (ID = 1 if party is independent and zero otherwise): PI × ID. This interaction assesses the differential effect of being an independent on the relation between political ideology and evaluation of one party's candidate.

The results of the regression analysis shown in Table 6.2 show that indeed both party affiliation and political ideology influence ratings of Bush. For example, for every unit increase in liberal political ideology, there is an approximate 5.8 unit decrease in rating (see the unstandardized coefficients or B weights). A similar effect occurs as one moves from being a Republican to an Independent (about sixteen units less favorable rating). However, the interaction between being an independent and political ideology also contributes to the prediction of Bush's rating. In particular, for Independents, each unit increase in liberal ideology results in a little over a two-unit decrease in rating, reflecting the more severe effect of ideology among Independents.

The t tests in the table are the ratios of the B weights to their standard errors. When t ratios are greater than 2.00 in absolute value in samples of at least moderate size (N > 60), they are significant at the .05 level. Most analyses using the NAES will easily exceed this sample size (as does this one, N = 8,118). The only coefficient that is not significant (at the .05 level) is the one for the dummy-coded variable representing independents (ID).

The standardized coefficients (Betas) in the table represent the regression weights for the variables when they are transformed into standard scores (Z scores) that have the same standard deviation (1). Betas permit ready interpretation of differences in the sizes of the coefficients. In this analysis, party is the most influential predictor, followed by ideology.

This analysis shows that Independents treat the candidates differently from the way party affiliates do. In addition, it appears that conservatives were less influenced by their party identification than were liberals. How-

TABLE 6.2 Regression Analysis of Bush Favorability Rating (Thermometer) as a Function of Respondent Political Ideology, Party, and Interaction Between Party Independence and Ideology

| | UNSTANDARDIZED COEFFICIENTS | | STANDARDIZED COEFFICIENTS | | |
	B	Std. Error	Beta	t	Prob.
Constant	107.70	1.27		84.86	.00
Ideology (PI)	−5.83	.46	−.17	−12.66	.00
Party	−16.64	.44	−.41	−38.14	.00
Independents (ID)	3.01	2.08	.05	1.45	.15
PI × ID	−2.08	.70	−.10	−2.98	.00

ever, we have only examined half of the ideological spectrum. What would happen if we also looked at how respondents evaluate Gore?

To do so, we code a new dependent variable that assesses respondents' reactions to both candidates simultaneously, namely, by taking the difference between Bush (cA01) and Gore (cA11) on the same thermometer scale. This coding not only removes individual differences in scale usage but also allows us to examine the influence of party identification independent of the ideology of the candidate. When we combine the two parties and compare them against Independents, we find a symmetric pattern of evaluation for the difference between the two candidates (see Figure 6.4).

This result reveals that both liberals and conservatives are influenced by party identification when evaluating candidates, with Independents more likely than those of either major party to use their political ideology when assessing candidates for office. In comparing effects across the two analyses (Table 6.2 vs. 6.3), we also see that the **t** ratios are larger in the difference score analysis, a result indicating that the dependent variable is now more sensitively measured than it was when we only analyzed Bush's rating. Hence, using difference scores produces a more interpretable pattern of results and increases the power of the regression model.

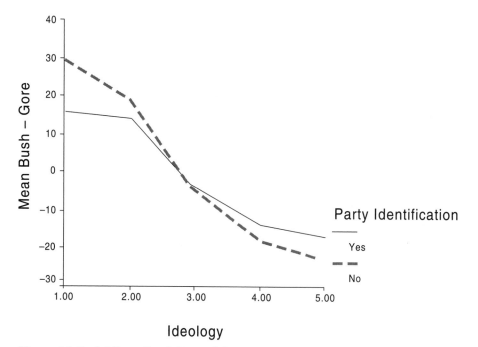

Figure 6.4 Bush Minus Gore's Favorability Rating as a Function of Respondent Party Identification (Democrat and Republican = Yes; Independent = No) and Political Ideology (1 = Very Conservative and 5 = Very Liberal)

TABLE 6.3 Regression Analysis of Bush-Gore Favorability Rating (Thermometer) as a Function of Respondent Political Ideology, Party, and Interaction Between Party Independence and Ideology

| | UNSTANDARDIZED COEFFICIENTS | | STANDARDIZED COEFFICIENTS | | |
	B	Std. Error	Beta	t	Prob.
Constant	105.92		2.05	51.77	.000
Ideology (PI)	−12.65	.74	−.22	−17.02	.000
Party	−34.33	.71	−.48	−48.69	.000
Independents (ID)	10.63	3.36	.10	3.17	.002
PI × ID	−3.95	1.13	−.11	−3.50	.000

Effects of Behavior on Political Outcomes

Cross-sectional data can also be used to examine the relation between self-reported behavior, such as news use, debate watching, and other forms of political participation, and political outcomes, such as learning about the candidates, attitudes toward the candidates, and vote intentions. For example, how does exposure to news about the election influence learning about the candidates? To illustrate an analysis of this question, we use the survey question that asks whether respondents feel they have learned enough about the candidates to make a choice in the election (cL10). We would expect that the more in the past week a respondent has used a major news source, such as a daily newspaper (cE13), the more opportunity the respondent would have to learn about candidates for office. In addition, we would expect that the more respondents reported exposure in the past week to election news in the newspaper (cE14), the more likely they would be to say that they had learned something about the candidates.

Figure 6.5 shows the relation between use of newspapers in the past week and reports of learning about the candidates for president for the same September period we analyzed earlier. In addition, the figure shows the effect of exposure to election news in the newspapers. To make the figure easier to comprehend, use of newspapers was recoded into a four-point scale (0, 1 days = 1; 2, 3 days = 2; 4, 5 days = 3; and 6, 7 days = 4). The pattern of curves suggests that use of newspapers increases learning about candidates. However, this is not true when respondents have not been exposed to news about the election (the lowest curve). As a result, one would expect a regression model to require the inclusion of an interaction term for the two exposure measures.

To test this hypothesis, we set up a regression model of learning as a function of newspaper use (NU), exposure to election news in newspapers (EN), and the interaction of the two newspaper variables (NU × EN). Exposure to election news was reverse coded so that its value increased with exposure.

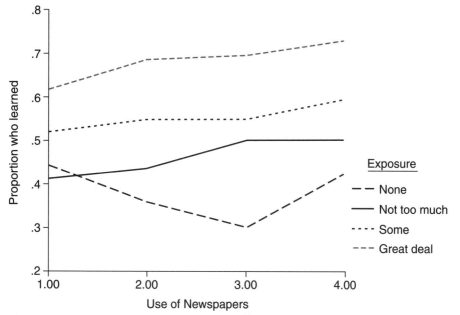

Figure 6.5 Proportion of Respondents Who Claimed to Have Learned Enough to Make a Choice Among the Presidential Candidates as a Function of Newspaper Use in the Past Week and Exposure to Election News in Newspapers

The results of this analysis, shown in Table 6.4, indicate that use of newspapers does not add much to predicting the learning outcome. However, exposure to election news and the interaction with use of newspapers does appear to increase learning, albeit at weak levels of statistical significance.

In addition to the weak results, one might question the validity of the analysis because exposure to election news and use of newspapers may be related to other background variables that are actually responsible for the

TABLE 6.4 Regression Analysis of Reported Learning about Candidates as a Function of Use of Newspapers, Exposure to Recent Election News in the Newspapers, and the Interaction of the Variables

Predictor	UNSTANDARDIZED COEFFICIENTS		STANDARDIZED COEFFICIENTS		
	B	Std. Error	Beta	t	Prob.
Constant	.327	.066		4.99	.000
Use of newspaper (UN)	−.015	.022	−.032	−.68	.500
Exposure to election news in newspapers (EN)	.051	.028	.097	1.85	.064
UN × EN	.015	.008	.143	1.82	.068

relations we observe. For example, more educated persons or older persons may use newspapers more and the findings might have more to do with demographic differences than with actual use of newspapers.

To evaluate this alternative explanation, we test the same model holding constant demographic variables in the equation. In particular, we add quantitative variables for age (cW02) and education (cW06). In addition, we add dummy variables for gender (cW01), Hispanic ethnicity (cW05), and various racial distinctions (black, Asian, and others not classified by white, black, or Asian categories) obtained from the question on racial identity (cW03).

As Table 6.5 indicates, the effects observed in the first analysis largely remain. The unstandardized coefficients in each analysis are about the same. Nevertheless, the probability levels are not statistically significant by usual standards ($p < .05$), suggesting that the estimates of the coefficients are not very reliable. This analysis also shows that age, education, and gender are related to reported learning about candidates. In particular, older, more educated, and male respondents were more likely to report having learned about the candidates at this time in the election period than were their younger, less educated, and female counterparts.

Both of these analyses used the linear regression model. This model assumes that the error variance is constant across all predicted values of Y and that the error is drawn from a normal distribution. However, these assumptions are not very plausible when the outcome is a two-valued (dichotomous) variable, such as "learned enough" or "did not learn enough" about the candidates. As the predicted score approaches either 1 or 0, the

TABLE 6.5 Regression Analysis of Reported Learning About Candidates, Including Demographic Variables in the Analysis

Predictor	UNSTANDARDIZED COEFFICIENTS		STANDARDIZED COEFFICIENTS		
	B	Std. Error	Beta	t	Prob.
Constant	.298	.076		3.921	.000
Use of newspaper (UN)	−.028	.022	−.061	−1.295	.196
Exposure to election news in newspapers (EN)	.048	.027	.092	1.779	.075
UN × EN	.013	.008	.125	1.607	.108
Gender	−.084	.017	−.084	−4.980	.000
Age	.028	.005	.094	5.145	.000
Hispanic ethnicity	−.053	.039	−.025	−1.369	.171
Black	.043	.032	.023	1.333	.183
Asian	−.125	.072	−.029	−1.724	.085
Other race	−.028	.037	−.014	−.753	.451
Education	.021	.004	.093	5.439	.000

error variance tends to depart significantly from normal. Hence, it is best to analyze data with a dichotomous outcome using a different analysis model called logistic regression. Before we illustrate a logistic regression solution with the present example, let's look briefly at how this model works.

The Logistic Regression Model

A more recent addition to the analysis arsenal, the logistic regression model is more difficult to estimate than OLS. However, with the advent of computers and maximum likelihood estimation procedures, these difficulties no longer pose a significant problem.

The logistic regression model is used to analyze dichotomous outcomes. When one analyzes such data, one expects the predicted scores to range between 0 and 1, the equivalent of a probability scale. The problem with doing this analysis using OLS is that the predicted scores need not stay within the 0–1 range. Indeed, OLS assumes that the relation between the predicted score and the dependent variable is linear. However, with a probability scale, the relation will look more like the curve in Figure 6.6. Because this relation is nonlinear, the linear regression model will fail to capture the relationship, especially as the probability of the outcome departs from .5.

Tests for interactions using OLS can be very misleading when the relationship actually conforms to the nonlinear pattern shown in Figure 6.6. To see this, consider the effect when one goes from 1 to 5 on the X axis. The change along the probability scale is only about .1 units. However, when one goes from 5 to 9 along X, the change in probability is about .3 units

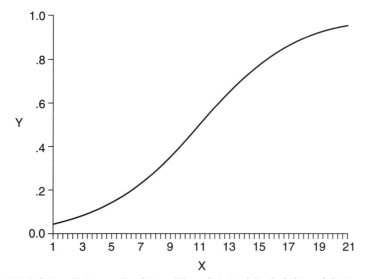

Figure 6.6 Relation Between Predictor (X) and Actual Probability of Outcome with a Dichotomous Outcome Variable (Y)

even though the change along X is the same in the two cases. As a result of the nonlinear relation between Y and X, apparent interactions between variables will occur that are the result of differential change along the probability scale.

The apparent interaction effect is illustrated in Figure 6.7. The effects of one independent variable X_1 are shown with a change of 4 units along the X axis. The effect of similar change in a second variable X_2 is shown for the two separate curves. The greater effect of X_1 when X_2 is larger is entirely attributable to the greater rise in probability that occurs as X_2 is added to X_1. Hence, the apparent interaction is purely the result of the nonlinear increase in Y as X increases (as illustrated in Figure 6.6).

Despite the nonlinearity of the relationship between X and Y, problems with using OLS are often not very serious, especially if the average predicted score is in the middle of the 0–1 scale. However, even if one does not report the use of a logistic regression analysis, one usually tries the analysis to make sure the findings are comparable. This caution is especially important when one is testing interaction predictions.

Interpreting Logistic Regression Weights

Many of the interpretations of logistic regression are the same as for OLS. The weights associated with the predictors represent the magnitude of the relationship with the dependent variable. When important predictors are left

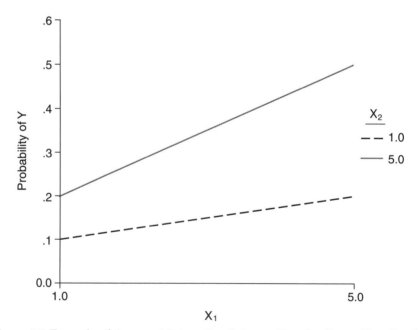

Figure 6.7 Example of Apparent Interaction Between Two Predictors That Results from Nonlinear Increase in Probability as a Function of Predictors

out of the model, the weights for the remaining predictors may be mis-specified. Coding of the predictors is done the same way as in OLS. However, the meaning of the coefficients in the model is different.

In logistic regression, the dependent variable is a function of the odds of the outcome:

$$\text{Odds} = P/(1 - P)$$

For example, if the probability of winning a lottery is .01, then the odds of winning are 1 to 99, or $.01/(1 - .01)$. Odds have the desirable property of ranging from zero to infinity. One benefit of the odds scale is that one can say that the odds are twice as great that something will happen no matter what the odds are. This is not possible with probabilities because they are bounded by zero and 1.

A further transformation of the odds ratio allows the scale to be unbounded for scores less than zero. The log of the odds is zero when $P = .5$ because the log of 1 (.5/.5) is zero. For values less than .5, the log of the odds is negative. Hence, the log odds can range from minus to plus infinity. Although the probability outcome looks like an S-shaped curve when plotted against a predictor, the log odds are linear with predictors.

The log odds, or **logit,** is the actual outcome that logistic regression estimates. Remember that the log of x equals the exponent to which the base of the log is raised in order to equal x.

$$\text{If Log } x = m, \text{ then } x = \text{base}^m.$$

As a result, the log of any base raised to a power (m) is simply m.

The base is arbitrary. Some people like to use 10. In statistical applications, the base is usually *e*, which is approximately 2.72. In addition, the log to the base *e* is usually written as **ln.**

Any product can be represented as the sum of two logs:

$$\text{If } Y = X\,Z, \text{ then } \text{Ln } Y = \text{Ln } X + \text{Ln } Y.$$

The log of e raised to a power is simply the exponent. For example,

$$\text{Ln } e^{b_0} = b_0$$

The coefficients in a logistic regression are part of an exponential expression of the form

$$P/(1 - P) = e^{b_0} e^{b_1 X_1} \ldots e^{b_k X_k},$$

or $\quad \text{Ln } [P/(1 - P)] = b_0 + b_1 X_1 + \cdots + b_k X_k + e$

The coefficients in the above version of the logistic regression model can be translated into an odds ratio. For example, if X_1 is 1 when the respondent is a Republican and zero otherwise, and b_1 is 1.30, then $e^{1.3} = 3.67$ for Republicans and $e^0 = 1$ for everyone else. This means that odds of the response are more than three times greater for Republicans than for people in other parties.

When a coefficient is zero, then the exponential function is 1. In this case, the odds are no different for one group than for the others.

If the independent variable is coded as a continuous variable, such as age or political ideology, then the coefficient is typically small and represents the increase in odds for a unit change in the variable. However, a simpler interpretation uses the following formula:

$$100(e^b - 1) = \% \text{ change for a unit increase in X}$$

For example, if $e^b = 1.1$, then a unit change in X produces a 10% change in the odds of the outcome.

An Example of Logistic Regression

We can now conduct a regression analysis using logistic regression and compare it with the results of linear regression. Let's look at the example we just presented predicting learning about the presidential candidates based on demographic variables and use of newspapers.

The results of this analysis, shown in Table 6.6, indicate that only exposure to election stories in the newspapers is related to learning about the candidates. The B weight of .283 translates into an odds ratio of 1.33 (Exp. B in the table), which means that an increase of one unit on the exposure scale increases the odds of learning about the candidates by 33% [100(1.33 − 1.0)]. The Wald test for each coefficient in the analysis is similar to the t test in OLS in that it represents the ratio of the unstandardized coefficient divided by its standard error. However, it is the square of this ratio, and it uses a different distribution to evaluate statistical significance (the Chi-square distribution). As a result, values greater than 3.84 are significant at the .05 probability level for a single degree of freedom test.

TABLE 6.6 Logistic Regression Analysis of Learning About the Presidential Candidates

Predictor	B	S.E.	Wald	df	Prob.	Exp(B)
Use of newspapers (NP)	−.021	.043	.232	1	.630	.979
Exposure to election stories in newspaper (EP)	.283	.116	6.002	1	.014	1.328
NP × EP	.031	.035	.761	1	.383	1.031
Gender	−.361	.073	24.175	1	.000	.697
Age	.118	.023	25.347	1	.000	1.125
Hispanic ethnicity	−.229	.168	1.844	1	.175	.796
Black	.192	.139	1.915	1	.166	1.212
Asian	−.541	.312	2.996	1	.083	.582
Other race	−.124	.161	.592	1	.442	.883
Education	.089	.016	29.404	1	.000	1.093
Constant	−1.109	.270	16.910	1	.000	.330

Another difference between the logistic and linear regression models is the measure of goodness of fit. In logistic regression analysis programs, the estimation procedure does not minimize the error variance. Rather, it attempts to maximize the likelihood that the model matches the data. A measure of this maximization is usually given in computer outputs as $-2 \times$ the log likelihood or $-2LL$ for short. This value should get **smaller** the better the fit of the model.

As one adds variables to a logistic regression model, $-2LL$ gets smaller. One can assess the significance of the added prediction by subtracting the value of the smaller score from the larger one. This value can be tested using a Chi-square test with k degrees of freedom representing the number of predictors that have been added to the equation. By this procedure, adding a single predictor to a logistic regression equation should reduce the $-2LL$ by at least 3.84 if the variable is to be regarded as adding significant prediction to the model. In the Statistical Package for the Social Sciences (SPSS), this test is called the omnibus test of model coefficients.

The logistic regression analysis does not find much evidence of interaction between use of newspapers and exposure to election stories. It seems to indicate that the only variable with importance is actual exposure to election stories in the press. That is, it does not seem to matter whether respondents read newspapers a lot or a little; their confidence that they have learned enough about the candidates only increases as exposure to election stories increases.

The analysis does confirm the findings from OLS with regard to the other predictors. Male, older, and more educated respondents were more likely to report confidence that they had learned enough to make a decision about the candidates.

TIME AS A PREDICTOR IN REPEATED CROSS-SECTIONAL DATASETS

Our examples of analyses using cross-sectional data have focused on the use of a time slice (e.g., September) in the national rolling cross-sectional database. However, the NAES also has the potential for repeated cross-sectional analyses with time as a predictor. One potential model for analyzing the data in this design is

$$Y_i = b_1 + b_2 TIME + BX + e_i$$

where Y_i is the measure of the critical outcome at different points in time (TIME = 1 to T). We can use this model to predict changes that occur as an election campaign progresses. For example, TIME might predict changes in awareness of a candidate or of the candidate's issue positions (see Figure 6.8).

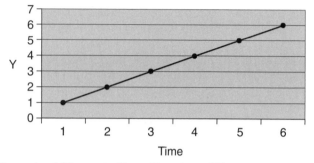

Figure 6.8 Example of Change in Y as a Function of Time

In this model, X is a matrix of demographic and other variables that we want to control in assessing changes that occur over time. B is a matrix of coefficients that weights the variables in X to predict Y. Including the X matrix is the best we can do to control for other variables that might be related to initial levels of Y at the individual level. It also can control for variables that might change with time but that are unrelated to the hypothesized causal process that occurs over TIME. For example, we might be interested in changes in support for a candidate over time controlling for the demographic characteristics of respondents. Fortunately, in the NAES, we do not expect major changes in demographic variables as a function of time because the sampling plan is designed to hold these differences relatively constant.

Nevertheless, holding constant X increases confidence that TIME is the causal factor and not other changes that might have occurred as well. In trying to understand changes that can occur during a campaign, the ability to study variables related to change is a major benefit of this design over the panel design.

Another feature of the repeated cross-sectional design is the ability to study causal factors that might interact with time. For example, one might be interested in the effects of exposure to news about the election. As time passes, heavy exposure to election news should produce greater learning about the candidates and their positions. The effect of news exposure should build over time and produce more learning among those who pay a lot of attention to news about the election than among those whose attention is minimal. Those who pay less attention to the news should display a weaker effect of time, since they will not benefit as much from their exposure to news. The cross-sectional design should allow one to observe these different trends.

An example of an interaction between time and a causal factor that should interact with time is shown in Figure 6.9. In this example, time is coded into 1, 2, 3, 4, 5 time periods, and attention to news about the election is coded as high = 1 versus low = 0. In this example, the interaction predicts that time will increase Y for people who pay attention to news about the elec-

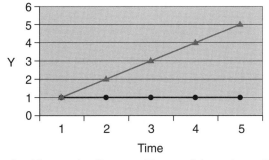

Figure 6.9 Example of Interaction Between Time and Attention to Election News in Affecting Y (triangles represent high exposure; circles represent low exposure)

tion but that time will make no difference for those who pay no attention to election news.

Analyzing Time in a Repeated Cross-Section

To illustrate the use of a repeated cross-sectional design, we will use the Super Tuesday file that contains data for the Super Tuesday states from January 4 to March 6, the last day before the primary on March 7. We can convert our rolling cross-section into a repeated cross-section by aggregating time periods. Our objective is reducing the number of time periods so that changes over time are sufficiently stable to enable an analysis of trends. If we choose time periods that are too large, we will minimize our ability to see change. On the other hand, if we choose periods that are too small, we will allow unsystematic changes to dominate the trend lines. We can begin by examining trends in weekly data points. Let's code each seven days into a single time point and create a variable called "Time" for this new predictor.

A frequency analysis of Time will tell us how many cases we have per time period. The data in Table 6.7 indicate that we have an increasing number of cases as time increases and that no time period has fewer than one hundred cases. This distribution should be adequate for analyzing change. However, we should withhold judgment until we have examined an outcome in which we are interested.

We will continue to pursue our example of learning about candidates. In addition, we will examine the influence of exposure to news about the election to see if it predicts change over time in learning about the candidates. Means of these variables as a function of time are shown in Table 6.8.

The first thing we note is that attention to election news was not assessed until the fourth week of the survey period. Nevertheless, we will be able to study the influence of news exposure for a period of six weeks. In addition, the question about learning was not asked of the entire

TABLE 6.7 Number of Cases in the Super Tuesday File Aggregated by Weeks

Time	Frequency	Percent	Valid Percent	Cumulative Percent
1.00	165	2.5	2.5	2.5
2.00	424	6.4	6.4	8.9
3.00	546	8.2	8.2	17.1
4.00	587	8.9	8.9	26.0
5.00	723	10.9	10.9	36.9
6.00	604	9.1	9.1	46.0
7.00	1,031	15.6	15.6	61.6
8.00	1,232	18.6	18.6	80.2
9.00	1,315	19.8	19.8	100.0
TOTAL	6,627	100.0	100.0	

TABLE 6.8 Means and Number of Cases for Three Variables Assessed in the Super Tuesday File

TIME		Learned Enough to Make a Choice	Attention to National Television News	Attention to Newspapers
1.00	Mean	.174		
	N	46		
2.00	Mean	.202		
	N	109		
3.00	Mean	.271		
	N	144		
4.00	Mean	.234	2.394	2.135
	N	137	348	348
5.00	Mean	.249	2.477	2.213
	N	193	723	723
6.00	Mean	.295	2.492	2.247
	N	156	604	604
7.00	Mean	.313	2.467	2.263
	N	243	1031	1031
8.00	Mean	.335	2.517	2.252
	N	296	1232	1232
9.00	Mean	.356	2.503	2.289
	N	315	1315	1315
TOTAL	Mean	.294	2.487	2.250
	N	1,639	5,253	5,253

sample. However, there are sufficient numbers of respondents at each time period to permit an analysis of this dependent variable. Our preliminary analysis indicates that we can proceed with the analysis of learning during the primary.

To determine whether the time periods we have created are sufficiently stable to permit identification of trends, we can plot the data by time period. This plot in Figure 6.10 indicates that the time trend is quite stable and is linear, especially from weeks 4–9.

Although the data are suggestive, we are still examining the entire universe of respondents, including those who have no intention of voting in the primary. By restricting our analysis to those who report an interest in voting in the primary (cR07), we isolate a still smaller universe (N = 998 vs. 1,639). Fortunately, there are still sufficient respondents to observe time trends even if we restrict the analysis to those who report an intention to vote in the primary (see Table 6.9). Furthermore, the time trend for this group of respondents (Figure 6.11) is stronger than the trend for the entire sample (Figure 6.10), which is not surprising in view of our selection of respondents who have expressed an interest in voting.

We can now examine the relation between time and learning about candidates controlling for attention to news about the primary election. The plot in Figure 6.12 indicates that learning increased primarily for those who devoted a "great deal" of attention to news on network and cable television about the election. Time had little or no impact on those who devoted less attention to news.

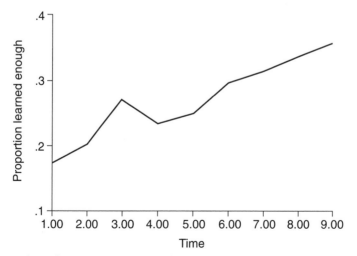

Figure 6.10 Growth in Learning About the Candidates for the Primary in the Super Tuesday States

TABLE 6.9 Means and Number of Cases for Three Variables Assessed in the Super Tuesday File Among Those Who Planned to Vote in the Primary

TIME		Learned Enough to Make a Choice	Attention to National Television News	Attention to Newspapers
1.00	Mean	.172		
	N	29		
2.00	Mean	.250		
	N	72		
3.00	Mean	.280		
	N	75		
4.00	Mean	.212	2.524	2.262
	N	85	233	233
5.00	Mean	.288	2.665	2.377
	N	125	475	475
6.00	Mean	.324	2.655	2.419
	N	105	377	377
7.00	Mean	.378	2.595	2.399
	N	156	671	671
8.00	Mean	.387	2.678	2.396
	N	173	772	772
9.00	Mean	.416	2.676	2.464
	N	178	756	756
TOTAL	Mean	.333	2.645	2.403
	N	998	3,284	3,284

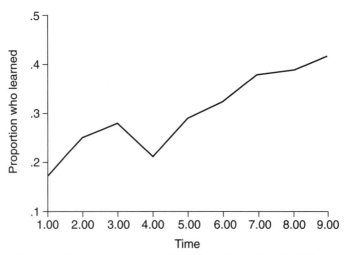

Figure 6.11 Relation Between Time and Learning About the Candidates in the Super Tuesday Primary States

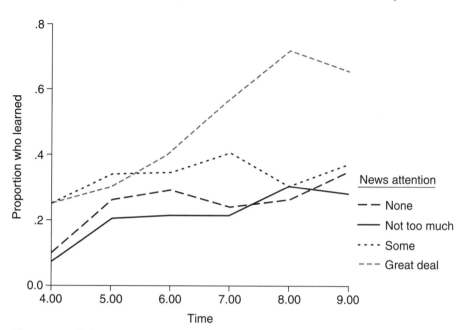

Figure 6.12 Relation Between Attention to Network and Cable Television News and Reports of Learning Enough About the Candidates in the Super Tuesday Primary Election (Time Is in Weeks Leading Up to March 7)

To assess this prediction, we create a new variable to represent the interaction between attention and time. We create a dummy variable that has the value of 1 when attention is the highest (a great deal) and zero otherwise. We can also create dummy variables for two other levels of attention to news: some and not too much. We then multiply the dummy variable for high attention by Time. This interaction essentially says that when attention is highest, there is an added effect of time over and above that produced by Time alone. We can also test the other interactions between lower levels of attention to news and time to see if they contribute to the model.

The results of this logistic regression, shown in Table 6.10, indicate that the best prediction of learning is the joint influence of time and intense attention to the news. Neither time nor attention alone is sufficient to increase learning. In addition, neither medium or low levels of attention to national television news in interaction with time affected learning to an appreciable degree.

We can add other predictors to the model to challenge the finding, but in this case demographic changes are less likely to account for the effect of time or attention to news. The results of this analysis, shown in Table 6.11 indicate that the interaction between time and news exposure remains significant despite the inclusion of demographic variables.

TABLE 6.10 Logistic Regression Analysis of Learning About Candidates

Variable	B	S.E.	Wald	df	Prob.	Exp(B)
Time	.052	.047	1.230	1	.267	1.053
High attention to news (AH)	−1.500	.832	3.251	1	.071	.223
Medium attention to news (AM)	.317	.604	.276	1	.599	1.374
Low attention to news (AL)	−1.182	.888	1.772	1	.183	.307
AH × Time	.365	.120	9.299	1	.002	1.441
AM × Time	−.005	.090	.003	1	.953	.995
AL × Time	.131	.125	1.099	1	.295	1.139
Constant	−1.277	.246	26.957	1	.000	.279

TABLE 6.11 Logistic Regression of Learning About Candidates with Demographic Variables Included

Variable	B	S.E.	Wald	df	Prob.	Exp(B)
Time	.056	.048	1.401	1	.237	1.058
High attention to news (AH)	−1.840	.850	4.685	1	.030	.159
Medium attention to news (AM)	.387	.617	.394	1	.530	1.473
Low attention to news (AL)	−1.137	.907	1.572	1	.210	.321
AH × Time	.395	.122	10.471	1	.001	1.484
AM × Time	−0.12	.092	.017	1	.897	.988
AL × Time	.141	.128	1.217	1	.270	1.151
Gender	−.514	.143	12.890	1	.000	.598
Age	.113	.045	6.369	1	.012	1.120
Hispanic	−.251	.314	.640	1	.424	.778
Black	.167	.234	.513	1	.474	1.182
Asian	−.199	.493	.163	1	.686	.819
Other race	.198	.334	.352	1	.553	1.220
Education	.083	.032	6.634	1	.010	1.086
Constant	−1.457	.432	11.389	1	.001	.233

SUMMARY

The major use of the simple cross-sectional design is to assess the relation between background variables and political outcomes, such as perceptions of the candidates. A more dynamic picture of the influence of behavior, such as exposure to election news or other political activity, can best be determined by the repeated cross-sectional design.

OLS regression is a valuable technique for assessing the relation between predictors and outcomes. However, logistic regression is also valuable when the outcome is measured dichotomously at the individual level. Logistic regression is particularly valuable for assessing interaction effects with a probabilistic response scale.

EXERCISES

Analyze news exposure during the month of October to see if it behaves the same as during September.

Analyze the effect of news exposure to newspapers rather than television to see if the same pattern appears during the Super Tuesday primary period.

Analyze the effect of news exposure on vote choice during the Super Tuesday primary period.

REFERENCE

Turner, J. T. 1987. Rediscovering the social group: A social categorization theory of group behavior. New York: Blackwell.

Analysis of Panel Data

Kate Kenski
Daniel Romer

In the last chapter, we described the use of cross-sectional data to analyze change during an election period. This chapter approaches the same problem using another analysis strategy, the panel design. The NAES contains several panel datasets to permit analysis of the same individuals before and after major election events such as primaries (e.g., Super Tuesday) and presidential debates. In this chapter, we will illustrate panel data analysis using the NAES's first presidential debate panel to shed light on changes in individuals' political talk and their opinions about the debate performances of Bush and Gore.

The layout of data in a panel design is similar to that of the repeated cross-section. As seen in Table 7.1, the major difference is that the same individuals (i = 1 to n) are interviewed at each wave of data collection (t). One dependent variable (Y) and two independent variables (X_1, X_2) are shown for purposes of illustration with subscripts for waves of data collection (t) and respondents (i). Scores for the dependent variable are represented as Y_{ti} while scores for the first independent variable are represented as X_{1ti}.

The time window between waves is selected to allow important events during the election period to occur so that the effects of those events on individuals can be assessed. In the 1980 NES, for example, a panel was created and interviewed at four time points during the election year: January, June, September, and November. This structure made possible analyses of changes that occurred as the election year unfolded.

Analysis of panel data uses the following equation for a two-wave design (omitting the respondent's subscript):

$$Y_2 = b_0 + b_1 Y_1 + b_2 X_{11} + b_3 X_{12} + e_2$$

The initial status of Y is entered into the model along with the prior status of a variable X_{11} that is predicted to cause change in Y_2 over the time interval between waves of the survey. The final status of X is also included in the model to control for any changes that might have occurred to the presumed causal variable subsequent to its assessment at time 1.

TABLE 7.1 Data Layout in a Panel Design with Four Waves

	WAVES (t)			
Individuals (i)	1	2	3	4
1	Y_{11}, X_{111}, X_{211}	Y_{21}, X_{121}, X_{212}	Y_{31}, X_{131}, X_{231}	Y_{41}, X_{141}, X_{241}
2	Y_{12}, X_{112}, X_{212}	Y_{22}, X_{122}, X_{222}	Y_{32}, X_{132}, X_{232}	Y_{42}, X_{142}, X_{242}
i	Y_{1i}, X_{11i}, X_{21i}	Y_{2i}, X_{12i}, X_{22i}	Y_{3i}, X_{13i}, X_{23i}	Y_{4i}, X_{14i}, X_{24i}
n-1	$Y_{1n-1}, X_{11n-1}, X_{21n-1}$	$Y_{2n-1}, X_{12n-1}, X_{22n-1}$	$Y_{3n-1}, X_{13n-1}, X_{23n-1}$	$Y_{4n-1}, X_{14n-1}, X_{24n-1}$
n	Y_{1n}, X_{11n}, X_{21n}	Y_{2n}, X_{12n}, X_{22n}	Y_{3n}, X_{13}, X_{23n}	Y_{4n}, X_{14n}, X_{24n}

The coefficient b_1 represents stability from time 1 to 2 in the status of Y; b_2 represents the causal effect of X_1 on change in Y; b_3 represents any contemporaneous relation between X and Y at time 2 that is unrelated to the causal effect of X at time 1; and e_2 represents a random component in Y at time 2 that is unrelated to any of the X predictors. The constant b_0 represents all of the influences on Y that are not captured by the other components of the model. Writing the equation in a slightly different way emphasizes that it is change in Y that is being predicted in this model:

$$Y_2 - b_1Y_1 = b_0 + b_2X_{11} + b_3X_{12} + e_{i2}$$

The difference score $(Y_2 - b_1Y_1)$ represents the part of Y that remains after the initial status of Y has been removed. Because b_1 is typically less than 1, the model only removes that part of Y_1 that is reliably related to Y_2. If we were simply to use the raw difference score $(Y_2 - Y_1)$, we would assume that b_1 were exactly 1, which is unlikely. Since we can estimate b_1, there is no reason to make this assumption.

A similar situation exists in the representation of X at both time periods. It might be tempting to use the difference score between X at both time periods $(X_{12} - X_{11})$ to assess its effect on change in Y. This, however, also forces the stability coefficient for X to be 1. The best model is one that allows both stability coefficients to be estimated from the data.

A major benefit of the panel design is the ability to assess change at the level of individual respondents. This is not possible in the cross-sectional design where we can only assess change at the group level. In the rolling cross-sectional design, we have the benefit of knowing that demographic differences are held constant across waves of the study. Nevertheless, we can only examine changes as a function of such group characteristics as demographics or behavior (see Chapter 6 for examples of these analyses).

Assessing change at the individual level also permits more sensitive measurement of change because all of the reliable individual variation in Y at time 1 is controlled. This situation results in smaller standard errors of prediction for analyses that attempt to predict change in Y. For example, consider the hypothetical data in Table 7.2. If the cases in this data table represented different individuals at each time period, then we would have to

TABLE 7.2 Hypothetical Data for Change in Y at
Two Time Points

Case	Y_1	Y_2	$Y_2 - Y_1$
1	1	3	2
2	2	4	2
3	3	4	1
4	4	4	0
5	5	5	0
Mean	3	4	1

measure change by comparing the means of Y_1 and Y_2, which in this example indicates a change of one unit. The standard error for this analysis depends on the standard deviations of the scores at each time period.[1] If the cases represented the same individuals at each time period, however, change could be estimated for each individual. Notice that although this estimate of change is the same as for the difference between means at each time point, the variation surrounding the individual difference score is smaller than the total variation in the two measures of Y. In practice, because individual scores will be correlated across time, the variation in difference scores will be smaller than the variation across the scores at each time point. As a result, change can be estimated with less error if the same individuals are assessed at each time period.

A second benefit of the panel design is that it allows us to analyze potential causes of change at the individual level. For example, if X at time 1 can predict change in Y_2, this is strong evidence for a possible causal role of X. This feature is not available in the cross-sectional design.

Despite the benefits of the panel design, there are some drawbacks to its use. First, selecting the time period between waves is an important decision because the ability to observe change and potential predictors of that change will depend on the choice of the time lag. If the lag is too long, then the causal effect of a variable may no longer be evident. If it is too short, then the time window may not be long enough to permit enough measurable change to occur. Furthermore, once a time lag is selected, then all of the variables in the dataset will be subject to analysis with that lag. If some vari-

---

[1] The standard error of the difference between means is SQRT[$(s_1)^2/n_1 + (s_2)^2/n_2$] where $(s_t)^2$ is the estimate of the variance for time t and n_t is the sample size at time t. The corresponding standard error for difference scores is SQRT[s^2/n], where s^2 is the variance estimate of the differences and n is the sample size. Inserting the values for our example in Table 7.2 produces a standard error of .77 for the difference between independent samples versus a value of .45 for the differences in matched scores. The standard error is over 70% larger in the independent samples compared to the matched sample.

ables have short causal lags while others have longer lags, it will not be possible to conduct useful analyses with all of the variables in the dataset.

A second possible drawback is the potential for sensitization to the survey questions. The cross-sectional study always interviews respondents who have not been previously exposed to the survey. By contrast, panel respondents are interviewed at two or more times. There is considerable evidence, however, that respondents can respond differently to the same questions depending on the content of prior questions (Sudman, Bradburn, and Schwarz 1996). This factor can make the interpretation of changes in survey responses somewhat problematic. Was the change produced by the events that occurred between waves, or is it the result of repeated questioning of survey respondents? We will discuss some strategies for controlling survey sensitization in the analysis of individual change. There may not be a good control for effects that influence the entire sample other than pairing the subsequent waves of a panel with separate cross-sectional samples.

CAUSAL INTERPRETATION OF PANEL DATA

To appreciate the factors that enter into a causal interpretation of panel data, it is helpful to use a causal diagram to consider the relation between the variables (see also Finkel 1995 for a discussion of the causal relations underlying panel data).

The causal diagram in Figure 7.1 is revealing because it shows that both Y and X at time 2 are influenced by errors of measurement (e_x, e_y) as well as by unknown components, U_x and U_y. We do not get estimates of these separate components when we conduct regression analyses. Their influence is represented in the constant term and the random component of the model. Nevertheless, they may affect the outcomes of the analysis. The correlation between X_1 and Y_1 (a) reflects the fact that the variables including their unknown components may initially be related. However, we are able to estimate paths from time 1 to time 2 holding constant those interrelations at time 1. Indeed, X_1 may directly influence Y_2. Although we assume that the unknown components are not related to each other or to the other predictors in the model, this is merely an assumption. If they are related to the prior status of X or Y, then we will get incorrect estimates of the effects of those variables. For this reason, one should control for important variables that might be related to X and Y.

The major challenge to analyzing the panel model is to rule out alternative interpretations for any observed relation between X_1 and Y_2. There are at least two ways that X_1 may appear to predict Y_2: (1) if X_2 directly affects Y_2 or (2) if the unknown components are related to each other ($c \neq 0$) and X_1 is related to X_2. In the latter case, the path from X_1 to Y_2 will include the correlation between the unknown components. One possible source of correlation between the variables at time 2 in the panel design is sensitization

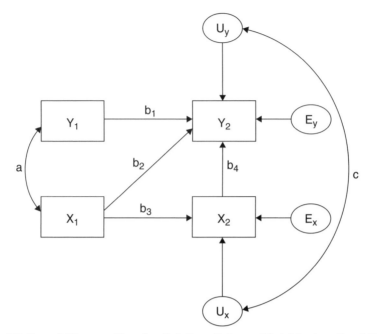

Figure 7.1 Causal Diagram Showing Relations Between Variables in a Panel Design

of the respondents to the content of the variables. For example, if asking about party affiliation and evaluation of the candidates prompts respondents to think more about being consistent with their party, this increased attention to the relation between the variables might encourage them to synchronize their evaluation of candidates with their party. As a result, party affiliation at time 1 would predict candidate evaluation at time 2. The source of this relation, however, would be the result of sensitization to the questions and not of increasing congruence with party affiliation over time. If this was the case, a cross-sectional survey would not find increasing correlation between party and candidate evaluation over time because respondents would not have been previously exposed to the items.

Errors of measurement may also be correlated in the panel design, but this source of relation between variables is also present in the cross-sectional design. The only way to identify this source of misspecification would be to use different types of measures for each variable in the survey. Unfortunately, we seldom have the luxury of including more than one type of measure of any variable in a large survey such as the NAES. Hence, we make the assumption that even if the errors of measurement are correlated, this source of error is not so large that it will account for significant relations between variables.

One way to handle the problem of correlation between unknown components in the variables at time 2 is to hold constant X_2 in the regression model. Doing this will control for the relation between X_2 and Y_2 that is unrelated to the direct effect of X_1 on Y_2. This strategy will work as long as X_1 and X_2 are not so highly related that they are indistinguishable from each other. If the correlation between them is very high (because they have not changed much), then this strategy may introduce collinearity and defeat the purpose of the analysis.

Another strategy to demonstrate that changes over time are not the result of sensitization is to show that the effect does not occur for everyone in the survey. For example, if prior party affiliation is hypothesized to predict changes in candidate evaluations after an event (such as a debate), then the effect should only occur for those who have been exposed to the debate. In this case, one would predict that the causal effect of X_1 would only occur for those who reported exposure to the debate. One could then create a dummy variable for debate exposure and use the product of this variable and X_1 to predict Y_2. If the hypothesis is correct, then party identification should predict subsequent candidate evaluation better for those who were exposed to the debate than for those who missed the event.

NAES PRESIDENTIAL DEBATE PANEL EXAMPLES

To illustrate some of the ways in which panels can be analyzed, we will take a look at the NAES October 3 presidential debate panel (N = 1,514). In wave 1, pre-debate interviews took place between September 21 and October 2. The post-debate follow-up, wave 2, occurred between October 4 and October 10.

Debates give members of the electorate the opportunity to compare candidates and issue positions. Do debates stimulate individuals' levels of political engagement? One way in which people engage in politics is by talking about politics with others. For a deliberative democracy to work effectively, political discussion within the citizenry is essential. NAES respondents were asked how many days they had talked about politics with friends and family and how many days they talked with coworkers or online in the past week. A random half of panel respondents were asked these questions both before and after the debate. Paired sample t-tests were conducted to see whether there was change in the amount of time that people talked about politics. While respondents reported talking about politics with friends and family 2.36 days in the past week on average, after the debate this increased to 2.63 days. The difference between the pre-debate and post-debate amounts of political discussion in our panel was statistically significant (t = −4.34, df = 779, p < .001). The reported amounts of political discussion with coworkers or online, however, did not change significantly. On average, respondents said they had talked with coworkers or online .87 days per week before the debate compared to .91 days per week after the debate (t = −.76, df = 778, p = .446).

While we observed differences in the amounts of political discussion with friends and family comparing the pre-debate and post-debate responses, it is unclear that watching the debate contributed to the differences in these individuals. One way that we can test the impact of debate-watching on political discussion is by constructing a model that uses debate-watching to predict talking about politics with friends and family. After the first presidential debate, NAES respondents were asked: "Did you happen to watch the presidential debate October 3 between George W. Bush and Al Gore? If yes, Did you watch all, most, or just some of it?" These responses were recoded so that those who did not watch the debate could be compared to individuals who watched some, most, or all of it.

Using the post-debate variable on political talk with friends and family as the dependent variable, we can determine whether watching the debate had an impact. Other variables should be taken into account as well. NAES respondents were asked about their interest in politics:

> Some people seem to follow what is going on in government and public affairs most of the time, whether there is an election or not. Others are not that interested. Would you say you follow what is going on in government and public affairs most of the time, some of the time, only now and then, or hardly at all?

This response was recoded into a dichotomous variable so that those who said they were interested in politics most of the time could be compared to those less interested in politics. To test whether debate-watching caused an increase in talking about politics with friends and family, a multivariate model was created allowing us to control for political interest and pre-debate responses to the political talk question.

Let's return to our initial equation for a two-wave design:

$$Y_2 = b_0 + b_1Y_1 + b_2X_{11} + b_3X_{12} + e_2$$

In this example, Y_2 represents post-debate political talk with friends and family, and Y_1 represents pre-debate political talk. X_{11} stands for political interest before the debate interview, and X_{12} stands for political interest after the debate. To this equation, we add another independent variable (X_{21}), having watched the debate. Our new equation can be expressed as follows:

$$Y_2 = b_0 + b_1Y_1 + b_2X_{11} + b_3X_{12} + b_4X_{21} + e_2$$

Table 7.3 shows the results of regression analyses using this model and some modified versions of it. Model 1 is a simple regression using pre-debate political talk to predict post-debate political talk. Not surprisingly, pre-debate political talk is statistically significant, capturing 50% of the variation in post-debate political talk as demonstrated by the R-square.[2] Model 2

---

[2] The R-square statistic tells us how much of the variation in the dependent variable the model explains. It is important to note that "a sizable R^2 does not necessarily mean we have a *causal* explanation for the dependent variable; instead, we may merely have provided a *statistical* explanation" (Lewis-Beck 1980, 24).

TABLE 7.3 Regression Models Predicting Post-Debate Political Discussion with Friends and Family in the Past Week

	MODEL 1		MODEL 2		MODEL 3		MODEL 4	
	B (SE)	Beta	B (SE)	Beta	B (SE)	Beta	B (SE)	Beta
Constant	.919***		.755***		.368***		.350***	
	(.085)		(.091)		(.108)		(.107)	
Pre-debate political talk with friends and family (0 to 7 days)	.728*** (.026)	.709	.673*** (.028)	.655	.635*** (.028)	.619	.606*** (.028)	.591
Pre-debate political interest (interested most of the time = 1, not interested, interested now and then, or only some of the time = 0)			.663*** (.128)	.140	.549*** (.126)	.116	.275# (.144)	.058
Watched October 3 debate (Yes = 1, No = 0)					.815*** (.127)	.165	.785*** (.126)	.159
Post-debate political interest (coding same as pre-debate)							.577*** (.150)	.120
R-square	.502		.518		.541		.550	
Adjusted R-square	.502		.517		.539		.548	
N	780		776		774		773	

#p < .10 *p < .05 **p < .01 ***p < .001.

includes pre-debate political interest. Model 3 adds our primary variable of concern, debate-watching. All three independent variables in this model are statistically significant. Model 4 best represents the equation just given. Even when controlling for pre-debate political talk, pre-debate political interest, and post-debate political interest, having watched the first presidential debate is a significant predictor of talking about politics with friends and family (post-debate). This model explains 55% of the variation in post-debate political talk.

As already mentioned, collinearity between variables can be a problem if the independent variables are highly correlated. One might expect collinearity problems, for example, when different versions of the same variable are put into a model, as is the case with political interest at time 1 and time 2. In this example, however, the collinearity diagnostics revealed that the independent variables were not multicollinear.

The debate panels can be used to answer other questions as well. Rather than focusing on the change in a particular variable, we may be interested in predicting a variable at time 2 based on data gathered at time 1. For example, did watching the debate affect which candidate, Bush or Gore, respondents thought performed better in the debate? Individuals who watched the debate and individuals who had not but had heard about the debate were asked: "(From what you have heard or read) who do you think performed best in this debate, George W. Bush or Al Gore?" Around 42.6% of respondents said that Gore had performed better in the October 3 debate, 37.0% said that Bush had performed better, and 20.4% said that there was no difference between them.[3] This variable was recoded into a dichotomy where those who said that Bush had performed better were compared to those who either thought that Gore had performed better or saw no difference between them.

Table 7.4 presents the results of a logistic regression predicting the opinion that Bush had performed better. Since party identification frequently influences people's opinions about candidates, the pre-debate party identifications were put into the model. Controlling for education and party identification, those who watched the debate were more likely to say that Bush had performed better in the debate. Watching the debate was a statistically significant predictor of opinion about Bush's debate performance.

As previously mentioned, prior questioning (survey sensitization) can influence survey results. One could argue that the significant relationships involving party identification and debate watching in Table 7.4 are due in part to survey sensitization. Perhaps respondents became sensitized to their party affiliation in the pre-debate wave and this influenced their evaluation of the debate in the post-wave.

How might we demonstrate that the results from Table 7.4 are not due to sensitization? One way is to run the model on a cross-section of respondents who have not previously been surveyed. Using the NAES national RCS, we can take respondents interviewed during the same period that the post-debate panel respondents were interviewed (October 4 to October 10) and see if similar patterns appear in these data. We know that sensitization to party affiliation is less likely to have affected responses to the debate evaluation question in the cross-section because party identification is asked at the end of the survey.

Table 7.5 reveals that party identification and debate-watching were significant predictors of respondents' opinions about debate performance in the October 3 debate. Indeed, the effect of watching the debate was slightly stronger in the cross-sectional sample (.477 versus .388). In addition, the effects of party identification were comparable in the two surveys. These findings suggest that pre-debate sensitization was not responsible for the effects of party identification or reports of debate watching. Independent of party identification, respondents who had watched the debate were more likely to say that Bush had won the debate.

One difference between the panel and RCS respondents was that education was not a significant predictor for the RCS respondents. This is not par-

---

[3] This dataset was not weighted.

TABLE 7.4 Binary Logistic Regression Predicting the Opinion That Bush Performed Better Than Gore in the October 3 Presidential Debate

	B	SE	Wald	Exp (B)
Constant	.069	.443	.024	1.071
Education (in years)	−.066*	.029	5.240	.936
Republican (Yes = 1, Else = 0)	1.160***	.149	60.903	3.191
Democrat (Yes = 1, Else = 0)	−1.554***	.201	59.697	.211
Watched October 3 debate (Yes = 1, No = 0)	.388*	.169	5.286	1.473
Cox and Snell R-square[1]			.196	
Nagelkerke R-square			.268	
N			1,157	

*p < .05 **p < .01 ***p < .001.

[1]These measures of R-square are designed to provide comparable information to estimates from OLS regression. They are based on the likelihood function rather than squared residuals and so should not be interpreted as variance explained. The Nagelkerke measure has an upper bound of 1 which makes it more comparable to R-square from OLS regression (see Allison, 1999, for a discussion of these statistics).

ticularly surprising considering that the effect was only significant at the .05-level for panel respondents. Another difference to note is that the RCS respondents were slightly different from those in the panel in a few key characteristics. While the panel and RCS respondents were not statistically different in their gender composition or strength of partisanship, the panel respondents were slightly more interested in politics and more educated than their RCS counterparts.

TABLE 7.5 Binary Logistic Regression Predicting the Opinion That Bush Performed Better Than Gore in the October 3 Presidential Debate Using National RCS Data from October 4 to October 10

	B	SE	Wald	Exp (B)
Constant	−.840*	.389	4.663	.432
Education (in years)	−.027	.025	1.188	.973
Republican (Yes = 1, Else = 0)	1.404***	.132	112.748	4.071
Democrat (Yes = 1, Else = 0)	−1.180***	.168	49.325	.307
Watched October 3 Debate (Yes = 1, No = 0)	.477***	.143	11.196	1.611
Cox and Snell R-square			.178	
Nagelkerke R-square			.247	
N			1,571	

*p < .05 **p < .01 ***p < .001.

ADDITIONAL USES FOR THE PANELS IN RCS ANALYSES

Johnston and Brady (2002) argue that the RCS design "necessitates an estimation strategy that distinguishes time-series from cross-sectional effects" (283). They make the case for a method in which a post-election panel can be used as a control so that one can differentiate between time series and cross-sectional variation. Researchers interested in this approach should read Johnston and Brady's important article on the rolling cross-section design.

CONCLUSION

Unlike the repeated cross-section design, which can only track changes at the group level, panel data allow us to track changes in individuals. Using panel data, we can control the variation from responses at prior points in time. There are two risks in the panel design. First, researchers must anticipate the time points when they think significant events will occur. They must also decide how much time should pass before subsequent waves of data are collected. If these two judgments are not sound, the panel design will be costly and unproductive. Second, when respondents answer questions repeatedly, they may become sensitized to the questions and act differently than they would have if they had not answered an initial round of questions. Despite the drawbacks, researchers who want to make inferences about the causes of variables on individual-level processes must use data collected on the same individuals at more than one point in time.

REFERENCES

Allison, P. D. 1999. *Logistic regression: Using the SAS system.* Cary, NC: SAS Institute.

Finkel, S. E. 1995. *Causal analysis of panel data.* Thousand Oaks, CA: Sage.

Johnston, Richard, and Henry E. Brady. 2002. The rolling cross-section design. *Electoral Studies* 21: 283–95.

Lewis-Beck, Michael S. 1980. *Applied regression: An introduction.* Newbury Park, CA: Sage.

Sudman, S., N. M. Bradburn, and N. Schwarz. 1996. *Thinking about answers: The application of cognitive processes to survey methodology.* San Francisco: Jossey-Bass Publishers.

Time Series Models

Daniel Romer

I n this chapter we introduce methods for analyzing the data from the NAES that take advantage of the information contained in the daily observations made throughout the period of the survey. This analysis relies primarily on the quantitative methods introduced by economists for the study of time series data (see Chatfield 1996, Diebold 2001, Enders 1995, and Harvey 1993 for overviews of these methods). Because these techniques are less well known, our discussion is lengthier than that devoted to the methods in previous chapters.

In this chapter, we will review methods for uncovering cycles in the daily behavior of the U.S. electorate. We will also examine ways to study the influence of events that occurred during the election year using the daily reactions of the public. Finally, we will examine how the public's daily reactions to a candidate (e.g., learning the candidate's likelihood of victory) might affect their evaluation of the candidate.

WHAT IS A TIME SERIES?

A time series is a set of observations, Y_t, measured at regular intervals of time, $t = 1, 2, 3, \ldots T$. In this chapter, we analyze such series by looking at relations between values of Y at time t and at k prior time periods or **lags,** $t - k$, of Y. For example, we can calculate the average interest in the election on any given day and determine if that interest is related to the public's interest one day or two days earlier. Ordinarily when we correlate variables, we examine the relation between ordered pairs of values for two variables measured at the same time. In time series analysis, we examine relations between variables that are paired at different lags. As seen in Table 8.1, a series can be correlated with values of itself at different lags. In this example, a series with T periods of observations is paired with values of the same series one lag (Y_{t-1}) and two lags (Y_{t-2}) back in time. Note that each time the series is paired with a lag of itself, initial observations in the original series are no longer paired with the lagged versions. A series that is lagged k times will have k fewer observations paired with the original series.

TABLE 8.1 Example of Two Lags of a Time Series with T Time Periods

	TERM IN THE SERIES				
Lag	First	Second	Third	Fourth	Last
Y_t	Y_1	Y_2	Y_3	Y_4	Y_T
Y_{t-1}		Y_1	Y_2	Y_3	Y_{T-1}
Y_{t-2}			Y_1	Y_2	Y_{T-2}

Approaches that analyze time series as a function of lags of the original series focus on the **time domain** of a series. Another approach to analyzing time series involves the **frequency domain,** in which a series is analyzed in terms of recurring waves represented by trigonometric functions. Either approach can be applied to time series data, but we will restrict our analysis to the time domain because this approach is of more interest to the disciplines that study politics, such as political science, economics, sociology, and communication. For a discussion of time series analysis in the frequency domain, see Chatfield (1996).

THE PURELY RANDOM TIME SERIES

Before considering how to analyze a series in the time domain, it will be helpful to consider the simplest of all series, the purely random series. No matter what time series we examine, it will almost certainly have a random component that is uncorrelated between lags. In time series terminology, this series is known as **white noise.** A series composed of white noise has values that are uncorrelated with any other lags in the series, a mean of 0, and a constant standard deviation. In such a series, the observations at each time period are drawn at random from the same distribution of potential scores. These scores can be written as

$$Y_t = e_t$$

where e_t is the randomly drawn score at time t.

If the distribution from which e_t is drawn is normal, then the series is completely described by its mean and standard deviation. Each value is statistically independent of other values in the series. In the NAES, we can aggregate the scores from each day's interviews to obtain a set of means. According to the central limit theorem for means, these means will tend to be normally distributed as the sample size increases. So, we can also be relatively confident that the white noise in our series approximates a normal distribution.

Figure 8.1 shows a randomly generated series for one hundred time periods drawn from a normal distribution that was simulated using the random number generator in SPSS with a mean of zero and a standard deviation of 1 or ND(0, 1). The series fluctuates around the mean, and the

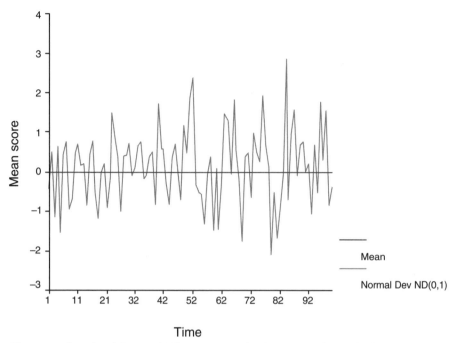

Figure 8.1 Simulated Series of White Noise with Mean = 0 and Standard Deviation = 1

fluctuations are relatively unsystematic. This series has no systematic relations across time periods because it was designed that way. Scores at one time period are unrelated to scores at other time periods.

These scores exhibit another important feature of time series data: covariance stationarity. A white noise series will have the same mean and standard deviation across all possible time periods. As a result, it also will have the same covariance between lags, which will be $C(Y_t, Y_{t-k}) = 0$ for any value of k. Although the covariance is theoretically zero, in practice as sampling error enters into the estimates, it will vary around zero.

Quite often in time series data, a series will have a constant mean and variance, but the scores at one time period will be systematically related to those of other time periods. These dependencies can take at least two forms, described by autoregressive (AR) and moving average (MA) models. Both models suppose that observations at time t are related to observations at different lags. But the form of the relation is different.

THE AUTOREGRESSIVE MODEL

In the simplest autoregressive model, the score at time t is based only on the immediately previous score:

$$Y_t - m = a_1 (Y_{t-1} - m) + e_t$$

where a_1 is a regression coefficient that is assumed to be between -1 and $+1$, m is the mean of the series, and e_t is a random variable representing white noise. The coefficient a_1 transfers the effect of Y at time $t - 1$ to Y at time t.

The restriction that the value of a_1 lies between -1 and $+1$ is important because the series would not be stationary unless this condition were met. You can see this by inserting the value of a_1Y repeatedly into each succeeding value of the series. Unless a_1 is less than 1 in absolute value, the series will change its mean dramatically and no longer be stationary. Later we will see what happens when the value of a_1 is exactly 1. In this case, the series is also not stationary because the variation around the mean may be unstable.

The autoregressive model is essentially a multiple regression model with the dependent variable predicted by a lagged value of itself, hence the term autoregressive process. It is called an AR(1) model because only one lag is involved in influencing the values of the series. The general model is an AR(p) process with up to p lags influencing the scores at any time period.

Although the AR model is akin to OLS regression, the values of the independent and dependent variables are the same sets of scores. The only difference is that the ordering has been shifted by one time period for each lag of Y that is related to Y.

Why Are Time Lags Related?

There are at least two reasons for the presence of lagged relations in time series data. The relation can be causal, in which case the observations at one time period influence the observations at a later time period. An example would be an imitative effect in which publicly observable events at time t lead to similar events at time $t + k$. For example, it is believed that some crimes lead to copycat behavior by others. If this is true, then crimes at one time period will produce similar behavior at a subsequent time period. Highly publicized suicide is discussed as subject to imitation. In the business world, the daily closing values of the stock market are well known to market participants and can influence trading on the succeeding day. Housing starts and other conspicuous forms of consumption may also lead to imitative effects such that a spurt in buying at one time period can lead to imitative effects at later time periods.

In addition to imitative effects, relations between lags may represent underlying changes that take time to unfold. Observations at nearby time periods may be related because people's feelings or perceptions at one time point carry over to succeeding ones. The relations may or may not be causal, but the effect at the level of observations is the same. Whether they are causally related or not, the autoregressive model assumes that characteristics of observations at previous time periods carry over to succeeding periods.

In political campaigns, an AR(1) model might mean that respondents at any point in time have the same reactions they had one period earlier in time. For example, people's feelings toward a candidate might be influenced by how they felt yesterday as well as by new, unrelated influences today. On the next day, their feelings from today will carry over to tomorrow along with tomorrow's new influences. If we assume that the mean of the observations stays the same over time and that the variability does as well, then these processes will tend to cycle. These cycles are important because we need to model them if we want to understand how people's feelings, knowledge, and perceptions change over time and possibly affect each other.

In addition to continuous cycles in an election time series, alterations in the campaign can introduce change that unfolds over time. But such influences are different from the cycles we are describing in an AR(p) process. An AR process will characterize a series for a relatively long period of time that is independent of sudden changes in the direction of a campaign (a new election strategy by a candidate) or of outside events that change the standing of the candidates in an election (economic or other events).

Figure 8.2 illustrates two AR(1) time series using the same set of random deviates that were shown in Figure 8.1. Notice that the two series are nearly identical and only vary in their dispersion around the mean of the series. The variance of an AR(1) process is

$$\sigma^2 / (1 - a_1^2)$$

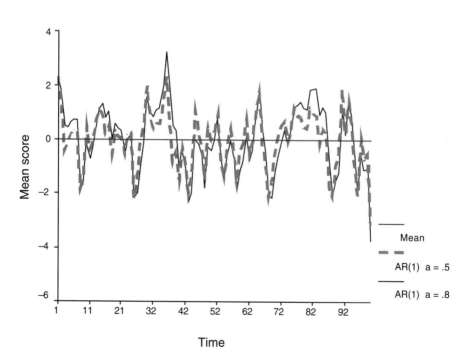

Figure 8.2 Two Autoregressive Models That Differ in the Regression Parameter, a_1.

in which σ^2 represents the variance of the white noise contained in the series. This equation indicates that the variance of the AR series grows larger as a_1 increases.

The Moving Average Model

A second model that has been widely studied is the moving average model. This series is different from an AR process in that the carryover from previous days is restricted to the random process rather than to the entire previous observed score. For example, in an MA(1) model, the equation looks like this:

$$Y_t - m = e_t + b_1 e_{t-1}$$

where the random process at the previous time point, e_{t-1}, carries over to the next time period, with a coefficient of b_1. The new score at time t is also influenced by the random process for that time period, e_t. The coefficient b_1 is also restricted to a value no greater than 1 in absolute value. In the MA model, the restriction in values of b_1 does not function to ensure stationarity. The MA series will be stationary even if b_1 is greater than 1. However, the restriction is maintained so that the MA model can be approximated by an AR model. Just like the AR model, the general MA process can also have any number of lags represented as an MA(q) model.

Unlike the AR model, the MA model is not based on observed scores because neither of the random processes is directly observed. In the AR (1) model, the random process can be estimated by subtracting the predicted score from the observed score:

$$e_t = Y_t - a_1 Y_{t-1} + m(1 - a_1).$$

In the MA (1) model, the random process can be written as

$$e_t = Y_t - b e_{t-1}, \text{ where the mean (m) is set to zero.}$$

This equation says that the current random score is a function of the immediately previous random score. But that score can be written as

$$e_{t-1} = Y_{t-1} - b e_{t-2}.$$

If you keep going with this line of reasoning, you will not get to an observed score until you arrive at the first score in the series. Despite this problem, we can see a pattern in the relations between different time lags in an MA(1) process. If we substitute equations for each prior value of e_t, we get the following result:

$$Y_t = e_t + b Y_{t-1} - b^2 Y_{t-2} + b^3 Y_{t-3} + \ldots - (-b)^j Y_{t-j}$$

where j equals different lagged values of the series. This result tells us that the relation between lags in an MA(1) process is positive for odd-numbered lags and negative for even-numbered lags. In addition, if **b** is less than 1 in absolute value, the coefficients decline in absolute size as lag size increases.

Diagnosing Model Type: The Correlogram

A very important way of diagnosing the characteristics of a time series is to examine the correlations between lags. The correlation coefficient is a standard measure of linear relationship that is equal to

$$r_{xy} = C(x,y)/(S(x)S(y))$$

where C stands for the covariance of two variables (x, y), and S(x) and S(y) stand for their respective standard deviations. The covariance measures the extent to which the two variables are linearly related. The more two variables are related, the greater the absolute size of the covariance. However, the covariance has no upper or lower bounds. Dividing the covariance by the product of the standard deviations produces a score that varies from -1 to $+1$. If x and y are perfectly correlated, then their covariance equals the product of their standard deviations. If they are positively related, then r will equal 1. If they are negatively related, r will equal -1.

When different lags of a time series are correlated with each other, we can observe systematic relations between successive lags. The **autocorrelation function** (**ACF** for short) is the name for the relation between the correlation coefficient at different lags (k) and the value of the lag. It is defined as

$$r_k = C(x_t - m, x_{t-k} - m)/V_x$$

where V_x represents the variance of the series.

One major difference between the AC coefficient and the regular correlation coefficient is that one assumes that the series is stationary when analyzing the ACF. Instead of using the mean of the series at each lag to calculate the difference scores, the mean **(m)** is fixed at the value of the entire series. In addition, the variance of the series is assumed to be constant. This allows the ACF to detect systematic patterns in the lag structure.

When the series has an AR structure and **a** is positive, it tends to produce an ACF that gradually dampens. The AC is always 1 at zero lag (the series correlated with itself). However, as the number of lags increases, the AC declines as the square of **a**. The resulting graph of the ACF is called the **correlogram** of the series (see Figure 8.3).

When a series has an MA structure and **b** is positive, it tends to produce an abrupt drop at the number of lags that carry over in the process. In the example in Figure 8.4, there is only one lag in the MA process, and so the ACF drops dramatically after one lag.

This difference in the pattern of the ACF makes sense, since the AR process brings with it the effects of previous lags at each time period. The MA process only carries information from the lags that influence the present time

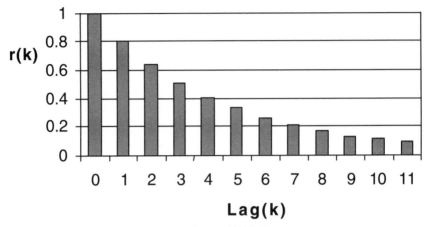

Figure 8.3 Autocorrelation Function for an AR(1) Process

period. In this sense, the AR process is said to have a longer **memory** than the MA process.

For example, consider what happens when you have an AR(1) process with a positive coefficient. In this case, the first three values of the series are

$$Y_1 = e_1$$
$$Y_2 = a_1 Y_1 + e_2$$
$$Y_3 = a_1 Y_2 + e_3$$

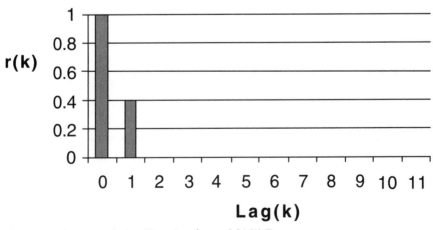

Figure 8.4 Autocorrelation Function for an MA(1) Process

If one inserts the equation for Y_2 into Y_3, one obtains

$$Y_3 = (a_1)^2 Y_1 + a_1 e_2 + e_{3s}$$

As is evident, time 3 is related to time 1 as the square of a_1, while time 2 is related to time 1 as a_1. So, time 3 is related to time 1, although at a weaker level than time 2 is related to time 1. If one continued this process for successive lags, the AC between Y_t and other lags would decline until it effectively reached zero. If a_1 is negative, then the relation would be negative for odd lags and positive for even lags.

Compare the AR(1) process with an MA(1) process. In the MA(1) case, we have the following relations across time periods:

$$Y_1 = e_1$$
$$Y_2 = e_2 + b_1 e_1$$
$$Y_3 = e_3 + b_1 e_2$$

But even if we recognize Y_1 in Y_2, there is still no carryover from Y_1 to Y_3. This produces a basic difference between the two series that can be observed in the ACF.

The Partial Autocorrelation Function

Another diagnostic tool for interpreting time series data is the **partial autocorrelation** at different lags. If we predict the series at lag 0 using successive lags in a stepwise multiple regression model, then the partial AC is the standardized regression coefficient for the series at lag p with $p - 1$ prior lags in the model. For the first lag, the partial AC is always equal to the AC at the first lag. As more lags are added to the model, earlier lags are held constant and the coefficient for the pth lag represents the additional prediction afforded by that lag once all earlier lags are held constant.

The partial acf (PACF) is the relation between the coefficients and their respective lag values. For an AR(p) process, the partial ACF will drop to zero after the pth lag. For an AR(1) process, the partial for the second lag should be zero, since the second lag produces no auto-correlation beyond that produced by the first lag.

For an MA(1) process, the PACF tends to oscillate around and to gradually approach zero. For larger orders ($q > 1$), the PACF can either oscillate or dampen gradually depending on the characteristics of the lag parameters. So, the characteristics of the PACF are the opposite of the ACF for the two types of series.

ANALYSIS OF TIME SERIES

Some Artificial Examples

Let's create an MA(1) series using $Y_t = .5(Z_{t-1}) + Z_t$, where Z is drawn from a normal distribution with a mean of 0 and standard deviation of 1 (ND(0,1)). First we can examine the ACF and partial ACF for the white noise series Z. We use the auto-correlation procedure in SPSS to produce the output shown in Table 8.2.

Because we created the series from white noise, we expect the ACF to show no significant values for any lag. There are two ways to assess this prediction.

Correlations lying outside the confidence bands defined by 2 times $1/\text{sqrt}(N)$ are regarded as significant at the .05 level. This is a helpful tool for quickly identifying significant relations between lags. The first several coefficients representing the nearest lags are usually the critical ones because we would expect them to be most related to the series at lag 0.

Another helpful tool for diagnosing the results of the ACF is the Box-Ljung test for independence across lags. If the time series has no serial dependence, the Box-Ljung statistic will be nonsignificant except for the occasional type I error. The Box-Ljung is a Chi-square test of the hypothesis that the first **P** lags in a time series have correlations equal to 0. It has **P** degrees of freedom and is calculated as

$$T(T + 2)\sum r_k^2/(T - k)$$

where k runs from 1 to **P**, **T** is the number of time periods in the series, and r_k is the autocorrelation at lag k.

Its value at each lag tests whether any correlations are significant up to and including that lag. The test is usually significant at early lags if some degree of autocorrelation is present. However, as the number of lags increases, the test tends to become nonsignificant because later lags are usually not as highly correlated as earlier ones.

We see that the Box-Ljung statistic is not significant at any lag. However, it approaches significance at lag 7. This lag also has an AC that lies outside the 95% confidence interval. This pattern illustrates that even a randomly generated series can have some dependencies by chance. If one encountered such a result for a series in the NAES dataset one would have to consider the possibility that the significant value at lag 7 merely represents a type I error. That is, something that happens by chance once every twenty times when one uses the .05 level of significance. However, another possibility is that behavior is dependent on the calendar, such that people's responses are similar on the same day of the week. Later we will discuss how to test for such a possibility.

We also see that the partial AC at lag 7 is significant, a result that again supports the possible presence of a relation between days one week apart.

TABLE 8.2 Autocorrelation Output from SPSS for a Simulated White Noise Series (Z)

```
     Auto- Stand.
Lag  Corr.  Err. -1  -.75  -.5 -.25   0   .25  .5   .75   1   Box-Ljung  Prob.
                  ├───┼────┼────┼────┼────┼────┼────┼────┤
  1   .053  .099                      .  |*  .                    .292    .589
  2  -.122  .098                      . **|  .                   1.841    .398
  3  -.141  .098                      .***|  .                   3.933    .269
  4   .016  .097                      .  |*  .                   3.962    .411
  5   .069  .097                      .  |*  .                   4.471    .484
  6   .045  .096                      .  |*  .                   4.687    .585
  7  -.261  .095                   *.***|  .                    12.177    .095
  8   .008  .095                      .  *  .                   12.184    .143
  9  -.084  .094                      . **|  .                  12.975    .164
 10   .004  .094                      .  *  .                   12.976    .225
 11   .025  .093                      .  *  .                   13.046    .290
 12  -.007  .093                      .  *  .                   13.051    .365
 13  -.027  .092                      . *|  .                   13.137    .437
 14   .029  .092                      .  |* .                   13.238    .508
 15   .093  .091                      .  |**.                   14.269    .505
 16   .103  .091                      .  |**.                   15.561    .484
```

Plot Symbols: Autocorrelations *   Two Standard Error Limits .

Total cases: 100   Computable first lags: 99

Partial Autocorrelations: Z   random variable drawn from ND(0,1)

```
     Pr-Aut- Stand.
Lag  Corr.   Err. -1  -.75  -.5 -.25   0   .25  .5   .75   1
                   ├───┼────┼────┼────┼────┼────┼────┼────┤
  1   .053   .100                     .  |*  .
  2  -.125   .100                     .***|  .
  3  -.129   .100                     .***|  .
  4   .016   .100                     .  *  .
  5   .036   .100                     .  |*  .
  6   .026   .100                     .  |*  .
  7  -.258   .100                   *.***|  .
  8   .059   .100                     .  |*  .
  9  -.150   .100                     .***|  .
 10  -.047   .100                     . *|  .
 11   .008   .100                     .  *  .
 12  -.028   .100                     . *|  .
 13  -.012   .100                     .  *  .
 14  -.038   .100                     . *|  .
 15   .131   .100                     .  |***.
 16   .025   .100                     .  |*  .
```

Plot Symbols: Autocorrelations *   Two Standard Error Limits .

Total cases: 100   Computable first lags: 99

The graph of the MA(1) series along with the random series Z is shown in Figure 8.5. The MA(1) series has a mean of 0 and a variance of 1.25 (1 + b^2), which is somewhat larger than the white noise series. As one would expect given the nature of an MA series, there is also evidence of greater carryover from one time period to the next.

The ACF and PACF for the MA(1) are shown in Table 8.3. The significant AC for the first lag is consistent with how we defined the series. Recall that the succeeding lags should drop off dramatically and should alternate in sign. As you can see, the second lag has negative value. In addition, we see the spuriously significant coefficient at lag 7. The partials show a significant coefficient at lag 1 and a significant negative coefficient for lag 2. The second coefficient is also spurious. It represents the characteristic pattern of the ACF for an MA process. Succeeding PACs will oscillate until they dampen to zero. The spurious coefficient at lag 7 introduces a relatively large coefficient that also oscillates from that point onward.

We now turn to an artificially created AR(1) series using the same random series Z as the basis for the series. In this case, the series is defined by $Y_t = .5(Y_{t-1}) + Z_t$. As the plot in Figure 8.6 indicates, the series looks very similar to the MA(1). This conclusion is also supported by examining the correlogram. The first coefficient is significant in the ACF and no others rise to significance except for the seventh, which is the same spurious lag we observed in the original random series. The ACF for the AR(1) series does not oscillate, and so the second coefficient is not as large as it was in the MA series. The PACFs show that the first coefficient is significant and that the seventh

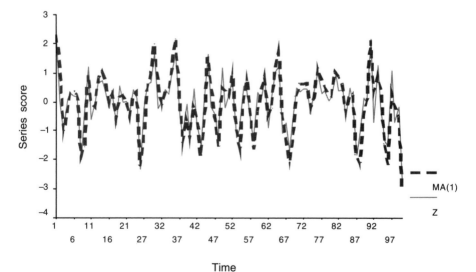

Figure 8.5 A Plot of the MA(1) Series Defined by $Y_t = .5(Z_{t-1}) + Z_t$ and White Noise Defined by Z_t

TABLE 8.3 Correlogram Analysis of Simulated MA(1) Series

```
Autocorrelations for series defined as:    Y = Z_t  +  .5Z_{t-1}
```

Lag	Auto- Corr.	Stand. Err.	-1 -.75 -.5 -.25 0 .25 .5 .75 1	Box-Ljung	Prob.
1	.356	.099	. |***.***	13.083	.000
2	-.160	.098	.***| .	15.750	.000
3	-.181	.098	****| .	19.193	.000
4	-.008	.097	. *| .	19.200	.001
5	.063	.097	. |* .	19.621	.001
6	-.051	.096	. *| .	19.899	.003
7	-.229	.095	* .***| .	25.673	.001
8	-.116	.095	. **| .	27.159	.001
9	-.073	.094	. *| .	27.758	.001
10	.009	.094	. *| .	27.766	.002
11	.023	.093	. |* .	27.828	.003
12	-.014	.093	. *| .	27.850	.006
13	-.046	.092	. *| .	28.093	.009
14	.030	.092	. |* .	28.203	.013
15	.146	.091	. |***.	30.755	.009
16	.112	.091	. |** .	32.279	.009

```
Plot Symbols:      Autocorrelations *     Two Standard Error Limits .

Total cases:  100     Computable first lags:  99


Partial Autocorrelations for series defined as:  Y = Z_t  +  .5Z_{t-1}
```

Lag	Pr-Aut- Corr.	Stand. Err.	-1 -.75 -.5 -.25 0 .25 .5 .75 1
1	.356	.100	. |***.***
2	-.329	.100	***.***| .
3	.015	.100	. *| .
4	.025	.100	. |* .
5	-.002	.100	. * .
6	-.100	.100	. **| .
7	-.186	.100	****| .
8	.047	.100	. |* .
9	-.189	.100	****| .
10	.062	.100	. |* .
11	-.055	.100	. *| .
12	-.024	.100	. *| .
13	-.060	.100	. *| .
14	.025	.100	. |* .
15	.119	.100	. |** .
16	-.064	.100	. *| .

```
Plot Symbols:      Autocorrelations *     Two Standard Error Limits .

Total cases:  100     Computable first lags:  99
```

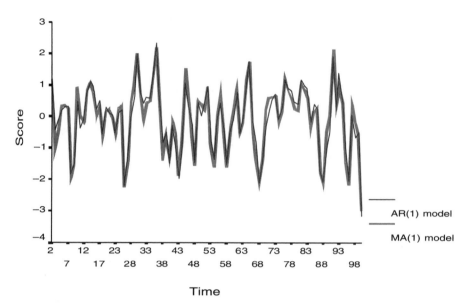

Figure 8.6 Comparison of Autoregressive (AR) and Moving Average (MA) Models

is as well. Unless one had a good reason to suppose that there was a seven-day lag, one would treat this coefficient with skepticism (see Table 8.4).

ACTUAL DATA FROM THE NAES

Let's now look at an actual data series from the NAES. In Figure 8.7, we plot the average favorability rating of Al Gore (cA11) using the thermometer scale during the months of January through April 2000. The series looks relatively stationary. There is no apparent change in the mean of the series or in the dispersion of values during this period. One important factor that could affect the dispersion of the series is the number of interviews done per day. However, during this period in the national sample, the number of interviews remained relatively stable at approximately eighty-five per day.

We can test the hypothesis that the series mean remained stable by subjecting the series to a curve-fitting analysis. The results of this analysis shown below indicate that neither linear nor quadratic trend terms are significant. Hence, we can be relatively confident that the series is stationary (see Table 8.5).

If we examine the ACF for this series, we find that there is no evidence of autocorrelation in the series. This suggests that people's ratings of Gore

TABLE 8.4 Correlogram Analysis of Simulated AR(1) Series

Autocorrelations for series defined as: $Y_t = .5(Y_{t-1}) + Z_t$

```
      Auto- Stand.
Lag   Corr.  Err. -1  -.75  -.5  -.25   0   .25  .5   .75   1    Box-Ljung   Prob.
                   |----+----+----+----+----+----+----+----|
  1    .422  .099                     . |*** .****               18.374      .000
  2    .055  .098                     . |*   .                    18.686      .000
  3   -.085  .098                   . **|    .                    19.441      .000
  4   -.019  .097                   .   *|   .                    19.480      .001
  5   -.022  .097                   .   *|   .                    19.533      .002
  6   -.103  .096                   . **|    .                    20.678      .002
  7   -.267  .095                 *.***|     .                    28.489      .000
  8   -.138  .095                  .***|     .                    30.587      .000
  9   -.126  .094                  .***|     .                    32.378      .000
 10   -.021  .094                   .  *|    .                    32.430      .000
 11    .003  .093                   .   *    .                    32.431      .001
 12   -.009  .093                   .   *    .                    32.441      .001
 13   -.020  .092                   .   *    .                    32.487      .002
 14    .039  .092                   . |*     .                    32.667      .003
 15    .124  .091                   . |**    .                    34.515      .003
 16    .121  .091                   . |**    .                    36.291      .003
```

Plot Symbols: Autocorrelations *   Two Standard Error Limits .

Total cases: 100   Computable first lags: 99

Partial Autocorrelations for series defined as: $Y_t = .5(Y_{t-1}) + Z_t$

```
      Pr-Aut- Stand.
Lag   Corr.   Err. -1  -.75  -.5  -.25   0   .25  .5   .75   1
                    |----+----+----+----+----+----+----+----|
  1    .422   .100                     . |*** .****
  2   -.150   .100                   .***|    .
  3   -.059   .100                   .  *|    .
  4    .066   .100                   .   |*   .
  5   -.057   .100                   .  *|    .
  6   -.105   .100                   . **|    .
  7   -.217   .100                 ****|     .
  8    .082   .100                   . |**    .
  9   -.160   .100                  .***|     .
 10    .051   .100                   . |*     .
 11   -.010   .100                   .   *    .
 12   -.053   .100                   .  *|    .
 13   -.024   .100                   .   *    .
 14   -.001   .100                   .   *    .
 15    .119   .100                   . |**    .
 16   -.052   .100                   .  *|    .
```

Plot Symbols: Autocorrelations *   Two Standard Error Limits .

Total cases: 100   Computable first lags: 99

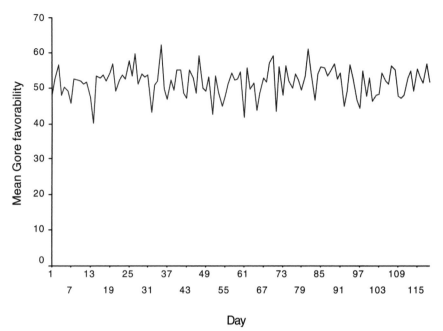

Figure 8.7 Ratings of Gore's Favorability Using the Thermomenter Scale, January 3 to April 30

during this period displayed no evidence of carryover from one day to the next. Each day's ratings by the interview sample represented an independent sample from the distribution of feelings that people had toward Gore during this time period (see Table 8.6).

The Effect of Sample Size on the Standard Error of the Mean

As we noted earlier, mean scores for interview data for each day will approximate a normal distribution. As a result, two parameters will completely specify the distribution of scores for a series defined on means: the mean and the standard deviation. However, the size of the sample that is observed each day will determine the size of the standard deviation. In general, the standard error of the mean is proportional to the standard deviation of

TABLE 8.5 Regression Analysis of Gore's Thermometer Rating Using Linear and Quadratic Trends as Predictors

Predictor	R^2	d.f.	t	Prob.
Linear	.001	117	.36	.714
Quadratic	.002	116	.30	.913

TABLE 8.6 Correlogram Analysis of Gore's Favorability Thermometer Rating from January 3 to April 30

```
Autocorrelations:   cAll   (Gore Favorability Rating)

        Auto- Stand.
Lag     Corr.  Err.  -1  -.75  -.5  -.25   0   .25   .5   .75   1    Box-Ljung  Prob.
                      ├──┼───┼───┼───┼───┼───┼───┼───┼──┤
  1    -.017  .091                        *    .                      .035     .851
  2    -.034  .090                  .    *|    .                      .180     .914
  3    -.014  .090                  .     *    .                      .206     .977
  4     .020  .089                  .     *    .                      .257     .992
  5     .086  .089                  .     |**  .                     1.190     .946
  6    -.002  .089                  .     *    .                     1.191     .977
  7     .034  .088                  .     |*   .                     1.339     .987
  8     .006  .088                  .     *    .                     1.344     .995
  9    -.028  .087                  .  *  |    .                     1.447     .998
 10     .161  .087                  .     |*** .                     4.857     .901
 11    -.144  .087               ***      .                          7.608     .748
 12     .086  .086                  .     |**. .                     8.609     .736
 13    -.054  .086                  . *   |    .                     9.005     .773
 14    -.034  .086                  . *   |    .                     9.164     .820
 15    -.091  .085                  . **  |    .                    10.317     .799
 16    -.212  .085               * .**    |    .                    16.576     .414

Plot Symbols:      Autocorrelations *      Two Standard Error Limits .

Total cases:  119     Computable first lags:  118

Partial Autocorrelations:   V201G_1   (Gore Favorability Rating)

        Pr-Aut- Stand.
Lag     Corr.   Err.  -1  -.75  -.5  -.25   0   .25   .5   .75   1
                      ├──┼───┼───┼───┼───┼───┼───┼───┼──┤
  1    -.017  .092                     .  *   .
  2    -.035  .092                     . *|   .
  3    -.016  .092                     .  *   .
  4     .019  .092                     .  *   .
  5     .086  .092                     .  |** .
  6     .002  .092                     .  *   .
  7     .041  .092                     .  |*  .
  8     .009  .092                     .  *   .
  9    -.029  .092                     . *|   .
 10     .155  .092                     .  |***.
 11    -.147  .092                  .***     .
 12     .094  .092                     .  |**.
 13    -.067  .092                     . *|   .
 14    -.034  .092                     . *|   .
 15    -.120  .092                  . **|   .
 16    -.211  .092                  ****|   .

Plot Symbols:      Autocorrelations *      Two Standard Error Limits .

Total cases:  119     Computable first lags:  118
```

the individual interview scores (σ) divided by the square root of the size of the sample (N):

$$\sigma / \sqrt{N}$$

If we assume that σ stays the same despite changes in sample size, then the standard error will decrease as the inverse of the square root of the sample size. The relation between the standard error and sample size is shown in Figure 8.8. The largest decrease occurs in the range from one to thirty. After sample size of thirty, the standard error changes relatively little. Nevertheless, differences in daily sample size will have an effect on the variability of a series.

The effect of sample size can be seen by comparing daily samples from the national survey from January 3 to April 30, 2000. Figure 8.9 shows the sample size for each day for the full sample and for a randomly selected half of the sample. One can see that the two series are parallel over this interview period and that the daily sample size increased heading into the March primaries and then declined during April. Nevertheless, the sample size remained at thirty or higher in the smaller of the two series at least until April, and so we would expect the variation to be greater in the half sample but not dramatically so.

Figure 8.10 compares mean daily thermometer ratings for the full sample and the random half. It is evident that the variation is larger in the half sample. Nevertheless, the two series are remarkably similar. They are expected

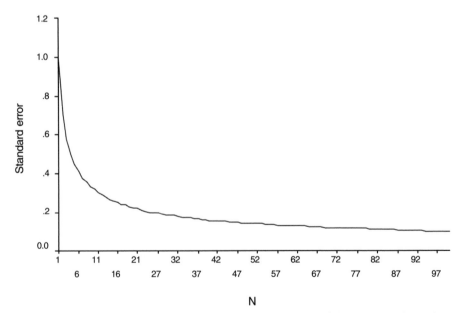

Figure 8.8 The Effect of Sample Size on the Standard Error of the Mean with a Value of 1 for σ

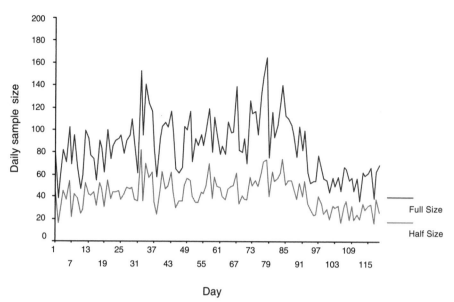

Figure 8.9 Comparison of Sample Sizes for January to April 2000: The Entire Daily National Sample and a Random Half of the National Sample

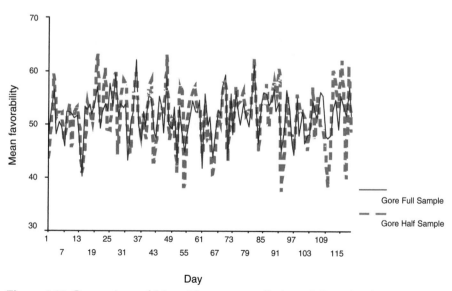

Figure 8.10 Comparison of Mean Thermometer Rating of Gore for the Entire National Sample and for a Random Half of the Sample from January to April 2000

to have the same mean and only slightly different standard deviations. Differences in variability are most evident in April when the sample size of the half sample dipped below thirty per day.

Describing a Time Series: Going Beyond Random Variation

In order to examine some of the basic characteristics of time series data, we first explored the simplest component of any time series, the random variation that enters at each time point. When this variation displays no relation to other time points, it is known as white noise. A second source of potential variation in a time series is the systematic cycles that are described by AR(p) and MA(q) processes. We now consider two other components that have not been discussed, namely, trends and seasonal or calendar effects. In total, we will see that there are four potential components of any time series:

1. Trends, such as linear, curvilinear, or exponential changes in the level of the series
2. Seasonal or calendar-related components, such as stable variation coinciding with days of the week or months of the year
3. AR(p) or MA(q) processes
4. White noise

Trends and seasonal changes can also introduce correlations between lags. To use the correlogram to detect AR or MA components, it is important to first remove all other trends in the series that introduce systematic departures from the mean and standard deviation over time. This strategy is an attempt to achieve covariance stationarity. For normally distributed data, covariance stationarity is achieved when a series has a constant mean and standard deviation. We can reduce considerable variation in the standard deviation by making sure that the number of interviews per day is relatively constant across days of the survey. If not, then a minimal condition is that the number of interviews is greater than thirty per day. Unless there is a true change in the variability of the time series over time, holding constant the number of interviews should achieve stationarity in the standard deviation.

If the series undergoes change in its mean, these changes are attributable either to trends or to seasonal variation. Furthermore, systematic changes in mean will introduce correlations between time periods, and these correlations will obscure our ability to identify AR or MA processes.

We have already seen covariance stationarity in examples of MA(1) and AR(1) models and in people's feelings toward Gore during the primary season. We will now use graphing and regression techniques to achieve stationarity in a series that has a trend component so that we can identify potential MA and AR processes.

Let's look at a time trend in the NAES. Voter awareness of John McCain grew steadily early in 2000 (Figure 8.11). Awareness of candidates can be assessed using responses to the favorability thermometer questions (which for McCain is cA21). When respondents were asked to rate their overall favor-

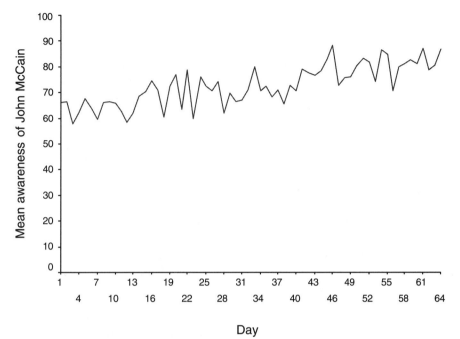

Figure 8.11 Awareness of John McCain (% Aware) in the National Sample, January 3 to March 6

ability toward candidates (on a 0 to 100 scale), they were given the option of saying that they did not know the candidate well enough to provide a rating (response 102). This measure of awareness was used to create the series plotted in Figure 8.11. We should be able to detect the linear trend in awareness and remove it from the awareness series.

McCain's awareness curve appears to exhibit a linear increase with time. If we fit a linear model to the awareness series, we should be able to remove the linear trend. The remaining or residual variation should then be stationary.

A regression analysis using days as the predictor indicates a significant linear component (see Table 8.7).

TABLE 8.7 Regression Analysis of McCain's Awareness as a Function of Day

Predictor	UNSTANDARDIZED COEFFICIENTS		STANDARDIZED COEFFICIENTS		
	B	Std. Error	Beta	t	Prob.
Constant	61.889	1.253		49.41	.000
Day	.334	.034	.784	9.96	.000

The regression analysis indicates that each day, a little over three tenths of a percentage point (.334) of Americans became aware of McCain. Although this rate of increase would eventually slow down as the total approached 100%, the pattern is relatively linear during this time period.

Once we remove the linear increase from McCain's series, we are left with the pattern shown in Figure 8.12. This series appears to be quite stationary. Indeed, we could attempt to fit other time trends to the series, but they would not add significant predictive power to the model.

We can now examine the correlogram for the residuals in McCain's awareness series (i.e., the awareness series after we have removed the linear trend component). The correlogram shows no systematic correlation across waves. It appears that aside from the dramatic increase in awareness in the national sample, the daily cycles in awareness are serially uncorrelated. There is no carryover in awareness from day to day other than the linear rise that is apparent in the daily trend (see Table 8.8).

With linear trend, each additional time period increases (or decreases) the outcome by a constant amount: $Y_t = Y_{t-1} + A$. This implies that increases will be a function of time: $Y_t = At + Y_0$.

As an exercise, find the ACF for the original series of McCain's awareness. You will see a dramatic difference compared with the residuals we just analyzed. The very dominant pattern of recurrent positive correlations across lags is indicative of a nonstationary series.

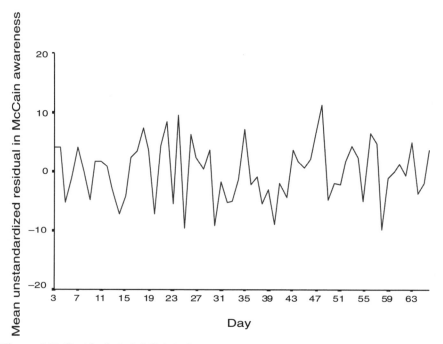

Figure 8.12 Residuals in McCain's Awareness

TABLE 8.8 Correlogram Analysis of Residuals in McCain Awareness After Removing Linear Trend

```
Autocorrelations:    Residuals in McCain Awareness:   Jan 3 to Mar 6

      Auto- Stand.
Lag   Corr.  Err. -1  -.75  -.5 -.25   0   .25  .5   .75   1    Box-Ljung  Prob.
                  ├────┼────┼────┼────┼────┼────┼────┼────┤
  1   -.067  .122                     .  *│  .                   .300      .584
  2   -.028  .121                     .  *│  .                   .354      .838
  3   -.021  .120                     .   *  .                   .386      .943
  4   -.082  .119                     . **│  .                   .863      .930
  5    .059  .118                     .  │*  .                  1.109      .953
  6   -.021  .117                     .  │*  .                  1.141      .980
  7   -.052  .116                     .  *│  .                  1.340      .987
  8   -.042  .115                     .  *│  .                  1.475      .993
  9    .116  .114                     .  │**  .                 2.512      .981
 10   -.015  .113                     .  *│  .                  2.530      .990
 11   -.029  .112                     .  *│  .                  2.597      .995
 12   -.160  .111                     .***│  .                  4.687      .968
 13   -.014  .110                     .  *│  .                  4.704      .981
 14   -.157  .109                     .***│  .                  6.783      .943
 15   -.053  .108                     .  *│  .                  7.028      .957
 16   -.118  .107                     . **│  .                  8.252      .941

Plot Symbols:       Autocorrelations *      Two Standard Error Limits .

Total cases:  64     Computable first lags:  63


Partial Autocorrelations:    Residuals in McCain Awareness:   Jan 3 to Mar 6

      Pr-Aut- Stand.
Lag   Corr.   Err. -1  -.75  -.5 -.25   0   .25  .5   .75   1
                   ├────┼────┼────┼────┼────┼────┼────┼────┤
  1   -.067   .125                     .  *│  .
  2   -.033   .125                     .  *│  .
  3   -.026   .125                     .  *│  .
  4   -.087   .125                     . **│  .
  5    .046   .125                     .  │*  .
  6   -.020   .125                     .  │*  .
  7   -.056   .125                     .  *│  .
  8   -.056   .125                     .  *│  .
  9    .116   .125                     .  │**  .
 10   -.012   .125                     .  │*  .
 11   -.035   .125                     .  *│  .
 12   -.168   .125                     . ***│  .
 13   -.016   .125                     .  │*  .
 14   -.202   .125                     .****│  .
 15   -.102   .125                     . **│  .
 16   -.187   .125                     .****│  .

Plot Symbols:       Autocorrelations *      Two Standard Error Limits .

Total cases:  64     Computable first lags:  63
```

Differencing as a Trend Removal Strategy

Another strategy for removing trends is to transform the series by taking differences between lags. The first order difference can be written as: $Y - L(Y)$, where $L(Y)$ represents the first lag of the series. Every score in the lag of Y is subtracted from its corresponding score in Y. Since each lagged score has a value that is A less than the next score on average, this operation removes the linear trend.

Differencing works especially well if the series is a "random walk." A random walk is so named because each step in the series is completely random with regard to the previous step. A random walk is the limiting case of an AR(1) when a_1 is 1,

$$Y_t = Y_{t-1} + e_t.$$

In this case, taking the difference score leaves only the random component in Y at each time point as the residual. This can be seen by examining three time periods in a random walk:

$$Y_3 = Y_2 + e_3 = e_1 + e_2 + e_3$$
$$Y_2 = Y_1 + e_2 = e_1 + e_2$$
$$Y_1 = e_1$$

Each time period adds a random component to the previous random components. When successive time periods are differenced, one is left with only the random component from each time period: $Y_t - Y_{t-1} = e_t$.

It may seem strange that so subtle a change in the AR model should lead to such dramatic differences in the behavior of a series. However, one must keep in mind that in a random walk the entire score from the previous day is carried over to the next day ($a_1 = 1$). Furthermore, a random walk is not stationary. It can exhibit widely varying variation over time.

The erratic behavior of a random walk in comparison to a stationary series is illustrated in Figure 8.13. In this example, we use the same simulated random series to construct an AR(1) with a coefficient of .5 and a random walk with a coefficient of 1. The random walk has the same expected value of zero, but it meanders widely from this value. The AR series tends to oscillate around its expected value with the same variability over time.

If a series is not a random walk, then differencing leaves a more complex pattern. For example, if we examine three time periods that contain a linear trend, we see that each time period acquires the trend plus a random component:

$$Y_3 = 2A + e_3$$
$$Y_2 = A + e_2$$
$$Y_1 = e_1.$$

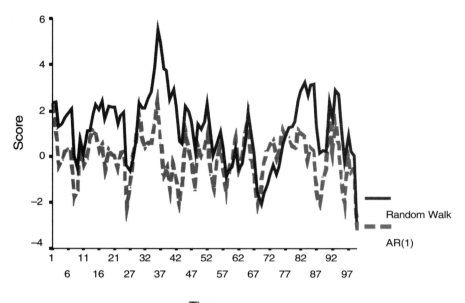

Figure 8.13 Comparison of a Random Walk with an AR(1) Series Using the Same Randomly Generated White Noise

When the series is differenced, the residual contains the average trend and the difference in random components for the present and previous time period:

$$Y_t - Y_{t-1} = A + e_t - e_{t-1}.$$

This differencing introduces an MA(1) process with a coefficient of -1.

Let's examine this outcome with McCain's awareness growth using the previously analyzed first sixty-four days of 2000. We have seen that the residual of the awareness series after removing the linear trend is essentially white noise. If instead we detrend the series using difference scores, we find that the correlogram for this series exhibits a large negative autocorrelation at lag 1. In addition, the partial correlations exhibit gradual decay. These patterns are characteristic of an MA(1) (see Table 8.9).

If we calculate the mean of the differenced series we see that it is about .3 units. This implies that the average increase per day is .3 percentage units (very similar to what we found in our earlier regression analysis). However, the correlogram tells us that the random components are now correlated.

In essence, by applying the difference operation, we have introduced an MA(1) into the series. Later we will see how we can remove the MA(1) introduced by first order differencing. However, you can see that removing the trend using the residuals from regression analysis takes care of the

TABLE 8.9 Correlogram Analysis of McCain's Differenced Awareness

Variable: Difference Score Missing cases: 1   Valid cases: 63

Autocorrelations: Difference Scores for McCain Awareness

```
      Auto- Stand.
Lag   Corr.  Err.  -1  -.75  -.5 -.25   0   .25  .5   .75   1    Box-Ljung  Prob.
                    |--+----+----+----+----+----+----+----+--|
  1   -.516  .123             ***** ****|      .              17.614    .000
  2    .029  .122                      .|*     .              17.669    .000
  3    .017  .121                      .|*     .              17.688    .001
  4   -.095  .120                    .**|      .              18.321    .001
  5    .107  .119                      .|**    .              19.135    .002
  6   -.016  .118                      .|*     .              19.153    .004
  7   -.026  .117                     .*|      .              19.202    .008
  8   -.061  .116                     .*|      .              19.476    .013
  9    .122  .115                      .|**    .              20.601    .015
 10   -.053  .114                     .*|      .              20.819    .022
 11    .074  .113                      .|*     .              21.255    .031
 12   -.144  .112                   .***|      .              22.911    .028
 13    .126  .110                      .|***.                 24.213    .029
 14   -.115  .109                    .**|      .              25.315    .032
 15    .079  .108                      .|**  .                25.848    .040
 16   -.087  .107                    .**|      .              26.512    .047
```

Plot Symbols: Autocorrelations *   Two Standard Error Limits .

Total cases: 64   Computable first lags: 62

Partial Autocorrelations: Difference Scores for McCain Awareness

```
      Pr-Aut- Stand.
Lag   Corr.   Err.  -1  -.75  -.5 -.25   0   .25  .5   .75   1
                     |--+----+----+----+----+----+----+----+--|
  1   -.516   .126            ***** ****|      .
  2   -.325   .126              * .****|      .
  3   -.200   .126                .****|      .
  4   -.274   .126               *****|      .
  5   -.154   .126                . ***|      .
  6   -.082   .126                .  **|      .
  7   -.081   .126                .  **|      .
  8   -.201   .126                .****|      .
  9   -.048   .126                .   *|      .
 10   -.027   .126                .   *|      .
 11    .104   .126                .   |**    .
 12   -.061   .126                .   *|      .
 13    .086   .126                .   |**    .
 14   -.053   .126                .  *|      .
 15   -.005   .126                .   *      .
 16   -.174   .126                . ***|     .
```

Plot Symbols: Autocorrelations *   Two Standard Error Limits .

Total cases: 64   Computable first lags: 62

problem of nonstationarity without introducing MA processes into the de-trended series. Because we do not expect to find evidence of random walks in the NAES, we will opt to remove trends using regression techniques rather than differencing.

Nonlinear Trend

In addition to linear trend, there is also the possibility of nonlinear trend. A commonly encountered set of nonlinear trends can be modeled using the exponential function. In this case, change is dependent on the previous value of Y. For example,

$$Y_t = Y_{t-1} + A Y_{t-1}.$$

Here, changes in Y are proportional to previous values of Y:

$$Y_t - Y_{t-1} = A Y_{t-1}.$$

This trend implies the following equation: $Y_t = Y_0 e^{At}$. Neverthless, one can write this model as a linear function of the log of Y_t:

$$Ln(Y_t) = ln(Y_0) + At.$$

One could easily transform such data by taking the log of Y and doing a linear regression with time as the predictor. Then one is predicting constant percentage changes at each time point. It can be noted that an exponential growth trend will also produce nonstationary standard deviations. If the standard deviation is proportional to the value of the series, then taking the log of the series will reduce this source of nonstationarity as well.

If one wanted to stay in the same metric, then one could calculate predicted scores using the conversion $Y = ke^{At}$ or by estimating this equation from the beginning. As an exercise, try fitting an exponential growth curve to the proportion of people who report that they have voted by absentee ballot prior to the general election (see Figure 5.6). The curve in that figure looks remarkably like the curve we show in Figure 8.14.

Another exponential trend is the inverse of exponential growth, known as exponential decay. In this case, the coefficient (A) is negative and reflects a constant percentage decline (Figure 8.15).

A milder form of exponential change that is likely in public opinion contexts is shown in Figure 8.16. This curve is a typical media diffusion model in which a constant proportion of previously unexposed people is exposed to a message at each time point. As the media message reaches more and more people, the proportion of people still available to learn the message at each time point declines.

One can estimate the parameters of this model using nonlinear regression and then predicting the trend. As an exercise, try fitting this model to McCain's awareness using the first four months of data in the NAES.

Figure 8.17 shows a decay function in which the growth is subtracted from a starting point. Compare this with the first model and you will see

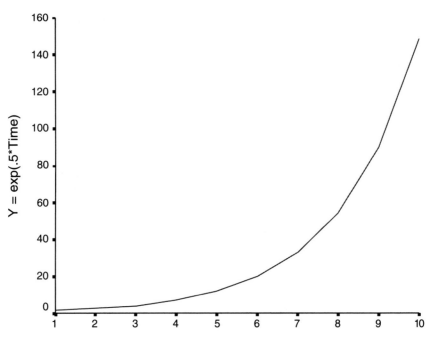

Figure 8.14 Example of Exponential Growth in Which Change at Each Time Period Is Proportional to the Value of the Previous Time Period; the Formula for Y Represents the Exponential Function (exp) Using e as the Base

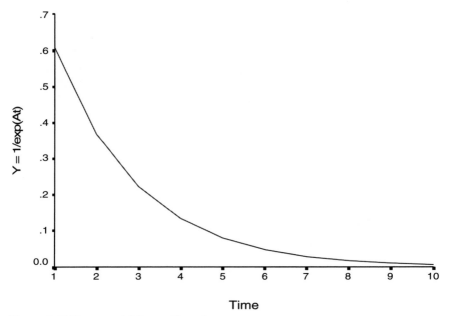

Figure 8.15 Exponential Decay Function

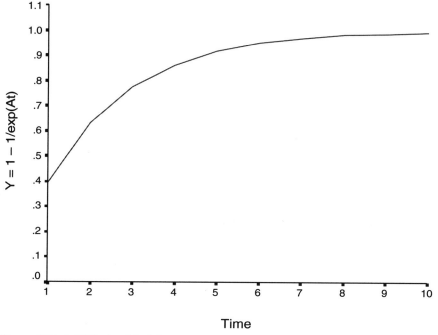

Figure 8.16 A Diffusion Model

that the decline is simply the inverse of exponential growth: slow at first, but then faster with time. This model can also be estimated using nonlinear regression.

Models with Powers of Time

Despite the beauty of exponential functions for modeling trend, a useful trend analysis tool is to fit a curve that uses powers of time as predictors of trend. The model for this analysis is

$$Y_t = K + a_1t + a_2t^2 + a_3t^3 + \cdots + a_nt^n.$$

For example, a curve that has a quadratic component will look like the curve in Figure 8.18.

This curve represents a trend that increases, reaches a peak, and then declines. This is a possible trend for support of a candidate or for interest in a news event. One can fit such a model using the curve-fitting program in SPSS (an example of this analysis was done earlier in our analysis of Gore's favorability rating) or by writing an OLS regression model with increasing powers of time as predictors.

We can illustrate the power of this curve-fitting technique by examining media use during the primary season of the 2000 election. Starting on day

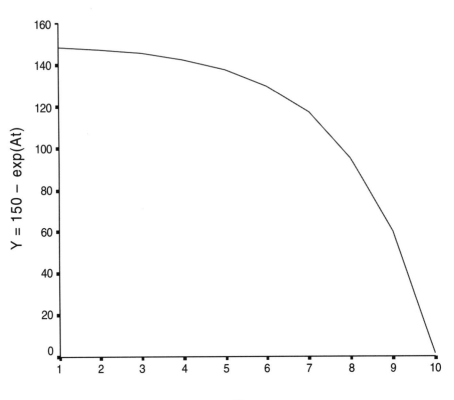

Figure 8.17 Inverse Exponential Decay

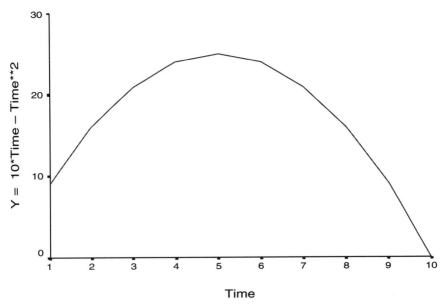

Figure 8.18 A Trend That Is a Quadratic Function of Time

26, the survey asked respondents if they were attending to news about the primaries on various news media. Figure 8.19 shows the average rating of attention to news about the primaries on national television news in the past week (cE03).

The series was subjected to a trend analysis that tested the linear, quadratic, and cubic components of the series. The results of this analysis showing the effect of each additional trend is in Table 8.10. All three components of the curve were significant predictors in the analysis. This is evident in the significant **t** values for each predictor that was added to the model. The increments in R^2 also indicate that the additional variation was substantial.

The fitted curve indicates that interest in the primaries peaked around day 50. It then gradually declined before leveling off and beginning to rise again around day 120. The series did not begin prior to day 26, so we cannot identify the trend prior to that day. Nevertheless, we can interpret this pattern as reflecting the effects of events during the primary period. The South Carolina and Michigan primaries occurred around day 50, and the American public was undoubtedly interested in the outcomes of these races.

Once the trend has been identified, we can examine the residuals in the series. The residuals of this detrended series are shown in Figure 8.20.

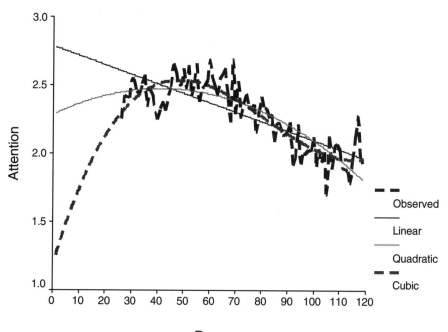

Figure 8.19 Observed and Predicted Time Series of National Television News Exposure to Stories about the Presidential Primaries (Attention to News Scored on a Scale from 1 = None, 2 = Not Too Much, 3 = Some, and 4 = A Great Deal).

TABLE 8.10 Three-Step Regression Analysis of Attention to Election News on National Television

	STEP 1			STEP 2			STEP 3		
Predictor	*B*	*t*	*Prob*	*B*	*t*	*Prob*	*B*	*t*	*Prob*
Day (Linear)	−.00687	−11.92	0.000	.00916	2.98	0.004	.06473	5.56	0.000
Day^2 (Quad.)				−.00011	−5.29	0.000	−.00095	−5.53	0.000
Day^3 (Cubic)							.000003	4.91	0.000
R^2		.607			.699			.763	

Examination of the correlogram (Table 8.11) indicates little evidence of systematic variation in the residuals. This finding suggests that once the cubic trend was removed, reports of weekly viewing of national television news for political information were relatively independent of reports on previous days. Nevertheless, this analysis tells us that attention to news exhibits rather dramatic changes as a function of events in the primary period.

Seasonal Influences

Another type of systematic trend is covariation attributable to seasonality or to the calendar. For example, one might hypothesize that respondents

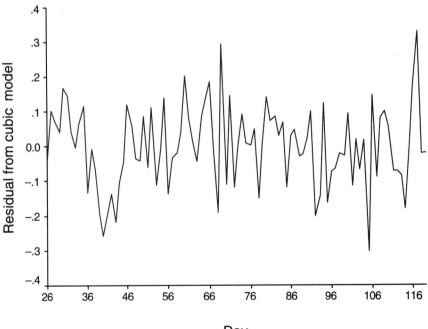

Figure 8.20 Residuals in Television News Interest During the Primaries

TABLE 8.11 Correlogram Analysis of Residuals in National TV News Attention to News About the Primary

Variable: Residuals Cubic Model   Missing cases: 25   Valid cases: 94

Autocorrelations: Residuals Cubic Model

Lag	Auto- Corr.	Stand. Err.	-1	-.75	-.5	-.25	0	.25	.5	.75	1	Box-Ljung	Prob.
1	.093	.102					**					.837	.360
2	.161	.101					***					3.384	.184
3	.048	.100					*					3.615	.306
4	.073	.100					*					4.151	.386
5	.009	.099					*					4.159	.527
6	.000	.099					*					4.159	.655
7	-.017	.098					*					4.188	.758
8	-.006	.098					*					4.192	.839
9	-.033	.097					*					4.305	.890
10	-.013	.096					*					4.324	.932
11	-.076	.096					**					4.959	.933
12	-.177	.095					****					8.425	.751
13	-.097	.095					**					9.476	.736
14	.001	.094					*					9.476	.799
15	.036	.094					*					9.626	.843
16	-.067	.093					*					10.151	.859

Plot Symbols: Autocorrelations *   Two Standard Error Limits .

Total cases: 119   Computable first lags: 93

Partial Autocorrelations: ERR_3   Error for NATTV with DAY from CURVEFIT,

Lag	Pr-Aut- Corr.	Stand. Err.	-1	-.75	-.5	-.25	0	.25	.5	.75	1
1	.093	.103					**				
2	.154	.103					***				
3	.022	.103					*				
4	.044	.103					*				
5	-.011	.103					*				
6	-.020	.103					*				
7	-.019	.103					*				
8	-.004	.103					*				
9	-.026	.103					*				
10	-.005	.103					*				
11	-.066	.103					*				
12	-.169	.103					***				
13	-.053	.103					*				
14	.070	.103					*				
15	.078	.103					**				
16	-.065	.103					*				

Plot Symbols: Autocorrelations *   Two Standard Error Limits .

Total cases: 119   Computable first lags: 93

behave differently on weekends from the way they do on weekdays. If this were true, one would see a pattern in the time series such that weekend days looked different from other days. In addition, the correlogram would show systematic correlation at lag 7 reflecting the fact that the series was similar to itself every week.

Figure 8.21 shows an example of a series that was constructed to be high on weekends and low on other days. The series begins on a Sunday and proceeds through five weeks. It is evident that weekends tend to have higher scores than weekdays.

The correlogram shows a significant lag at seven days (Table 8.12). There is also a significant lag at fourteen days, reflecting the fact that this is a weekly pattern. There is some evidence of negative correlations at lags 3 to 5, reflecting the fact that high scores on weekends are inversely related to scores on weekdays. This effect is also evident in the partial correlations where there is a significant partial at lag 5 as well as at lag 7.

To remove these weekend effects, one can regress the series on two dummy variables representing Saturday (D7) and Sunday (D1). The results of this analysis are shown in Table 8.13. With these predictors held constant, the residual series looks more stationary. The detrended series shown in Figure 8.22 is much less influenced by the weekend effect, and the correlogram no longer shows a significant pattern (see Table 8.14).

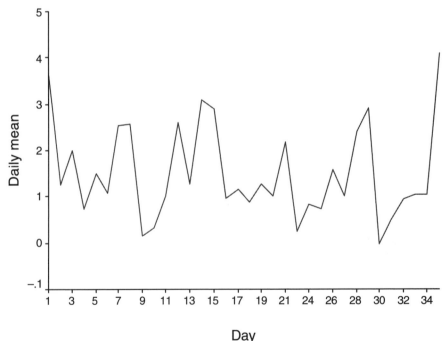

Figure 8.21 Example of a Series with Weekend Effects

TABLE 8.12 Correlogram Analysis of Simulated Series with Higher Scores on Weekends

```
Autocorrelations:   Weekend Series

      Auto- Stand.
Lag   Corr.  Err.  -1  -.75  -.5 -.25    0   .25   .5   .75    1    Box-Ljung  Prob.
                    ├──┼────┼───┼───┼────┼───┼───┼────┼───┤
  1   .049   .162                        .    *    .                    .092    .762
  2  -.153   .160                        . ***      .                  1.008    .604
  3  -.230   .157                        .*****     .                  3.154    .368
  4  -.208   .155                        . ****     .                  4.965    .291
  5  -.257   .152                        .*****     .                  7.813    .167
  6   .177   .150                        .     **** .                  9.208    .162
  7   .541   .147                        .     *****.*****            22.742    .002
  8  -.063   .144                        .   *      .                 22.933    .003
  9  -.156   .142                        . ***      .                 24.140    .004
 10  -.170   .139                        . ***      .                 25.645    .004
 11  -.118   .136                        .  **      .                 26.392    .006
 12  -.188   .133                        .****      .                 28.372    .005
 13   .193   .130                        .     ****.                  30.572    .004
 14   .434   .127                        .    ****.****               42.172    .000
 15  -.007   .124                        .    *     .                 42.175    .000
 16  -.137   .121                        . ***|     .                 43.462    .000

Plot Symbols:      Autocorrelations *      Two Standard Error Limits  .

Total cases:  35    Computable first lags:  34


Partial Autocorrelations:   Weekend Series

      Pr-Aut- Stand.
Lag   Corr.   Err.  -1  -.75  -.5 -.25    0   .25   .5   .75    1
                    ├──┼────┼───┼───┼────┼───┼───┼────┼───┤
  1   .049   .169                        .    *    .
  2  -.156   .169                        .   ***      .
  3  -.220   .169                        .  ****      .
  4  -.231   .169                        . *****      .
  5  -.370   .169                        .******|     .
  6   .015   .169                        .    *       .
  7   .431   .169                        .     |******.**
  8  -.204   .169                        .  ****      .
  9  -.152   .169                        .   ***      .
 10  -.072   .169                        .     *      .
 11   .042   .169                        .     |*     .
 12  -.087   .169                        .    **      .
 13  -.134   .169                        .   ***      .
 14   .193   .169                        .     |****  .
 15   .109   .169                        .     |**    .
 16  -.066   .169                        .     *|     .

Plot Symbols:      Autocorrelations *      Two Standard Error Limits  .

Total cases:  35    Computable first lags:  34
```

151

TABLE 8.13 Regression Analysis of Series with Weekend Effects

Predictor	UNSTANDARDIZED COEFFICIENTS		STANDARDIZED COEFFICIENTS		
	B	Std. Error	Beta	t	Prob.
Constant	.994	.111		8.981	.000
D7	1.861	.271	.640	6.867	.000
D1	1.984	.271	.682	7.321	.000

MAXIMUM LIKELIHOOD ESTIMATION OF ARMA MODELS

We have shown that it is possible to remove trends and seasonal components from time series using OLS regression. One of the cautions that has been emphasized in many treatments of time series data is the potential for violation of the assumptions of OLS regression. In particular, time series data can violate the assumption of independence between residuals, also known as the assumption of zero autocorrelation. The result is that estimates of the parameters in the equation may be inaccurate and the standard errors of the parameters may be underestimated.

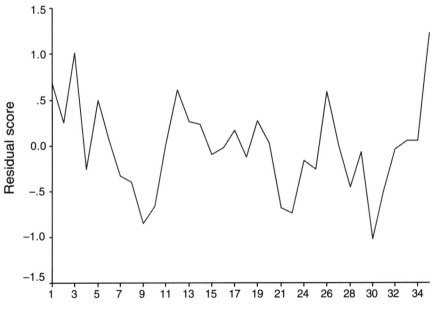

Figure 8.22 Adjusted Weekend Series After Controlling for Differences on Saturday and Sunday

TABLE 8.14 Correlogram Analysis of Weekend Series Following Removal of Weekend Trend.

Variable: Residuals in Weekend Series   Valid cases: 35

Autocorrelations: Weekend Series   Unstandardized Residual

Lag	Auto-Corr.	Stand. Err.	-1 -.75 -.5 -.25 0 .25 .5 .75 1	Box-Ljung	Prob.
1	.236	.162	. ***** .	2.115	.146
2	.164	.160	. *** .	3.171	.205
3	-.145	.157	. *** .	4.019	.259
4	-.275	.155	.***** .	7.175	.127
5	-.238	.152	.***** .	9.627	.087
6	-.094	.150	. ** .	10.020	.124
7	.044	.147	. * .	10.110	.182
8	-.061	.144	. * .	10.286	.246
9	.119	.142	. ** .	10.996	.276
10	-.013	.139	. * .	11.005	.357
11	-.012	.136	. * .	11.013	.442
12	-.035	.133	. * .	11.080	.522
13	.047	.130	. * .	11.208	.593
14	.109	.127	. ** .	11.940	.611
15	.045	.124	. * .	12.069	.674
16	-.033	.121	. * .	12.143	.734

Plot Symbols: Autocorrelations *   Two Standard Error Limits .

Total cases: 35   Computable first lags: 34

Partial Autocorrelations: Weekend Series   Unstandardized Residual

Lag	Pr-Aut-Corr.	Stand. Err.	-1 -.75 -.5 -.25 0 .25 .5 .75 1
1	.236	.169	. ***** .
2	.115	.169	. ** .
3	-.221	.169	. **** .
4	-.243	.169	. ***** .
5	-.091	.169	. ** .
6	.039	.169	. * .
7	.048	.169	. * .
8	-.211	.169	. **** .
9	.065	.169	. * .
10	-.019	.169	. * .
11	-.056	.169	. * .
12	-.049	.169	. * .
13	.079	.169	. ** .
14	.132	.169	. *** .
15	-.048	.169	. * .
16	-.166	.169	. *** .

Plot Symbols: Autocorrelations *   Two Standard Error Limits .

Total cases: 100   Computable first lags: 34

Despite these cautions, the effects of violating the autocorrelation assumption are complex and may be quite minimal in large samples ($T > 100$). In addition, when we use polynomial predictors of time trends and other error-free variables, such as dummy variables for seasonal components, OLS produces accurate estimates of parameters and standard errors. As a result, the caution against conducting OLS regression with time series is often not as serious as might be expected (Harvey 1994).

Even though OLS regression is often satisfactory for estimating time series models, it is generally recommended that one test for the presence of both AR and MA components in time series data. We know from our discussion of the MA process that it can be represented as an AR model if one is willing to estimate an infinite series of terms. Since this is not possible using OLS, we need to employ maximum likelihood estimation techniques. These techniques are available in programs used to estimate ARMA models that allow for the presence of both AR and MA components. In SPSS, this program is part of the trends package that can be added to the advanced statistics core.

The procedure for conducting an analysis of time series data is as follows:

1. Plot the series to identify potential trends or calendar effects.
2. Detrend the series with time or calendar predictors using OLS regression.
3. Conduct a correlogram analysis of the detrended series.
4. Test plausible models for AR and MA components in the detrended series.
5. Use goodness of fit statistics to evaluate the best model.
6. Combine the deterministic trends and the best fitting ARMA processes into a single model.

Goodness of Fit Measures

Building a model using the ARMA program often involves trying different combinations of AR and MA processes for the same model. Any dataset can be fit if you have enough parameters in a model. All else being equal, the best models are the simplest because they involve the fewest assumptions and are least likely to capitalize on chance or unique characteristics of a dataset. To do this, one needs a measure of goodness of fit. To help diagnose model fit, one can use two descriptive statistics that are sensitive to both the closeness of fit and the number of parameters that have been used to fit the data.

One of the best known (but no longer considered adequate) is the adjusted R^2. This is often provided in computer output for OLS regression (including SPSS). If we just used the unadjusted R^2, we would see that the fit always increased as the number of predictors in the model increased. The purpose of the adjusted R^2 is to make it harder for the fit measure to increase as more parameters are added to the model by introducing a penalty for each additional parameter included in the prediction equation. So, if one has a model with ten parameters that predicts as well as one with five, the one with five will have a higher adjusted R^2.

A similar correction is introduced in two other measures of fit: the Aikake (1974) information criterion (AIC) and the Schwartz (1978) information criterion (SIC). However, these measures include more stringent penalties for increasing the number of parameters.

The formula for the AIC is

$$AIC = e^{2k/T}\left[\frac{1}{T}\sum(e_t)^2\right]$$

where the summation is done over the entire set of residuals (e_t) in the model from 1 to T, and k represents the number of parameters estimated in the model. The summation term in the AIC, $[1/T\sum(e_t)^2]$, is actually the mean square error (MS_e) that is reported in OLS regression output. The standard error of the estimate, which is also reported in OLS output, is the square root of the MS_e. As a result, the AIC is a product of the exponential term and the MS_e. Even if MS_e declines as a result of adding more parameters (k) to a model, the exponential term ($e^{2k/T}$) will increase. The result is that the AIC can actually increase even if error of prediction declines. The goal in model fitting is to find a model that has no more parameters than necessary to explain the data. The lower the AIC, the better the model.

The SIC uses an even more stringent penalty for additional parameters:

$$SIC = T^{k/T}\left[\frac{1}{T}\sum(e_t)^2\right]$$

because $T^{k/T}$ increases more rapidly than $e^{2k/T}$ as k increases.

These fit measures provide some indication of the success of a model by allowing comparisons between alternative models. The AIC is designed to get **smaller** as the fit improves and to identify the best model if one has that model in one's consideration set. That is, if you are pretty sure that you have a correct model in your analysis pool, then the AIC will identify it.

However, if you do not know whether you have the correct model, then the SIC is designed to provide the better index because it will identify the best model of the ones you have. Often, the two will move consistently and give you the same conclusion. But sometimes they don't and you have to pick one of them as your guide. Because we seldom are confident about our models, many analysts use the SIC as the more diagnostic index (Diebold 2001).

As we examine different models from here on, we should keep track of the two criteria to see what they say about the fit of our models. SPSS does not provide the AIC or SIC for OLS regression, so you have to calculate it yourself. However, you can get it when using the ARMA program. Because the ARMA program uses maximum likelihood estimation, it uses a different measure of overall fit instead of the MS_e. This measure was discussed when we examined logistic regression analysis in Chapter 6. As a result, calculations of the AIC and SIC in the ARMA program are based on $-2LL$ (-2 times the log likelihood). However, the same interpretation is applied to these fit measures: the smaller the value, the better the fit.

Testing for Trends That Have Causal Interpretations

To illustrate the use of the ARMA program for model building, we will apply it to test causal hypotheses about the effects of external events. Let's look at the different types of external events that one might want to study.

One is just a variation on the trends we have already studied: the discontinuity or interrupted time series. This type of model assumes that there is an external event that dramatically changes the direction or elevation of a series. We usually know when the event occurred, and so we can test its effect on the series by comparing behavior before and after the event.

The simplest model for the interrupted time series is one in which we define a contrast that is -1 before the event and $+1$ after the event (Figure 8.23a). If we think that the event should change the slope of the series, then we can test a nonlinear component that represents this slope change (Figure 8.23b). If there are enough time points in the series, we can test this hypothesis without worrying about AR components in the series. You can see the reason for this by comparing the interrupted time series with a hypothetical series that has cycles but is stationary (Figure 8.23c). If there are insufficient time periods in the dataset, then one might mistake the cycle for a discontinuity in the time series. For example, going from time 2 to time 5 might give the impression that the series has changed its mean. However, with enough time periods, one should see that the series has not changed its trend. With fewer than one hundred time periods, one should consider fitting an ARMA model to the nontrend components and then jointly estimating the trends and cyclic effects.

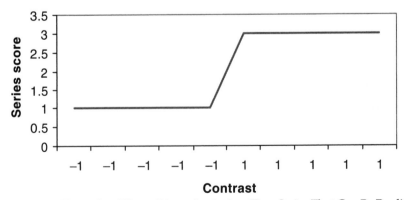

Figure 8.23a Example of Sharp Discontinuity in a Time Series That Can Be Predicted with a Simple Change Contrast

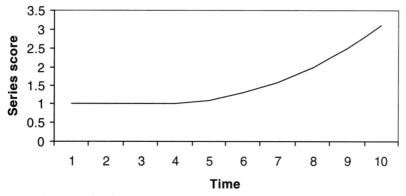

Figure 8.23b Example of Gradual Change in the Mean of a Time Series That Can Be Predicted Using a Nonlinear Curve-Fitting Procedure

Another type of external event is one that occurs repeatedly but only has a short-lived effect, perhaps for a few days or a week after the event. However, the effects of this event may be confused with regular cycles that occur in the time series apart from the effect of the event. As a result, it will be important to control for these cycles when testing for the effects of the event.

We can explore the potential existence of these components by examining the residuals of the regression following removal of the event trend. If the correlogram and Box-Ljung statistic indicate the presence of serial correlation in the residuals, we can then test models using the ARMA program in combination with changes in the AIC and SIC.

We illustrate the use of this procedure to analyze a somewhat complicated **set** of external events that can influence the series of interest both instantaneously and with a lag: the case of debates during the primary season.

We have two measures of debate awareness during the primary period, item cF01:

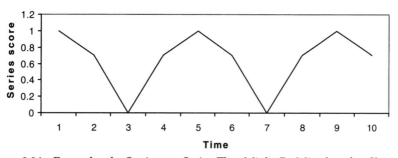

Figure 8.24c Example of a Stationary Series That Might Be Mistaken for Change in the Mean If a Small Time Segment Were Examined

Have you heard or read anything about any debates (Starting 12.14.1999: or town hall meetings) among the candidates for president?

1   Yes
2   No

and item cF02:

Have you watched any of these debates (Starting 12.14.1999: or town hall meetings)?

1   Yes
2   No (+ Unaware of debates in cF01)

To assess awareness and exposure to the debates, we can create a proportion for each day that represents the respondents who said they heard or saw a debate divided by the total number of respondents who were interviewed on that day.

We can also define a trend that takes on the value of 1 whenever a debate or town meeting took place and 0 otherwise. This variable registers twelve different debates from January 3 to April 3. A list of these debates is contained in the calendar of political and media events on your CD-ROM.

Plots of the two indexes are shown in Figures 8.24 and 8.25.

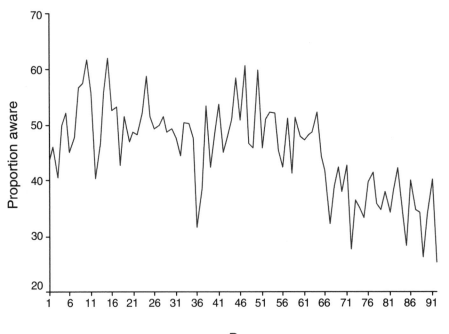

Figure 8.24 Proportion of Respondents Who Were Aware of Debates Between the Major Candidates During the Primary Period

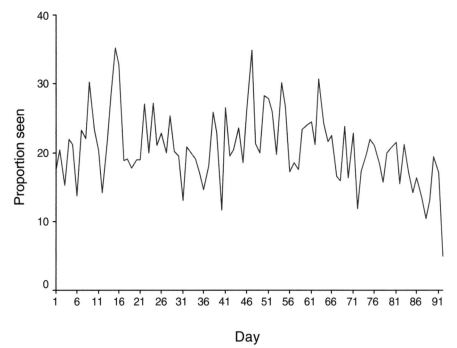

Figure 8.25 Proportion of Respondents Who Reported Watching or Listening to a Debate During the Primary Period

We begin with the awareness series by regressing the series on the debate predictor. However, we want to see if debates on any given day have effects that carry over to subsequent days. So, we create additional lagged versions of the debate variable that represent the delayed debate effect for up to six additional days. To do this, we use the lag transform in SPSS to create six versions of the debate variable representing six days of potentially delayed effects. It seems reasonable that the effect could last for a week. However, we could test alternative delay periods if we chose to do so.

We also want to rule out other calendar effects that might be related to the effects of debates. In particular, we can create dummy variables representing the six days of the week. If there was greater awareness of debates on certain days of the week, this could obscure or increase the actual effect of the debates.

Finally, we can also consider another effect, which is simply that awareness of debates declines as the primary period progresses. This effect would entail a significant predictor for the linear effect of days.

Entering all these variables into a multiple regression analysis yields the model shown in Table 8.15.

TABLE 8.15 Multiple Regression Analysis of Debate Awareness Using Linear Day, Day of Week (D1–D6) and Debate Event Predictor (Debates) with Lagged Versions for Six Days (Lag 1–Lag 6)

Predictor	UNSTANDARDIZED COEFFICIENTS		STANDARDIZED COEFFICIENTS		
	B	Std. Error	Beta	t	Prob.
Constant	51.175	2.619		19.540	.000
Day	−.191	.031	−.562	−6.066	.000
Debates	5.927	2.317	.204	2.557	.013
Lag 1	2.765	2.245	.100	1.232	.222
Lag 2	1.803	2.200	.069	.820	.415
Lag 3	3.060	2.148	.121	1.424	.159
Lag 4	.470	2.117	.019	.222	.825
Lag 5	−.316	2.089	−.013	−.151	.880
Lag 6	1.883	2.046	.077	.920	.361
D1	2.052	2.526	.084	.812	.419
D2	3.091	2.436	.127	1.269	.209
D3	1.779	2.431	.076	.732	.467
D4	1.798	2.450	.076	.734	.465
D5	.350	2.430	.014	.144	.886
D6	4.920	2.527	.202	1.947	.056

There appears to be a strong day of debate effect as well as general decline in debate awareness as time during the primaries progressed. In addition, there is some evidence of greater awareness of debates on Fridays (day 6).

This preliminary analysis enables us to obtain residuals that we can then examine for potential AR and MA components. A plot of these residuals is shown in Figure 8.26.

Examination of the correlogram for this series (Table 8.16) indicates the possible presence of an AR(1) and AR(5).

We therefore test an AR model with up to five lags using the ARMA program in SPSS. The solution in Table 8.17 indicates that debates have an immediate effect on the day they occur (debates) but that they also have a delayed effect three days later (debate_3). In particular, the solution indicates that there is an increase of 5.5 percentage points in awareness of debates on the day of the debate and an effect nearly as large three days later. We still see the Friday effect (D6) and a general decline in debate awareness as the primary period unfolded (Day). Finally, the analysis finds evidence of autoregression at lags 1 and 5.

We can try various alternative models with different numbers of lags in the autoregression function to see if the present model is the best solution.

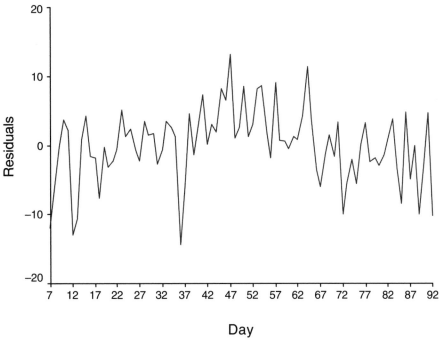

Figure 8.26 Residuals in Awareness of Debates

Table 8.18 shows values of the AIC and SIC for several alternative models. This analysis indicates that the present model is adequate (line in bold). Examination of the residuals from this model (Figure 8.27) also suggests that all cycles have been removed from the data.

The correlogram in Table 8.19 indicates a similar conclusion.

A comparison of the predicted and observed awareness series in Figure 8.28 indicates a fairly close fit.

Debates Seen

A similar analysis can be done for the measure of reported debate viewing. An initial regression analysis indicates that respondents report seeing the debate on the day it happens as well as the next day. However, the decline over time is much less dramatic (see Table 8.20).

Examination of the residuals from the regression solution indicates no evidence of autocorrelation. Hence we can try an ARMA model with just an AR(1) process. The solution to this equation is very similar to the OLS regression model (see Table 8.21). A comparison of the predicted and observed series (Figure 8.29) for this variable also indicates a fairly close fit.

TABLE 8.16 Correlogram Analysis of Residuals in Debate Awareness Following Removal of Trend Predictors

Valid cases: 86

Autocorrelations: Unstandardized Awareness Residual

Lag	Auto-Corr.	Stand. Err.	Plot	Box-Ljung	Prob.
1	.273	.106	***.*	6.612	.010
2	.040	.105	*	6.755	.034
3	.094	.105	**	7.563	.056
4	.156	.104	***.	9.807	.044
5	.327	.103	***.***	19.772	.001
6	.225	.103	***.*	24.580	.000
7	.199	.102	****	28.393	.000
8	.050	.102	*	28.635	.000
9	.053	.101	*	28.908	.001
10	.049	.100	*	29.144	.001
11	-.004	.100	*	29.146	.002
12	.139	.099	***.	31.133	.002
13	.057	.098	*	31.469	.003
14	.061	.098	*	31.866	.004
15	.009	.097	*	31.875	.007
16	-.050	.096	*|	32.145	.010

Plot Symbols: Autocorrelations *   Two Standard Error Limits .

Total cases: 119   Computable first lags: 85

Partial Autocorrelations: Unstandardized Awareness Residual

Lag	Pr-Aut-Corr.	Stand. Err.	Plot
1	.273	.108	***.*
2	-.037	.108	*
3	.101	.108	**
4	.114	.108	**
5	.283	.108	***.**
6	.086	.108	**
7	.153	.108	***.
8	-.076	.108	**|
9	.000	.108	*
10	-.117	.108	**|
11	-.121	.108	**|
12	.055	.108	*
13	-.034	.108	*|
14	.071	.108	|*
15	.007	.108	*
16	-.012	.108	*

Plot Symbols: Autocorrelations *   Two Standard Error Limits .

TABLE 8.17 Output from ARMA Program Assuming an AR(5) Model Along with Predictors for Effects of Debates (with Six Lags) and Days of the Week (D1–D6)

Number of residuals	86
Standard error	5.392536
Log likelihood	−257.28202
AIC	554.56405
SBC	603.65099

ANALYSIS OF VARIANCE

	DF Adj.	Sum of Squares	Residual Variance
Residuals	66	1939.1311	29.079445

VARIABLES IN THE MODEL

	B	SEB	T-ratio	Approx. Prob.
AR1	.249190	.1205550	2.067023	.04265805
AR2	−.099742	.1223744	−.815053	.41797338
AR3	.109485	.1247162	.877870	.38319867
AR4	.068516	.1286047	.532763	.59598717
AR5	.336001	.1213595	2.768638	.00729964
Debates	5.498159	2.2017062	2.497227	.01501909
Debate_1	2.447289	2.1950633	1.114906	.26893416
Debate_2	2.267104	2.0097166	1.128071	.26337392
Debate_3	4.296476	1.8806109	2.284617	.02555773
Debate_4	1.410350	1.9133170	.737123	.46366008
Debate_5	−.469452	1.9788334	−.237237	.81320779
Debate_6	1.925586	1.9784607	.973275	.33397033
D1	2.327928	1.9431369	1.198026	.23519166
D2	3.019802	1.9671391	1.535124	.12953372
D3	1.938067	1.9800741	.978785	.33126028
D4	2.162207	2.0041223	1.078880	.28456858
D5	.151871	1.9568838	.077609	.93837424
D6	4.888441	1.9282651	2.535150	.01361746
Day	−.181775	.0639086	−2.844288	.00592080
Constant	49.755520	4.2549350	11.693603	.00000000

TABLE 8.18 Values of AIC and SIC for Various Alternative Models of Debate Awareness

Model	AIC	SIC
AR(4)	560.69	607.33
AR(5)	**554.56**	**603.65**
AR(6)	555.83	607.37
AR(5) MA(1)	555.01	606.56
AR(6) MA(1)	559.64	613.63
MA(5)	557.28	606.37
MA(6)	555.70	607.25

TESTING HYPOTHESES ABOUT CAUSAL RELATIONS BETWEEN TIME SERIES

We have used the ARMA procedure to model the random component in an analysis of external events. However, we may be interested in a different problem, namely, the relation between two time series.

For example, if we were interested in the relation between a candidate's favorability thermometer rating and the candidate's perceived viability as a

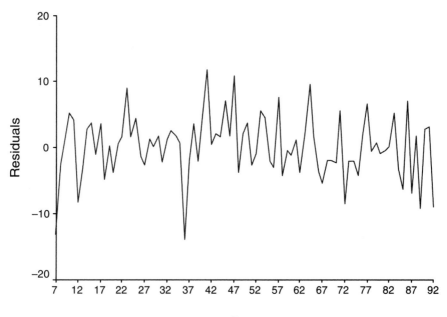

Figure 8.27 Residual Plot in Awareness of Debates Following Removal of Trends and AR(5) Model for Random Component

TABLE 8.19 Correlogram Analysis of Residuals from AR(5) Model Including Trends for Debates and Day of Week

```
Variable:  ERR_1          Valid cases:   86

Autocorrelations:   ERR_1    Error for cF01_1 from ARIMA, MOD_23 CON

       Auto- Stand.
Lag   Corr.  Err.  -1  -.75  -.5 -.25   0   .25  .5  .75   1   Box-Ljung  Prob.

  1  -.033  .106                      . *  .                    .094     .759
  2  -.056  .105                      . *  .                    .373     .830
  3  -.020  .105                      .  *  .                   .408     .939
  4  -.023  .104                      .  *  .                   .456     .978
  5   .009  .103                      .  *  .                   .464     .993
  6   .079  .103                      .  |** .                 1.061     .983
  7   .128  .102                      .  |***.                 2.630     .917
  8  -.029  .102                      . *  .                   2.711     .951
  9  -.040  .101                      . *  .                   2.868     .969
 10  -.029  .100                      . *  .                   2.950     .983
 11  -.122  .100                      . ** .                   4.461     .954
 12   .114  .099                      .  |** .                 5.796     .926
 13  -.008  .098                      .  *  .                   5.804     .953
 14  -.001  .098                      .  *  .                   5.804     .971
 15  -.012  .097                      .  *  .                   5.819     .983
 16  -.052  .096                      . *|  .                   6.108     .987
```

Plot Symbols: Autocorrelations *   Two Standard Error Limits .

Total cases: 119   Computable first lags: 85

```
Partial Autocorrelations:   ERR_1   Error for cF01_1 from ARIMA, MOD_23 CON

       Pr-Aut- Stand.
Lag   Corr.   Err.  -1  -.75  -.5 -.25   0   .25  .5  .75   1

  1  -.033  .108                      . *  .
  2  -.057  .108                      . *| .
  3  -.023  .108                      .  *  .
  4  -.028  .108                      . *| .
  5   .004  .108                      .  *  .
  6   .077  .108                      .  |** .
  7   .135  .108                      .  |***.
  8  -.010  .108                      . *  .
  9  -.024  .108                      .  *  .
 10  -.026  .108                      . *| .
 11  -.129  .108                   .***|  .
 12   .092  .108                      .  |** .
 13  -.037  .108                      . *| .
 14  -.009  .108                      .  *  .
 15  -.003  .108                      .  *  .
 16  -.038  .108                      . *| .
```

Plot Symbols: Autocorrelations *   Two Standard Error Limits .

Total cases: 119   Computable first lags: 85

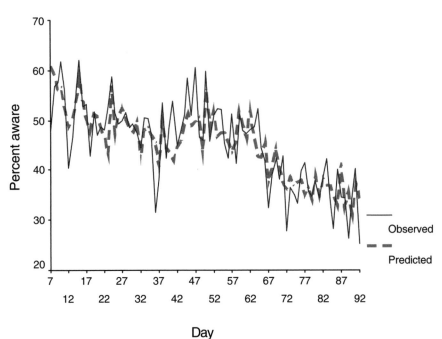

Figure 8.28 Plot of Predicted and Observed Scores for Debate Awareness

TABLE 8.20 Multiple Regression Analysis of Debates Seen Using Linear Day, Day of Week (D1–D6), and Debate Event Predictor and Its Lagged Version for Six Periods

Predictor	UNSTANDARDIZED COEFFICIENTS		STANDARDIZED COEFFICIENTS		
	B	Std. Error	Beta	t	Prob.
Constant	20.469	2.194		9.329	.000
Day	−3.99E-02	.026	−.187	−1.517	.134
Debates	4.463	1.941	.244	2.299	.024
Lag 1	3.726	1.881	.215	1.981	.051
Lag 2	1.526	1.843	.092	.828	.410
Lag 3	2.673	1.800	.168	1.485	.142
Lag 4	.958	1.773	.063	.540	.591
Lag 5	−.581	1.750	−.038	−.332	.741
Lag 6	6.84E-02	1.714	.004	.040	.968
D1	.677	2.116	.044	.320	.750
D2	2.454	2.041	.160	1.203	.233
D3	.911	2.036	.062	.447	.656
D4	.681	2.052	.046	.332	.741
D5	1.289	2.036	.084	.633	.529
D6	.777	2.117	.051	.367	.715

166

TABLE 8.21 ARMA Analysis Output of AR(1) Model with Debate and Day of Week Predictors

Number of residuals	86
Standard error	4.8429892
Log likelihood	−249.71171
AIC	531.42341
SBC	570.69297

ANALYSIS OF VARIANCE

	DF	Adj. Sum of Squares	Residual Variance
Residuals	70	1642.5327	23.454544

VARIABLES IN THE MODEL

	B	SEB	T-ratio	Approx. Prob.
AR1	.191652	.1237491	1.5487162	.12595953
Debates	4.598681	1.9248152	2.3891543	.01958561
Debate 1	3.665887	1.8657075	1.964877	.05339828
Debate 2	1.351867	1.8061725	.7484708	.45668376
Debate 3	2.590558	1.7498242	1.4804676	.14323558
Debate 4	1.019860	1.7339796	.5881614	.55831685
Debate 5	−.533180	1.7060894	−.3125156	.75557783
Debate 6	.103342	1.6976975	.0608717	.95163482
D1	.664782	1.9113218	.3478126	.72902465
D2	2.339439	2.0154008	1.1607812	.24967425
D3	.907861	2.0303516	.4471449	.65615095
D4	.648800	2.0430166	.3175697	.75175671
D5	1.072456	2.0131512	.5327250	.59591111
D6	.731573	1.9084263	.3833413	.70262845
Day	−.041309	.0317870	−1.2995410	.19802191
Constant	20.547952	2.4475168	8.3954282	.00000000

nominee for the party, should we regress one of these variables on the other? In particular, suppose we hypothesized that viability was a cause of rating. Could we create a series for each variable and do OLS regression analysis with rating as the dependent variable Y_t and viability as the independent variable X_t to see how they relate to each other over a period of interest? The model for this analysis would be

$$Y_t = aX_t + e_t$$

where e_t is the random component in series Y_t and **a** is the coefficient of the linear relation between the two series.

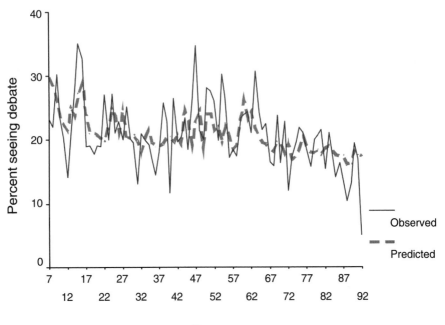

Figure 8.29 Comparison of Predicted and Observed Scores for Model of Debates Seen During the Primary Period

The first consideration is that if e_t has autoregressive (AR) or moving average (MA) components, then standard errors of the coefficients and the coefficients themselves may be biased. As a result, the confidence intervals may be incorrect, and we will end up with an invalid model.

There have been several solutions suggested to this problem over the years. One examines a statistic that is sensitive to the presence of AR(1) in the dependent variable: the Durbin Watson or d.

If we regress Y_t on X_t and calculate residuals from the regression model (e), then

$$d = \sum (e_t - e_{t-1})^2 / \sum (e_t)^2.$$

If the dependent variable contains an AR(1) process with a coefficient p, this statistic will equal

$$2(1 - p)$$

If there is no autocorrelation, then d = 2. If p is >0, then **d** falls in the range of from 0 to 2. If p is <0, then **d** is in the range from 2 to 4. The statistic has a complicated sampling distribution, but as it approaches either 0 or 4, one is advised to consider the presence of autocorrelation and hence to disregard the tests of coefficients for predictors.

Although the **d** statistic has long been associated with time series analysis, it is designed to have maximal power to detect only first order autocorrelation. If a series has no first order autocorrelation but does have higher order correlation, **d** may not detect it. We recommend the use of the Box-Ljung test and examination of the correlogram to determine presence of autocorrelation. But this procedure requires detrending the series to make it stationary before examining the correlogram.

The second thing to consider is that regressing one series on another is a very weak test of the relationship between them. Any number of explanations would predict a correlation between the two variables without there being a causal relation between them. The best evidence for causal influence in time series is the lag-lead relationship, in which a lagged value of a variable predicts the current value of another variable with the lagged value of the dependent variable held constant:

$$Y_t = b_1 Y_{t-1} + a_0 X_t + a_1 X_{t-1} + e_{1t}.$$

This model is similar to the panel study approach we examined in the section using OLS regression approaches to panel designs (Chapter 7). Furthermore, if the residual in the equation is normally distributed white noise, we can estimate the equation using OLS regression. However, this analysis requires both series to be stationary. To achieve this condition, we may either difference each series (if each represents a random walk) or, more likely, remove the time trend using OLS regression.

A second test of causal order is to regress X on previous values of itself and Y. If X causes Y, then earlier values of Y should not predict later values of X:

$$X_t = d_1 X_{t-1} + c_0 Y_t + c_1 Y_{t-1} + e_{2t}.$$

To pursue this analysis strategy, it is critical to know how many lags of each variable to introduce into the models predicting each variable. This is critical because the final models should have only white noise in their random terms. As a result, before exploring this method of analysis, we will examine another preliminary analytic technique known as the cross-correlation function. This analysis is similar to the autocorrelation; however, in this case, it is the relation between two detrended series (i.e., series that have been made stationary) that is correlated at different lags.

Let's look at an example that is constructed from simulated data. For one variable X, we have constructed a time series that is a direct function of time:

$$X_t = .5(\text{time}) + Z_t$$

where Z_t is a normal random deviate $(0,1)$. The trend variable was then used as a component in a second series, Y_t:

$$Y_t = .2X_t + W_t$$

where W_t is a normal random deviate $(0,1)$. The Y series can be contrasted with another series $Y(AR)_t$ that also has an AR(1) component:

$$Y(AR)_t = .2X + .5(LAG\ Y) + W_t.$$

A comparison of these two series plotted against time for $t = 1$ to 100 indicates that they follow a very similar path (see Figure 8.30).

If we detrend each series by removing time as a component of each series, we obtain two stationary series (Figure 8.31).

We can now use the cross-correlation function to observe relations between the series at different lags. This function tells us how the series relate to each other both as lagged and lead functions. However, one can only use this procedure if both series are stationary, which is to say that they have their trends removed.

The cross-correlation function is read as showing the correlation between the series at different lags for each series. At lag 0, we have the correlation between the series with no difference in lags. As the analysis indicates, the two series are highly related at lag 0 ($r = .80$). The confidence bands use the standard error of the correlation $2*(1/\sqrt{N})$ to indicate potentially significant relations between series. The significant relation at lag -1 refers to the fact that if one were to correlate the second series (Y) at lag 1 with the other series at lag 0, the correlation would be .459, a value close to the value of .5 that was used to construct the AR(1) relation for $Y(AR)$. This says that $Y(AR)$

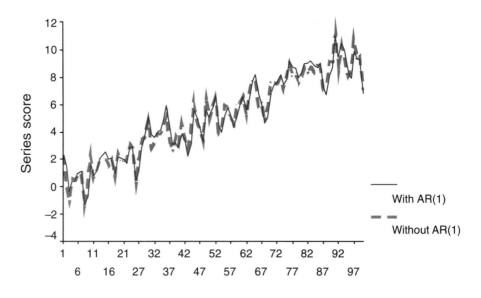

Figure 8.30 Plot of Each Series, One with an AR(1) and One Without It

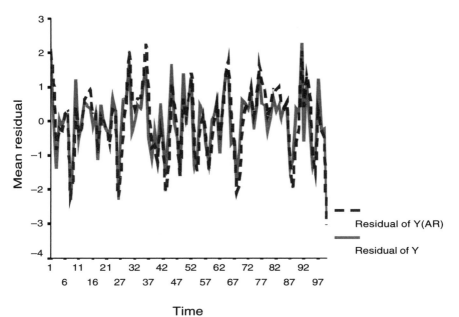

Figure 8.31 Plot of Two Detrended Series

leads Y by one lag, as it should since it was constructed to have the lagged relation (see Table 8.22).

This analysis is a helpful initial procedure to determine potential relations between series. It will tell us if they have a contemporaneous relation (the zero lag case cross-correlation) and if they have lagged relations.

We will want to test the relations in both directions to see if we can find evidence of causal priority. If there are only instantaneous relations, then we will be left with an ambiguous situation. Nevertheless, we will know that the series are related and that we can isolate their relationship without the problem of nonstationarity.

Interpretations of Contemporaneous Relations Between Time Series

Our strategy of detrending time series to create stationary series often raises questions in the minds of readers who are new to time series analysis. One question that is asked concerns the validity of the remaining variation in the series. If we correlate time series with each other after detrending, we often find sizeable relations between them. For example, all three measures of attention to news (on national television, local television, and newspapers) about the presidential primaries exhibited a similar time path during the primary period (see Figure 8.32).

TABLE 8.22 *Cross* Correlation Ouput from SPSS for Analysis of Residuals in Y and Y(AR)

```
Cross Correlations:    RES_1    Residual of Y(AR) from Time
                       RES_2    Residual of Y with Time


       Cross Stand.
Lag    Corr.  Err.  -1  -.75  -.5 -.25   0   .25   .5   .75    1
                    |---+---+----+----+----+----+----+----+----|

 -7   -.182   .104                    ****   .
 -6    .055   .103                 .       *   .
 -5    .062   .103                 .       *   .
 -4   -.060   .102                 .     *     .
 -3   -.097   .102                 .    **     .
 -2    .044   .101                 .       *   .
 -1    .459   .101                 .       *** .*****
  0    .885   .100                 .       *** .**************
  1   -.014   .101                 .       *     .
  2   -.218   .101              ****|       .
  3   -.117   .102                 .   **   .
  4   -.004   .102                 .       *     .
  5    .059   .103                 .       *   .
  6   -.075   .103                 .   **   .
  7   -.234   .104             *.***        .


Plot Symbols:      Autocorrelations  *     Two Standard Error Limits

Total cases:   100    Computable 0-order correlations:   100
```

After detrending each series using the procedure followed earlier, we obtained three series that still appear to follow the same time trends. Indeed, the correlation between local and national television news was .55 (p < .01) (see Figure 8.33).

An important question is whether the remaining covariation in these measures could merely reflect measurement error rather than anything substantive. To answer this question, we can examine the causal diagram shown in Figure 8.34.

This diagram represents a plausible interpretation of the relations between two news measures (attention to election news on network and on local television news) and the effects of time during the primary period. We assume that with the approach of a major primary, news media will create stories about it. These stories will increase in intensity as the primary approaches and will come to the attention of television news viewers. As a result, respondents will report seeing more of those stories on both types of news sources (paths a and b). At the same time, people's overall use of television news may also be related to time (path c) and this in turn may influence

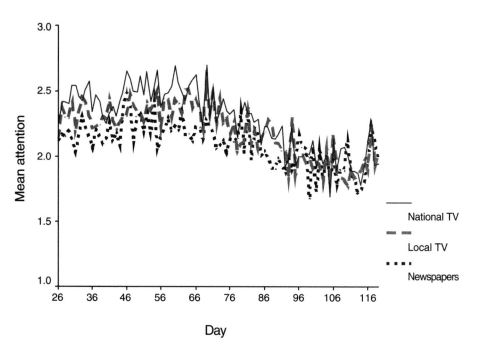

Figure 8.32 Time Series of Attention to News About the Presidential Primary on National (cE03) and Local Television News (cE07) and in Newspapers (cE14) from January 3 to April 30

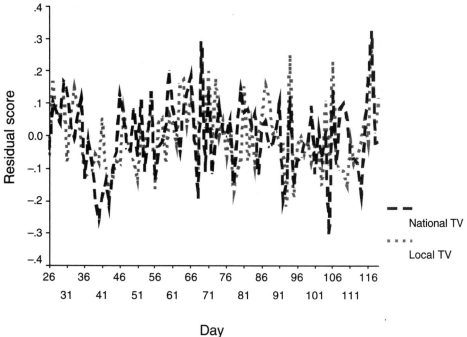

Figure 8.33 Residual Series in Attention to News on Television

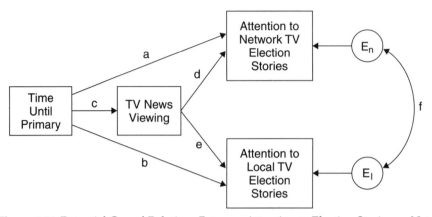

Figure 8.34 Potential Causal Relations Between Attention to Election Stories on Network and Local Television News

attention to news about the election (paths d and e). As a result, another influence on attention to election news is the sheer amount of time that people spend watching either news source. When time is taken out of the trend in exposure to campaign news in each news source, one source of correlation between attention to the two news sources may be errors of measurement in each variable (path f). Another may be correlation produced by valid influence on each news source. Unless we have a direct measure of potential influence on the two news sources, we cannot separate correlation between the unknown components and measurement error. Fortunately, one potential source of correlation is news viewing in general (paths d and e).

On each day of the survey, we may see variation in news viewing. The trends shown in Figure 8.35 suggest a pattern of slowly declining news use during the primary period. The detrended series for each type of television news (Figure 8.36) follows a similar time path. Indeed, they are correlated very highly: $r = .61$, $p < .01$. If detrended viewing of television news predicts detrended variation in the two election news measures, then the correlations we find between different measures of exposure to election news could represent this source of valid news use. If, however, the correlations are the result of measurement error, then the residuals in each news measure will be unrelated to attention to television news in general.

When we combine the residuals in national and local television news use to create a general television news viewing index, we see that this score correlates with both measures of attention to news about the primary: $r = .36$, with detrended attention to primary stories on national television news, and $r = .57$ with the same detrended attention to local television news. As a result, news viewing on television accounts for about 20% of the relation between the attention to primary election stories on the two television news sources.

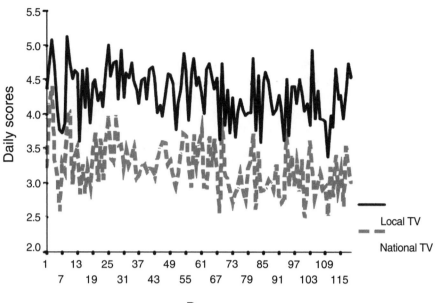

Figure 8.35 Time Series for Days in the Last Week That News Was Obtained from Three Sources: National Television News (cE01), Local Television News (cE06), and Daily Newspapers (cD13)

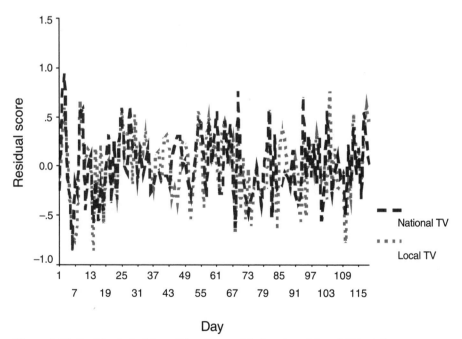

Figure 8.36 Residuals in News Viewing on National and Local Television

This analysis suggests that the relation between residual scores in attention to news stories about the primary is valid variation that could be explained by other factors, such as general use of news sources. The more people pay attention to television news, the more likely they are to be exposed to stories about the primary.

It is plausible therefore that correlations between residual scores in the NAES reflect sources of valid variation unrelated to time trends. Indeed, we are going to use this variation to isolate causal relations between time series.

The Strategy for Isolating Causal Relations between Time Series

The diagram in Figure 8.37 shows potential relations that might underlie a causal relation between two detrended times series, X and Y. Just as in the panel design, we are going to use the prior status of X as represented by the L operator to predict the subsequent status of Y.

The paths from the lagged versions of each variable to their unlagged versions (at lag 0) represent the potential for AR processes in each series. Our analysis will hold constant these AR processes so that the relation between series is not mediated by the prior relation between X and Y at the first lag (r_1). If X leads Y by one lag, then L(X) will predict Y. This path can be called

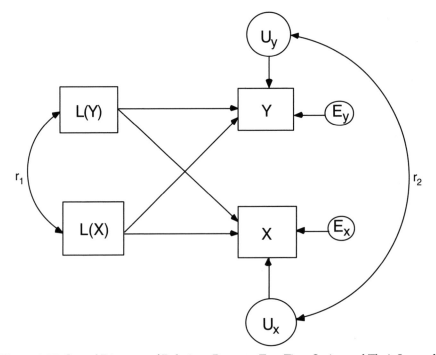

Figure 8.37 Causal Diagram of Relations Between Two Time Series and Their Lagged Values

the **cross-correlation** between the lag of X and Y. In addition, if the relation is unidirectional, then L(Y) will not predict X. This is a stronger requirement that rules out the possibility that X and Y are either jointly determined by some other factor or that they each affect the other, a result that is called **feedback.**

This type of causal pattern is called Granger causality in the economic literature, after the person who first identified it (Granger 1969). Lazarsfeld pioneered a similar approach in the analysis of political data (1948). In psychology, the approach is very similar to the cross-lagged panel correlation identified by Campbell (1963). In any case, the idea is that causality from X to Y implies that prior information in X will predict subsequent status of Y holding constant prior information in Y.

There is no path directly linking X and Y in Figure 8.37. If either X or Y causes the other contemporaneously (within the limits of the time periods used to measure the variables), then there is also the possibility of contemporaneous causality in the system. Since the purpose of the analysis is to find evidence of Granger causality between the variables, it is best not to make any assumptions about contemporaneous relations between them. However, the diagram does allow the possibility that the unknown components in X and Y are correlated (r_2). This assumption is weaker because it predicts that X and Y are correlated but not necessarily because of a causal relation between them.

To summarize the possible relations between two time series, one can distinguish four possible combinations of outcomes in a Granger causality analysis: (1) X can Granger cause Y; (2) Y can Granger cause X; (3) both X and Y can Granger cause each other (feedback); and (4) either X or Y may cause the other contemporaneously.

Analysis of Granger Causality

In the model shown in Figure 8.37 for the possible relation between two variables, X and Y, we can estimate the relations between the variables using a procedure known as vector autoregression, or VAR for short. The most basic model is one with a VAR(1) structure. The procedure involves estimating one regression equation for each variable in the system. Since in our example there are two variables, we will have two equations:

$$Y_t = b_1 Y_{t-1} + a_1 X_{t-1} + e_{1,t}$$
$$X_t = c_1 Y_{t-1} + d_1 X_{t-1} + e_{2,t}$$

The residual terms in these equations, $e_{1,t}$ and $e_{2,t}$, are assumed to be white noise processes with means of 0 and standard deviations of σ_1 and σ_2. They can be treated as white noise because the model includes all sources of autocorrelation in each variable. At the same time, the residual terms can be correlated with each other. This condition is likely when Y_t and X_t are correlated.

Considerations in Fitting a VAR System

There are two issues in estimating a VAR system. One concerns the number of lags to include in the model. To help identify a plausible start for a VAR model, we will use the partial autocorrelation function (PACF) for each variable to define the minimum number of lags to include in the system. In addition, we will use the cross-correlation function that is available in SPSS to determine if the two series are correlated across the lags of either variable.

The cross-correlation function should only be used on detrended series that are stationary. Otherwise, it will give misleading results. The function will provide some evidence of the range of lags that are potentially influencing each series. This is a good first step for defining the model that we will use to identify potential causal lags in time series.

A second issue that must be resolved in constructing a VAR model is the interpretation of the correlation between the residual terms in the model (r_2 in Figure 8.37). If the correlation between the series is 0, then problems in interpretation are minimal. However, the two series are often correlated at lag 0 apart from any causal influence that earlier lags introduce. In this case, it is unclear whether the correlation is the result of third causes that influence each series or of a contemporaneous causal relation between the series at lag 0. Of course, the whole point of conducting the VAR analysis is to gain an understanding of potential causal relations between the series. If we have to make assumptions about such causal relations, we are putting the cart before the horse.

Fortunately, there is one case in which a relation between the series at lag 0 ($r_2 \neq 0$) is not problematic. If neither series contains any AR processes, then the interpretation of the VAR analysis is more straightforward. As seen in Figure 8.37, AR relations between lags of the same series are a potential path of influence if correlation at lag 0 is present. To see this, consider the path from L(Y) to Y to X. This sequence of paths is not a direct influence of L(Y) on X, but it could be the source of any observed effect of L(Y) on X in a VAR analysis. However, if the relation between L(Y) and Y is zero (there is no AR(1) in Y), then this path does not exist and will not contribute to the relation between L(Y) and X.

When any series in a VAR has AR processes, its apparent influence on the other series may be misleading. If one took the outcome of the analysis at face value, one would conclude that Y causes X in the Granger sense when in actuality, it only predicts itself by virtue of an AR relation (also see Mark 1979 for a discussion of this problem).

If one only wants to test for the presence of Granger causality, then one can hold constant the contemporaneous relation between the variables. For the case in Figure 8.37, this would eliminate the relation between L(Y) and X even if there were an AR(1) in Y.

Let's use an example that is relevant during the primaries: estimates of candidate viability (likelihood of gaining the party's nomination) and respondent feelings of favorability toward the candidate (thermometer ratings). Bartels (1988) argues that perceptions of viability are important factors in primaries because they influence the likelihood that we will consider a candidate and increase our attraction to the candidate. His approach would suggest that changes in viability should increase attraction to a candidate.

We can test this prediction using the primary period in the NAES dataset. Figure 8.38 shows mean thermometer ratings for Bush (cA01) and McCain (cA21) from January 3 to April 30, and Figure 8.39 shows the viability ratings of each candidate for the same period (cN01 and cN02).

There is not much evidence in these plots to suggest that viability drives ratings of either Bush or McCain. But first let's take differences of each pair of measures so we can see changes in the relative standing of the two candidates (see Figure 8.40).

Figure 8.40 suggests that the candidates did not differ very much in their thermometer ratings over this period. However, Bush always had higher viability ratings, especially after Super Tuesday.

An examination of the thermometer series suggests no change in either the mean or variability of the series; hence it seems likely that the series is already stationary. But before examining the viability correlogram, we first have to detrend the series.

In examining the viability curve, it is apparent that there are at least four turning points in the viability status of the two candidates. Bush remains high until the New Hampshire primary, when he drops precipitously until

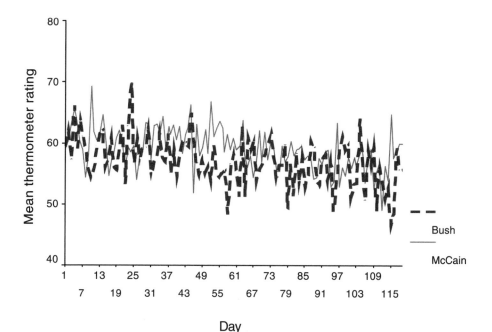

Figure 8.38 Time Series for Bush and McCain Thermometer Ratings from January 3 to April 30

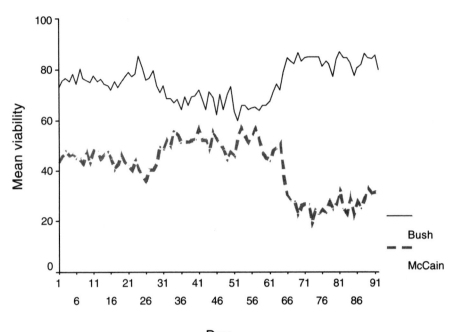

Figure 8.39 Time Series for Bush and McCain Viability Chances for Receiving the Nomination of the Republican Party

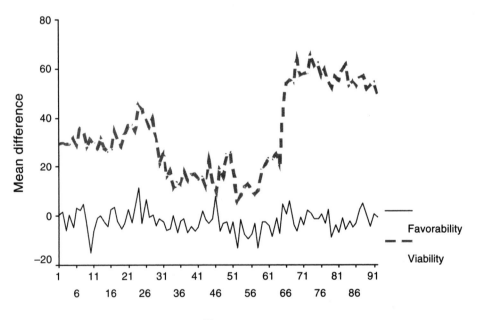

Figure 8.40 Time Series for Differences in Thermometer Ratings and Viability Estimates for Bush and McCain (Bush − McCain)

TABLE 8.23 Regression Analysis of Viability Difference Score with Powers of Day in the Series as Predictors

Predictor	UNSTANDARDIZED COEFFICIENTS		STANDARDIZED COEFFICIENTS		
	B	Std. Error	Beta	t	Prob.
Constant	17.034	4.169		4.086	.000
Day	3.445	.560	5.390	6.147	.000
Day^2	−.178	.021	−26.769	−8.409	.000
Day^3	2.433E-03	.000	32.173	9.641	.000
Day^5	−1.026E-07	.000	−10.293	−9.987	.000

Super Tuesday, when he quickly bounces back. From then on his viability advantage is so great that the survey does not continue to measure differences in the viability of the candidates.

To estimate the trend in the viability series, a polynomial regression model of order 5 was fit to the data. The regression solution shown in Table 8.23 produced a good fit to the series, $R^2 = .798$.

The coefficient for Day^4 was dropped from the model because it was collinear with the other predictors. A plot of the residuals of the trend model and the original series is shown in Figure 8.41.

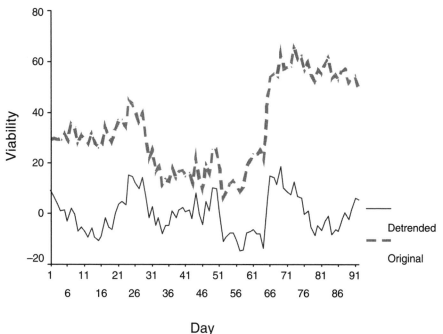

Figure 8.41 Comparison of Original and Detrended Viability Series

The detrended series contains the same basic cycles as the original series, but it is now stationary.

A comparison of the standardized thermometer and viability series is shown in Figure 8.42. There is some indication that thermometer differences lead viability differences. However, the two series are correlated, r = .308, p < .01.

An examination of the correlogram for the viability series suggests an AR(1) with some potential for later lags (Table 8.24).

The correlogram for the thermometer series indicates very little evidence of any serial correlation in the series (Table 8.25).

The cross-correlation function shows evidence of correlation between the series at the contemporaneous period (lag 0). In addition, there is evidence that lags in the viability estimate are also related to thermometer ratings. Finally, there is a correlation between viability at lag −1 and thermometer suggesting that thermometer ratings predict viability (Table 8.26).

The next step is to generate lagged versions of both variables so we can enter them into a vector autoregression model for each dependent variable. There is some uncertainty about the number of lags to include in this analysis. The cross-correlation function suggests that at least three lags may be involved, so we can begin with a VAR(3). We also know that there is a large

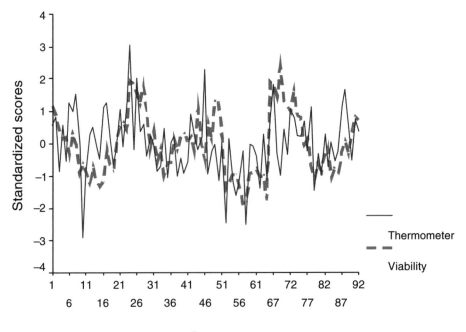

Figure 8.42 Standardized Values of the Residual Viability Series and the Thermometer Series

TABLE 8.24 Correlogram Analysis of Detrended Viability

```
Variable:  RES_3          Missing cases:  27     Valid cases:  92


Autocorrelations:  Unstandardized Residuals (Viability)

       Auto- Stand.
Lag    Corr.  Err. -1  -.75  -.5 -.25   0   .25   .5   .75   1    Box-Ljung  Prob.
```

Lag	Auto- Corr.	Stand. Err.	plot	Box-Ljung	Prob.
1	.760	.103	*** .***********	54.945	.000
2	.592	.102	*** .********	88.671	.000
3	.458	.101	*** .*****	109.041	.000
4	.331	.101	*** .***	119.826	.000
5	.163	.100	*** .	122.461	.000
6	.035	.100	* .	122.586	.000
7	-.113	.099	. **	123.878	.000
8	-.288	.099	** .***	132.436	.000
9	-.405	.098	**** .***	149.530	.000
10	-.469	.097	***** .***	172.758	.000
11	-.497	.097	****** .***	199.165	.000
12	-.531	.096	******* .***	229.690	.000
13	-.559	.096	******* .***	263.853	.000
14	-.494	.095	****** .***	290.886	.000
15	-.392	.094	**** .***	308.118	.000
16	-.225	.094	* .***	313.897	.000

```
Plot Symbols:     Autocorrelations *     Two Standard Error Limits  .

Total cases:  119     Computable first lags:  91


        Partial Autocorrelations:   Unstandardized Residuals:  Viability

        Pr-Aut- Stand.
        Lag   Corr.  Err. -1  -.75  -.5 -.25   0   .25   .5   .75   1
```

Lag	Pr-Aut- Corr.	Stand. Err.	plot
1	.760	.104	*** .***********
2	.034	.104	* .
3	-.007	.104	* .
4	-.054	.104	. *
5	-.184	.104	****
6	-.061	.104	. *
7	-.172	.104	.***
8	-.243	.104	* .***
9	-.097	.104	. **
10	-.072	.104	. *
11	-.035	.104	. *
12	-.121	.104	. **
13	-.176	.104	****
14	.045	.104	* .
15	.033	.104	* .
16	.164	.104	***.

```
Plot Symbols:     Autocorrelations *     Two Standard Error Limits  .

Total cases:  119     Computable first lags:  91
```

TABLE 8.25 Correlogram for Thermometer Ratings

Autocorrelations: Thermometer Ratings

```
     Auto- Stand.
Lag  Corr.  Err. -1  -.75  -.5 -.25   0   .25  .5  .75   1   Box-Ljung  Prob.
       ├────┼─────┼────┼────┼────┼────┼────┼────┤
 1   .101   .091                       .  ** .                 1.247     .264
 2   .104   .090                       .  ** .                 2.584     .275
 3   .058   .090                       .  * .                  3.005     .391
 4   .010   .089                       . *  .                  3.017     .555
 5   .108   .089                       .  ** .                 4.482     .482
 6   .016   .089                       .  * .                  4.514     .607
 7  -.007   .088                       .  * .                  4.521     .718
 8  -.048   .088                       . *|  .                 4.822     .776
 9  -.061   .087                       . *|  .                 5.306     .807
10   .116   .087                       .  **.                  7.092     .717
11  -.066   .087                       . *|  .                 7.681     .742
12  -.028   .086                       . *|  .                 7.788     .801
13  -.083   .086                       .**|  .                 8.718     .794
14  -.120   .085                       .**|  .                10.693     .710
15  -.005   .085                       . *|  .                10.697     .774
16  -.124   .085                       .**|  .                12.831     .685
```

Plot Symbols: Autocorrelations *   Two Standard Error Limits .

Total cases: 119   Computable first lags: 118

Partial Autocorrelations: Thermometer Ratings

```
     Pr-Aut- Stand.
Lag  Corr.   Err. -1  -.75  -.5 -.25   0   .25  .5  .75   1
         ├────┼─────┼────┼────┼────┼────┼────┼────┤
 1   .101   .092                       .  ** .
 2   .095   .092                       .  ** .
 3   .040   .092                       .  * .
 4  -.009   .092                       . *  .
 5   .100   .092                       .  ** .
 6  -.005   .092                       .  * .
 7  -.029   .092                       . *|  .
 8  -.057   .092                       . *|  .
 9  -.049   .092                       . *|  .
10   .131   .092                       .  ***.
11  -.079   .092                       . **|  .
12  -.032   .092                       . *|  .
13  -.068   .092                       . *|  .
14  -.085   .092                       . **|  .
15   .005   .092                       .  * .
16  -.100   .092                       . **|  .
```

Plot Symbols: Autocorrelations *   Two Standard Error Limits .

Total cases: 119   Computable first lags: 118

TABLE 8.26 Cross Correlation Analysis between Thermometer Rating Difference and Detrended Viability Rating

Listwise deletion.　　　Missing cases:　27　　　Valid cases:　92

Cross Correlations:　　Thermometer Rating
　　　　　　　　　　　　　Unstandardized Residual of Viability Rating

Lag	Cross Corr.	Stand. Err.	-1 -.75 -.5 -.25 0 .25 .5 .75 1
-7	-.130	.108	.***
-6	.001	.108	.* .
-5	.027	.107	.|* .
-4	.084	.107	.|** .
-3	.041	.106	.|* .
-2	.151	.105	.|***.
-1	.261	.105	.|***.*
0	.393	.104	.|***.****
1	.412	.105	.|***.****
2	.372	.105	.|***.***
3	.326	.106	.|***.***
4	.293	.107	.|***.**
5	.245	.107	.|***.*
6	.105	.108	.|** .
7	.034	.108	.|* .

Plot Symbols:　　　Autocorrelations *　　　Two Standard Error Limits

Total cases:　119　　Computable 0-order correlations:　92

AR(1) in the viability series. If correlations for later lags were in evidence (aside from some very distant lags at time 8 and 13), we would enter these in the model as well.

To determine the correct order of the VAR, we can compare goodness of fit indices for VAR models with one, two, and three lags. Table 8.27 shows that for the AIC and SIC, the solution with one lag seems to provide the best fit to the data. The adjusted R^2 index is the least sensitive of the three in that it does not distinguish between one and two lags for the model with the thermometer as dependent variable.

The results of the regressions for VAR(1) shown in Table 8.28 indicate that the lagged version of viability predicts thermometer ratings (p = .032) and that the reverse is also true: Lagged thermometer ratings predict viability (p = .066). In addition, there is evidence of a large AR(1) in viability.

TABLE 8.27 Goodness of Fit Indices for Three Different VAR Models

Lag Number/Index	Viability as Dependent Variable	Thermometer as Dependent Variable
1 Lag		
Adj. R^2	.597	.045
AIC	25.14	20.33
SIC	27.32	22.09
2 Lags		
Adj. R^2	.590	.045
AIC	26.81	21.61
SIC	30.80	24.83
3 Lags		
Adj. R^2	.581	.032
AIC	28.89	22.71
SIC	35.09	27.59

Because the two series are correlated at lag 0 ($r = .308$) and viability has a large AR(1), the significant cross-lag 1 coefficient for viability is suspect. To determine if this relation is spurious, we enter contemporaneous values in the models. The solutions to these equations indicate that the coefficient for viability at lag 1 is no longer significant (Table 8.29). However, the coefficient for the cross-lag 1 thermometer rating remains nearly significant ($p < .068$). Hence, the interpretation of this analysis is that only thermometer ratings have a causal influence in the Granger sense. The effect of viability on thermometer is potentially spurious, resulting from the AR(1) in viability, which carries over to the current day through its contemporaneous relation with favorability.

One could also argue that the contemporaneous relation between the series reflects true causal feedback, indicating that people's estimates of a candidate's viability affect their favorability toward the candidate and vice versa. However, the results clearly show that only one variable's prior status (thermometer ratings) influences the later status of the other. Since this is what is meant by Granger causality, one could argue that only thermometer ratings fully exhibit this characteristic. Furthermore, the pattern of the original time series in Figure 8.42 indicates that viability undergoes dramatic changes that are not mirrored in thermometer ratings. As a result, there is evidence in both the original series and the detrended versions that viability does not influence attraction to a candidate during the primary period.

One is still left with the question: What causes the contemporaneous relation between viability and favorability? Further analyses could be conducted with other detrended variables to determine if they predict the sta-

TABLE 8.28 Regression Analysis of Viability and Thermometer Variables

| Model | UNSTANDARDIZED COEFFICIENTS | | STANDARDIZED COEFFICIENTST | | |
	B	Std. Error	Beta	t	Prob.
Viability as dependent (Constant)	.418	.568		.736	.463
LAG (Viability)	.712	.072	.716	9.848	.000
LAG (Thermometer)	.231	.124	.135	1.864	.066
Thermometer as dependent					
(Constant)	−2.033	.508		−4.000	.000
LAG (Viability)	.141	.065	.243	2.177	.032
LAG (Thermometer)	.032	.111	.032	.289	.773

tus of both variables (as we illustrated in the case of attention to election news on different news media). For example, one could test the role of knowledge about the candidates, endorsements of the candidates by important groups or newspapers, and other perceived traits of the candidates. Once plausible variables have been identified, further analyses of Granger causation could be conducted.

TABLE 8.29 Regression Analysis of Viability and Thermometer Variables Holding Contemporaneous Scores Constant

| Model | UNSTANDARDIZED COEFFICIENTS | | STANDARDIZED COEFFICIENTS | | |
	B	Std. Error	Beta	t	Prob.
Viability as dependent					
(Constant)	1.090	.589		1.851	.068
LAG (Viability)	.663	.071	.666	9.312	.000
LAG (Thermometer)	.220	.119	.129	1.850	.068
Contemporaneous Thermometer	.338	.113	.198	2.979	.004
Thermometer as dependent					
(Constant)	−2.104	.492		−4.281	.000
LAG (Viability)	−.050	.090	−.086	−.553	.582
LAG (Thermometer)	−.030	.109	−.030	−.277	.783
Contemporaneous viability	.274	.092	.468	2.979	.004

SUMMARY

Our review of time series analysis indicates that we can decompose daily variation in NAES variables into white noise, AR and MA components, as well as trends attributable to external events (e.g., debates). We can also examine relations between series to identify Granger causality. We have argued that it is critical to detrend a series before detecting AR or MA components. It is also critical to include potential AR and MA components in any models that test for external events. The VAR approach can be used to test for Granger causality between time series. However, care must be taken to evaluate the effects of AR components that might appear to give a series the ability to predict the status of another series by going through contemporaneous relations at lag 0.

EXERCISES

Analyze the public's awareness and viewing of the presidential debates using the same techniques employed to study the influence of debates during the primaries.

Analyze the relation between viability perceptions of Bush and McCain and favorability ratings using the Super Tuesday file.

Analyze the relation between viability perceptions of Bush and McCain and vote intentions using the Super Tuesday file.

REFERENCES

Aikake, H. 1974. A new look at the statistical model identification. *IEEE Transactions on Automatic Control* AC-19:716–23.

Bartels, L. M. 1988. *Presidential primaries and the dynamics of public choice.* Princeton, NJ: Princeton University Press.

Campbell, D. T. 1963. From description to experimentation: Interpreting trends as quasi-experiments. *Problems in measuring change,* ed. C. W. Harris. Madison: University of Wisconsin Press.

Chatfield, C. 1996. *The analysis of time series: An introduction.* New York: Chapman & Hall/CRC.

Diebold, F. X. 2001. *Elements of forecasting.* 2d ed. Cincinnati, OH: South-Western.

Enders, W. 1995. *Applied econometric time series.* New York: John Wiley.

Granger, C. W. J. 1969. Investigating causal relations by econometric models and cross-spectral methods. *Econometrica* 37:424–38.

Harvey, A. C. 1990. *The econometric analysis of time series.* Boston: Philip Alan, Hemel Hempstead, and MT Press.

Harvey, A. C. 1993. *Time series models*. Cambridge, MA: The MIT Press.

Lazarsfeld, P. F. 1948. The use of panels in social research. *Proceedings of the American Philosophical Society* 92:405–10.

Mark, M. M. 1979. The causal analysis of concomitancies in time series. In *Quasi-experimentation: Design and analysis issues for field settings,* ed. T. D. Cook & D. T. Campbell. Boston: Houghton Mifflin.

Schwarz, G. 1978. Estimating the dimension of a model. Annals of Statistics 6:461–64.

Appendix of Technical Terms

CHAPTERS 3 AND 4

Descriptive research questions   Questions focus on the characteristics of a population based on the sample. The emphasis is on the accuracy of the estimate. For example, what proportion of the public intended to vote for Bush in the 2000 presidential election, and how much error surrounds the estimate? This is often the focus of press reports about elections.

Associative research questions   These questions ask whether there is a relationship between two variables. For example, is intention to vote for Bush related to age?

Causal research questions   These questions ask whether change in one variable affects or causes change in another. For example, does age affect intention to vote for Bush?

Variable   An entity that takes on two or more values. These values can be quantitative (e.g., political ideology) or qualitative (e.g., party identification).

Constant   An entity that has only one value. It does not vary.

Independent variable   A variable that is thought to be the cause or predictor of another variable.

Dependent variable   A variable that is analyzed as the result or outcome of another variable.

Covariation   Relation between two variables usually indexed by the covariance or the correlation coefficient.

Confounding variables   Variables that may explain the relationship between other variables but that are not explicitly acknowledged in an analysis. For example, level of education may explain why readers of newspapers have more knowledge about politics. Unless education were held constant, the relation between newspaper use and knowledge may be misleading.

Intervening variables Variables that help explain the causal relation between two variables. The independent variable causes variation in the intervening variable, which in turn produces variation in the dependent one. For example, the finding that men know more about the issue positions of the candidates than women may be explained by their greater tendency to discuss politics with friends. People who engage in more discussion about politics tend to have better recall of political information than those who do not. As a result, the relation between gender and political knowledge can be explained in part by the intervening variable of discussion. Holding constant people's discussion with others will reduce the relation between gender and ability to accurately recall the positions of candidates.

Operationalization The method by which variables are defined in measurement in distinction to their meaning in theory. In surveys such as the NAES, decisions are made about how to ask questions that assess such variables as knowledge of the candidates, perceptions of the candidate's personalities, and importance of certain issues. The survey questions used to assess these variables are operationalizations of the concepts they are intended to measure.

Reliability The ability of a measure to give the same results if nothing has changed in the underlying variable. In the NAES, the reliability of a question is the extent to which it would give the same answer if it were asked again a short time later. A measure that gives researchers different results on different occasions even though nothing else has changed is not reliable.

Validity The ability of an operationalization to measure the concept it is intended to capture. A valid measure is one that adequately assesses the meaning of the variable the researcher wants to measure. Validity can be demonstrated by showing that a variable correlates with other measures that should be related to the concept. For example, we are confident that measures of knowledge about the candidates' positions have validity because people who pay more attention to news about the election score better on the knowledge measures.

Content validity Asks whether the measures used in the study appear on their face to correspond with the concepts they are intended to measure. Sometimes called face validity.

Construct validity This type of validity concerns the adequacy with which our measures actually assess the concept we are measuring. To the degree different measures of a variable correlate with each other, we have increased confidence that they assess the same variable.

Random error   Error that does not occur in a systematic way. To the degree random error influences a score, it will as likely increase the score as decrease it. As a result, averaging across observations will tend to cancel out random errors and make estimates less subject to the influence of random error. Error will be reduced as the number of observations increases.

Bias   Error that influences scores systematically. Averaging observations will not remove this source of error from estimates. For example, if people overstate their previous voting behavior, then our estimates of this behavior will be biased upward no matter how large our sample.

Internal validity   The accuracy of a claim that one variable causes another. In analyses of the NAES, we find that respondents' party identification influences their evaluations of the candidates. To the extent this finding is based on sound measurement, analyses, and statistical inference, we can say that it has internal validity.

External validity   The ability to generalize a finding to alternate ways of measuring the concepts and across people, times, and settings. In our example of party identification affecting candidate evaluation (see earlier), if this finding generalizes across different measures of party identification and candidate evaluation and, in addition, if it represents the way different people behave no matter where or when they are questioned, then the finding has external validity. If, however, there were something in our survey procedures that produced this finding that would not be found using different procedures, then the finding's external validity might be questioned. A finding may have internal validity, but may lack external validity.

Census   A study or survey of an entire population.

Sample   A subset of a population that is selected for study.

Random sample   A subset of a population that is selected for study based on a sampling plan that gives each population member an equal chance of being selected.

Sample frame   Members from a population who have a chance of being selected into the sample.

Nonresponse bias   A bias that occurs when the individuals who have been selected for interviewing decline to participate in the survey or participate but do not complete the entire survey and differ from those individuals who do complete it. In the NAES, missing data are infrequent. However, it is wise when conducting analyses with variables that have missing scores (e.g., income) either to use a valid method of imputation for missing data or to ensure that the missing scores do not bias one's analyses. Response rates in the NAES are comparable to other major national telephone surveys (about 30%). Although the rate is relatively low, the survey is still relatively representative of the U.S. population (see Chapter 2) and should produce generalizable results.

Statistical conclusion validity The ability of a study to draw conclusions about the data based on the size of the sample, the sensitivity of the measurement, and the appropriateness of the statistical tests used to make inferences about the data. The larger the sample, the more sensitive the measurement, and the more appropriate the statistical tests, the greater the statistical conclusion validity.

Cross-section Data that have been collected at a single point in time.

Repeated cross-sectional design A design in which the data have been collected at two or more points in time. The collected data are different samples drawn from the same population.

Panel design A design in which the same individuals are interviewed at two or more points in time.

Rolling cross-section (RCS) design A design that involves taking a series of cross-sections over a period of time and employing a sampling protocol used to ensure that each cross-section is equally representative of the population. Each cross-section is equally spaced across the time period of interest. In the NAES, every effort was made to keep response rates and respondent characteristics constant across each day of interviewing. Hence the data can be analyzed by day without controlling for sampling variability. It is important to note that the interviews were conducted at the end of the day, so each day's data are the result of previous days and the effects of what happened during the daytime and early evening of the interview date.

Ecological fallacy Making potentially invalid inferences about individual-level process from group-level data.

Replicates Random subsamples of the telephone numbers targeted for interviewing in a rolling cross-sectional study such as the NAES.

CHAPTER 5

Smoothing A graphical presentation technique that permits examination of daily variation in a time series while minimizing the contribution of random variation. Smoothed scores are not typically analyzed using regression or other quantitative techniques. To analyze a time series quantitatively, it is recommended that the regression procedures discussed in Chapters 6 and 8 be employed.

Centered moving average   A smoothing technique that pools data by calculating an average for a given point in time with a specified number of values surrounding it. For example, a seven-day centered moving average for a given day is the value of that day plus the values of the three days preceding it and the values of the three days following it divided by seven.

Prior moving average   A smoothing technique that pools data by calculating an average for a given point in time with a specified number of values preceding it. For example, a seven-day prior moving average for a given day is the value of that day plus the values of the six days preceding it in the series divided by seven.

CHAPTERS 6 AND 7

Ordinary least squares (OLS)   A method of parameter estimation in linear regression for dependent variables that are measured on quantitative scales, such as ratings of candidates. The method identifies parameter values that minimize the variance of prediction errors (mean squared error).

Logistic regression analysis   A method of parameter estimation for dependent variables that are dichotomous at the individual level, such as yes versus no responses. The method uses maximum likelihood estimation procedures to identify predictors of the log of the odds of a response. These procedures maximize the log likelihood of the prediction function, and this value is frequently provided in computer output from the procedure.

Log likelihood   A measure of fit that is maximized in the method of maximum likelihood estimation. A transform of this measure, $-2 \times$ log likelihood ($-2LL$), is used to evaluate goodness of fit and to test the significance of additional parameters in a model. When prediction residuals are normally distributed, maximum likelihood and ordinary least squares estimation produce identical results.

Residuals   Deviations from prediction in a regression model. They contain both measurement error and effects of unknown variables. A common assumption is that the residuals are normally distributed. If they are, one can use standard tests of significance on the parameters, such as t-tests. Residuals that are not normally distributed can be estimated using maximum likelihood techniques, such as in the case of logistic regression.

Variance   A measure of dispersion for a set of scores calculated by summing the squared deviations of each score from the mean, $(X_i - M)^2$, or other predicted value of the score, and then taking the mean of this sum. The square root of the variance is the **standard deviation.**

Covariance   A measure of relation between two sets of paired scores calculated by summing the product of the deviations of each pair of scores from its mean, $(X_i - M_x)(Y_i - M_y)$, and then taking the mean of this sum. A covariance of zero means the variables are not linearly related.

Correlation   A measure of relation between two variables that have been standardized to a mean of zero and a standard deviation of 1 (**z scores**). The correlation is the mean of the products of the paired z scores, $Z_x Z_y$. The correlation ranges from -1 to $+1$. A score of 1 means that the variables are perfectly linearly related. A score of zero means they are not linearly related.

Mean squared error (MS$_e$)   The variance of the residuals in a regression model. OLS regression minimizes this value to identify the parameters of the model. The **standard error of the regression** is simply the standard deviation of the MS$_e$. Both statistics are typically contained in regression analysis output.

R^2   A measure of goodness of fit ranging between zero and 1 for OLS linear regression models. It is the square of the correlation between the predicted and observed scores. It increases as the mean square error of the prediction equation declines. The larger its value, the better the fit. Computer programs also provide estimates of R^2 for logistic regression models. These values provide an estimate of goodness of fit, but they do not have the same interpretation regarding mean square error.

Unknown regression components   Factors in a regression model that are not measured but that influence the scores in the model. Because they are not measured in the model, their weights are unknown and they might influence the weights of the known predictors if they were included. Unknown components may also produce correlations between the residuals of dependent variables.

Measurement error   Unmeasured random variation in a regression model that is attributable to unstable components in the measurement of the dependent variable. This source of variation is often assumed to be uncorrelated across dependent variables. In the NAES, measurement error could reflect unstable reactions to questions because the respondent is not paying attention to a question or samples recollections from memory that are not stable. See also random error in Chapters 3 and 4.

Contrast-coded variable   A transformation of an independent variable such that the mean of the variable is zero. The transformation enables easier interpretation of the coefficients in a regression model.

Dummy-coded variable   A variable in a regression model that is coded to the value of 1 to represent the value of a subclass and zero for all other members of the class. For example, one could recode political party into two dummy variables: 1 for Republicans and zero for everyone else, and 1 for Democrats and zero for everyone else. Any class of J members can have $J - 1$ dummy variables to represent its effects in a regression model.

Interaction variable   Variables created from existing variables in a regression model to represent predictions for any variable that depend on the values of other variables. Often the product of two variables is used to represent the effect of an interaction between them. A variable that interacts with another is often called a **moderator** of the effects of the other variable.

B weight   The unstandardized coefficient of a variable in a regression equation. It measures the change in the dependent variable as a function of a one-unit change in the independent variable. The constant term is also a B weight; however, it is simply a parameter in the model. Each B weight (other than the constant term) has a corresponding **Beta** weight that is the value of the coefficient applied to the variables when they are standardized (z scores).

Standard error (SE)   A deviation measure that defines the range of likely values that a parameter in a model can assume. The smaller the SE, the more sensitively the parameter can be estimated. The larger the sample size and the value of R^2 for the model, the smaller the SE. The ratio of the parameter to the SE in OLS regression defines the **t** test that is used to measure the probability that the parameter is in the range of zero. A **p** value of .05 is usually taken as a cutoff for defining a statistically significant result, although this is only a convention.

t-test   A test of statistical significance defined by the ratio of a parameter to its standard error. The test is used in linear regression analysis to identify significant B weights in the model. Values greater than 2 in absolute size identify parameters that are significant at the $p < .05$ level in samples greater than size 60.

Wald test   A test of statistical significance defined by the square of the ratio of a parameter to its standard error. The test is used in logistic regression analyses to identify significant B values. A value of 3.84 is significant at $p <$ .05 for a single parameter.

CHAPTER 8

Autocorrelation   The correlation between a series at lag 0 and the same series at a different lag.

ACF   Autocorrelation function, a graph of the autocorrelation for successive lags of the same series is called the ACF. The analysis should only be
conducted with detrended series.

Partial auto-correlation (PAC)   The standardized regression coefficient for
the pth lag holding constant all earlier lags.

PACF   Partial autocorrelation function, the graph that shows successive values of the PAC. In an AR(p) model, all PACs greater than lag p will be zero
because by controlling the earlier lags, there will be no significant relation
between the series remaining.

MA(q)   The moving average time series model with q lags, a function of
the present and q previous random components. It has no memory beyond
the q lags of previous influence. Its coefficients are restricted to values less
than 1 in absolute value.

AR(p)   The autoregressive time series model with p lags, a function of the
present random component and p previous lags of the series. Its memory
can extend beyond the p lags that directly influence its value because each
lag contains information from all previous lags. Its coefficients are restricted
to values less than 1 in absolute value.

White noise   A time series that is entirely composed of successive random
components with a mean of zero, constant variance, and no relation between
terms.

Stationary series   A time series that has a constant mean, standard deviation, and covariance between lags. White noise is an example of a stationary series. AR and MA processes are stationary as well. Any series with a
trend that changes the mean or variability of the series is not stationary.

Random walk   An AR(1) series in which the autoregressive weight is 1. A
random walk is not stationary, but taking the first difference of the series
will produce a series that is stationary.

Box-Ljung test   A Chi-square test that assesses the presence of autocorrelation for the first p lags of the ACF. For example, if one evaluates autocorrelation for the first three lags of a series, then the Box-Ljung test is evalu-
ated with three degrees of freedom.

Correlogram The ACF graph with confidence bands for the values of the autocorrelations. A correlogram analysis is an examination of the ACF and PACF.

Standard error bands A pair of lines in the SPSS correlogram output that defines the range of the autocorrelation that is within two standard-error deviations of zero. Values that lie outside of the band are individually significant predictors of the series at the $p < .05$ level of significance.

Lag In correlating a time series with prior values of itself, the lag refers to the number of prior time periods in the correlation. A lag of one refers to a series one time period back in time. A lag of zero is simply the series itself. Negative lags refer to the number of succeeding time periods that are correlated with a series. Negative lags are used in the output of the cross-correlation program in SPSS. The **lag operator** L moves a series ahead one time period so it can be compared with the original at lag 0. In this case, lag is used as a verb. To lag a series one time period is to perform the lag operation on the series. In SPSS, one can create a lagged version of a series using the time series transforms.

Cross-correlation function An analysis of the correlations between different lags of two series. The output in SPSS shows a graphic representation of the correlations and their confidence bands to allow ready detection of significant correlations at different lags of either series. The analysis should only be conducted on detrended series.

Adjusted R^2 A measure of goodness of fit based on R^2 that ranges between zero and 1. It adjusts for the number of parameters in the model to take account of increases in R^2 that can occur simply because additional parameters have been added to the model. Hence, the larger its value, the better the fit.

ARMA analysis A program that uses maximum likelihood estimation of AR and MA components in a time series and that allows simultaneous estimation of seasonal and other trends.

AIC The Aikake information criterion, a measure of goodness of fit for regression models that declines as the fit improves. It uses a harsher penalty for the addition of parameters than the adjusted R^2, and hence is regarded as a more sensitive test of model fit. In combination with the SIC, it allows one to evaluate alternative models for time series using either OLS regression or ARMA analysis.

SIC The Schwarz information criterion, a measure of goodness of fit for regression models that also declines as the fit improves. It uses an even harsher penalty than the AIC. It is regarded as more sensitive to model adequacy especially when little is known about the modeling domain. In combination with the AIC, it allows one to evaluate alternative models for time series using either OLS regression or ARMA analysis.

Durbin Watson statistic, d   A statistic that has been used to assess the presence of first order autocorrelation in the residuals of time series data. Presence of autocorrelation in the residuals has been taken as a signal that the solution may be biased. However, it is limited in its ability to detect higher-order correlation in time series. A value less than 2 in the range between 2 and zero is regarded as a sign of positive autocorrelation.

Granger causality   A concept of causation applied to time series analysis in which one series X is said to Granger cause the other Y, if information contained in the lags of X can predict Y holding constant comparable lags in Y.

Feedback in Granger causality   A possible outcome of Granger causality tests in which both series can predict the future status of the other.

Contemporaneous causality   A possible situation in Granger causality testing in which either series can cause the other at lag 0. It is a possibility whenever the two series are correlated even after removing all cross-correlation from lags of each variable.

INDEX

Page references followed by f and t refer to figures and tables, respectively.